# Gaelic Identities
## Aithne na nGael

# Gaelic Identities
## Aithne na nGael

EDITED BY
GORDON McCOY WITH
MAOLCHOLAIM SCOTT

Institute of Irish Studies
Queen's University Belfast

Iontaobhas ULTACH/ULTACH Trust

First published in 2000

The Institute of Irish Studies
Queen's University Belfast
8 Fitzwilliam Street
Belfast BT9 6AW
www.qub.ac.uk/iis/publications.html

Iontaobhas ULTACH/ULTACH Trust
Fountain House
19 Donegall Place
Belfast BT1 5AB

British Library Cataloguing-in-Publication Data
A catalogue record for this book is available from the British Library.


ISBN 0 85389 766 2

Typeset in Garamond 11.5pt

Printed by ColourBooks Ltd, Dublin
Cover design by Dunbar Design

# CONTENTS

Contributors      vii

Introduction      1
GORDON MCCOY WITH MAOLCHOLAIM SCOTT

Ireland and Scotland: The Foundations of a Relationship      19
MÁIRE HERBERT

God and Gaelic: The Highland Churches and
Gaelic Cultural Identity      28
DONALD E MEEK

Evangelicalism, Culture and the Gaelic Tradition in Ireland      48
ALWYN THOMSON

The Politics of Gaelic Development in Scotland      53
TORMOD CAIMBEUL

Legal and Institutional Aspects of Gaelic Development      67
ROBERT DUNBAR

Taig Talk      88
AODÁN MAC PÓILIN

Creating Culture      96
ANNE LORNE GILLIES

Parallel Universes:
Gaelic Arts Development in Scotland, 1985–2000      105
MALCOLM MACLEAN

The Gael is Dead; Long Live the Gaelic: The Changing
Relationship between Native and Learner Gaelic Users      126
PEADAR MORGAN

Irish Language Enthusiasts and Native Speakers:
An Uneasy Relationship                                             133
LARS KABEL


Aithne na nGael: Life after Death?                                 139
PHILIP GAWNE


Neighbours in Persistence: Prospects for Gaelic
Maintenance in a Globalising English World                         144
KENNETH MACKINNON
Tables 12.1, 12.2 and 12.3                                         153


Bibliography                                                       156

# Contributors

*Tormod Caimbeul* has been a journalist for the last ten years. From 1991 to 1992, and 1994 to April 2000, he was Western Isles reporter for the BBC's Gaelic service, Radio nan Gàidheal. In May 2000 he was appointed its political correspondent and is now based at the Scottish Parliament in Edinburgh. He graduated in Celtic and English Literature from Glasgow University in 1989 and also spent a year on the University of Wales, Cardiff College's journalism course.

*Robert Dunbar* is a Canadian now working as a lecturer in law in the School of Law, the University of Glasgow, where among his academic interests are the rights of minorities, particularly linguistic minorities. He holds an LLB from Osgoode Hall Law School and an LLM from the University of London. A descendant of Scottish Gaels who settled in Nova Scotia, he is himself a fluent Gaelic speaker.

*Philip Gawne* is a former chairman and treasurer of Yn Cheshaght Ghailckagh, the Manx Language Society. As chairman of Mooinjer Veggey, the Manx Preschool Organisation, he has been instrumental in promoting the concept of Gaelic-medium education and pre-school groups in Man. He is currently employed by the Manx Heritage Foundation and Manx National Heritage as a Manx Language Development Officer, yn Greinneyder.

*Anne Lorne Gillies* is a freelance singer, educationist and writer. Raised on a croft in Argyll, she is a graduate of Edinburgh University, trained to teach at both primary and secondary levels. She has a PhD from the University of Glasgow and an honorary doctorate from the University of Edinburgh. Until recently she lectured in Strathclyde University, training Gaelic-medium primary teachers.

*Máire Herbert* is Associate Professor in the Department of Early and Medieval Irish, University College, Cork. She is author of *Iona, Kells and Derry: The History and Hagiography of the monastic familia of Columba* (Oxford 1988, repr. Dublin 1996), and co-author/co-editor of *Betha Adamnain: The Irish Life of Adamnan, Irish Biblical Apocrypha: Selected Texts in Translation*, and the *Catalogue of Irish Manuscripts in Cambridge Libraries*. She has published many articles on early Irish literature and history.

*Lars Kabel*, was born in Germany and studied European ethnology/cultural anthropology, Celtic studies and German linguistics at the University of Freiburg, University College Galway and Queen's University, Belfast. He wrote an MA thesis on Belfast's Irish language movement for the University of Freiburg. He has taught Irish language night classes in Germany and wrote a pocket guide to the Irish language in German. From 1998 to 2000, he taught German at the University of Limerick. He is currently working on a PhD thesis on German immigrants in rural Ireland for the University of Freiburg.

*Gordon McCoy* studied for a degree in Celtic and Social Anthropology from Queen's University Belfast, and afterwards remained at the university to examine Protestant learners of Irish for a doctoral thesis in the Department of Social Anthropology. He is currently employed as a cross-community worker with the ULTACH Trust.

*Kenneth MacKinnon* read economics and sociology for a first degree at the London School of Economics. He was head of department of General and Social Studies at Barking College of Technology in the East End of London. He undertook higher degrees in education and sociolinguistics at the University of London Institute of Education and became Reader in the Sociology of Language at Hatfield Polytechnic. He is currently Visiting Professor and Emeritus Reader in the Sociology of Language at the University of Hertfordshire, Honorary Research Fellow in Celtic at the University of Edinburgh and an Associate Lecturer of the Open University in Education and Social Sciences. He works as a higher education consultant from his home base in the Black Isle in the Highlands of Scotland.

*Malcolm MacLean* is a Glasgow Gael who has lived in the Western Isles since 1975. He was educated at Bellahouston Academy, Govan, and is a graduate of Gray's School of Art, Aberdeen College of Education and the Open University. In 1987 he became the first Director of Scotland's national development agency for the Gaelic arts, Pròiseact nan Ealan (PNE)/The Gaelic Arts Agency. Malcolm has been involved in developing Scottish/Irish arts and cultural links since the early 1990s and with the national and international committees of Iomairt Chaluim Chille since its inception in 1997.

*Aodán Mac Póilin* was born in Belfast and was educated by the Christian Brothers and at the University of Ulster. He has been involved in the Irish language movement since 1971, and was an Irish language teacher and former chairman of the first Irish-medium school in Northern Ireland. He is currently director of the ULTACH Trust.

*Donald E Meek* is a native of Tiree in the Inner Hebrides. He has taught at the universities of Glasgow and Edinburgh, and has been Professor of Celtic at Aberdeen since 1993. His many interests include medieval Gaelic literature (especially the fiannaíocht), the 16th-century Scottish manuscript called the Book of the Dean of Lismore, Gaelic religious verse of all periods, and the Gaelic literature, prose and verse, of the 19th century. He also studies the relationship between the Christian faith and Gaelic culture. He has published numerous articles and several books, among them *The Scottish Highlands: The Churches and Gaelic Culture* (Geneva 1996), *Tuath is Tighearna: Tenants and Landlords* (Edinburgh 1995), and the *Quest for Celtic Christianity* (Book of Garten, 2000).

*Peadar Morgan* has been the Director of CLI (Comann an Luchd Ionnsachaidh), the membership charity for learners and supporters of Scots Gaelic, since 1995, following three years as a learners officer with Comunn na Gàidhlig. After graduating in history and international relations from Aberdeen University, he learned Gaelic before taking a Gaelic-medium diploma at Sabhal Mòr Ostaig. He has also worked as a journalist and with the Gaelic Terminology Database, and is on the committee of the Scottish Place-Name Society.

*Maolcholaim Scott* has taught English in Sudan, worked for the Irish language paper, *Lá*, and for the Cultural Diversity Programme of the Northern Ireland Community Relations Council. He was formerly Irish Language Development Officer with Newry and Mourne District Council, and is currently project officer with the Iomairt Cholm Cille/The Columba Initiative. He holds degrees in Irish studies and linguistics.

*Alwyn Thomson* is Research Officer with ECONI (Evangelical Contribution On Northern Ireland). He is currently conducting research into religion and identity in the Protestant tradition. During a recent sabbatical he spent some time in Scotland looking at the impact of social and political change on Scottish churches. Born and raised in Belfast, he currently lives in Dundonald, County Down.

# Introduction

## Gaelic Identities:
## Two Countries, Two Cultures?

GORDON MCCOY WITH MAOLCHOLAIM SCOTT

The Scottish Gaelic scene is both strange and familiar to Irish speakers. Gaelic movements on both sides of the Irish Sea have much in common: the language classes and learners' culture, struggles for increased status, and the contrasts between urban and rural Gaelic speakers.[1] Yet so much in Scotland is unfamiliar to Irish speakers: Gaelic choirs as a focus for learners' activities; ceilidhs held in British Legion halls; the lack of overt nationalism in the revival movement; a business-like revival seemingly without some of the trappings of a counter-culture; and what appears most unusual – Free Presbyterians who worship in Gaelic.

This book is the result of a conference in March 1998 which explored the commonalities and contrasts within the Gaelic world. The Aithne na nGael/Gaelic Identities conference was organised jointly by the ULTACH Trust and the Cultural Diversity Programme of the Community Relations Council.[2] The proposal for the event came during the commemorative year of Colm Cille in 1997. When the conference took place, another product of this year, Iomairt Cholm Cille, or the Columba Initiative, was beginning to take shape. This gave an added relevance to the conference theme, as the aim of the Columba Initiative was to strengthen the links between Gaelic speakers in Ireland and Scotland.

A major objective of the conference was to inform an Irish audience about the Scottish Gaelic revival. However, there was a significant contribution from Irish speakers, and from a speaker of Manx, often in the form of

---

1. The self-appellations of the Q-Celtic languages, Irish Gaeilge, Scottish Gàidhlig, and Manx Gaelg, have contributed the term 'Gaelic' to the English language; in English, 'Gaelic' is more commonly applied to the Scottish Celtic language than the Irish one. However, in this introduction we use the term to refer to both Irish and Scottish languages, given their similar histories.
2. ULTACH is an Irish language organisation which carries out research, provides grants to voluntary Irish language groups, and promotes the language on a cross-community (involving both Protestants and Catholics) basis. The Community Relations Council is a state-funded body which addresses the sectarian divisions within Northern Ireland.

responses to the Scottish delegates. This publication consists of the edited proceedings of the conference, including the responses, where they were available in written form.[3] This volume represents the first comprehensive account of the Scottish Gaelic renaissance. We hope that the work will contribute to the debates within language revival movements and inform the general reader of the Gaelic world in Ireland, Scotland, and the Isle of Man.

This introduction will provide a historical background for the reader, exploring some themes of the Irish and Scottish Gaelic revivals,[4] setting them within their historical and contemporary contexts. We also include a short sketch of the Irish language revival, which will balance the account of the Scottish Gaelic renaissance in succeeding chapters.[5]

## The rise and decline of the Gaelic languages

No-one is certain when Gaelic was first spoken in Ireland. Archaeological evidence suggests that a Celtic language arrived in Ireland during the last millennium BC; Celtic place-names are recorded by the geographer Ptolemy in the 2nd century BC (Mallory and McNeill 1995: 173). Gaelic was certainly spoken throughout the island by the 5th century AD, as attested by the survival of ogham stones, which commemorated the death of important individuals in Irish. From the 4th century AD Irish settlers travelled to the Isle of Man and western Scotland, taking their language with them. Around 1000 AD Irish speakers achieved pre-eminence throughout present-day Scotland, Cumbria and Northumberland, as evidenced by surviving place-names. Gaelic was spoken in all of Ireland and most of Scotland, and was the language of the state, learning, and the church in both countries. In the succeeding centuries Gaelic-speaking populations were divided and marginalised by Norse incursions and the development of English-speaking kingdoms. These processes contributed to the divergence of Irish, Manx and Scottish Gaelic; hitherto the learned classes of the three regions spoke a common variety of language, classical Irish, which eased mutual intelligibility.[6]

---

3. Lars Kabel's paper is an exception, as he did not attend the conference, but his research on the relevant topic prompted us to invite him to contribute to this volume.

4. Some enthusiasts prefer the word 'renaissance' as Gaelic never 'died' in Scotland, and therefore the term 'revival' is deemed inappropriate. The term 'Gaelic renaissance' seems to have been first used in the 1970s to refer to 20th-century Gaelic poetry (Macdonald 1997: 25).

5. According to Professor Kenneth Jackson the differences between Scottish Gaelic and Manx on the one hand and Irish on the other first appeared in the 10th century, and they 'continued to be one language, sharing many new developments in common, from the tenth until the thirteenth century' (1951: 91–2). The Ulster dialect of Irish shares features with Scottish Gaelic which are not found in the Irish of Munster and Connaught.

6. There are 'murder' and 'suicide' theories of the Irish and Scottish Gaelic languages. Some nationalist commentators emphasise the negative impact of English rule and parliamentary edicts. Critics of this approach highlight the active participation of Gaelic speakers in the decline of the language. See Macdonald (1997: 47–9) for a summary of these positions.

Thus Irish and Scottish Gaelic suffered a loss of status, and began a tran-
sition from state languages to peasant vernaculars. Unlike the Irish case,
whereby Gaelic was opposed by a colonial power, the campaign against Gaelic
in Scotland was waged by many who considered themselves thoroughly
Scottish in nationality. State-sponsored attacks on Scottish Gaelic began in
earnest after 1350, when the Scottish people won their independence from
England. In the 15th century Lowland commentators conceptually distanced
Gaelic and its speakers from the centre of Scottish life by referring to them
as 'Irish' or 'Erse' (Macdonald 1997: 39, 43). The mainly Lowland Protestant
Reformation of 1560 exacerbated the division; Lowlanders equated Gaelic
speakers with Catholicism and Jacobitism (Durkacz 1996: 52). These stereotypes persisted into the 18th century, although by the 1690s Protestantism in
its Presbyterian and Episcopalian forms had overtaken Catholicism in the
Highlands. The varieties of Gaelic were denigrated as well as their speakers.
For many, Irish and Scottish Gaelic became languages of backwardness and
poverty, incapable of expressing abstract or scientific concepts; at worst they
were languages of sedition, and at best antiquarian pursuits, suitable vehicles
only for emotional poetry and folklore. The English language, embodying
advancement and modernity, became the language of administration and
commerce. Negative attitudes to Irish and Scottish Gaelic were internalised
by many speakers of the languages, who were anxious that their children
should learn English, abandoning Gaelic in the process.

## Religion

Following the loss of political status, Gaelic remained the medium of a folk
culture in Ireland and Scotland, and Gaelic speakers became the object of
'improving' missions, both secular and religious. In Ireland, the monarch was
the leader of the Anglican church as well as the head of state; thus loyalty to
the state became part of the tradition of the Church of Ireland. The view that
politics and religion should be intertwined, constituting a moral government
of the word of God, meant that it was desirable to convert Scottish and Irish
Catholics to Protestantism for both theological and political reasons. Some
Protestant religious organisations attempted to proselytise the Catholics of
Ireland and Scotland through Gaelic, with dramatically different results.

Presbyterian and Anglican churches brought Gaelic-speaking preachers to
Ireland from Scotland, and established a tradition of publishing and preaching in Irish. Yet despite the efforts of many missionaries, Gaelic-speaking or
otherwise, relatively few Irish Catholics converted to Protestantism. The government and Protestant churches doubted that many conversions could be
effected, and refused to contribute substantial sums for the purposes of pros-

elytism. The militant anti-Catholicism of the Irish missionaries outraged Catholic congregations and their priests. For the Catholic Irish, Protestantism was the religion of conquest, dispossession and discrimination, and Catholicism the ancestral religion of sacrifice, suffering, and resistance to an alien invader (Barnard 1993).

The first half of the 19th century saw an evangelical revival, and a substantial effort by Protestant churches and bible societies to preach and educate through the medium of Irish. Yet the resurgence of self-assured and politically active Catholicism in the second half of the century left Protestantism on the retreat in the south and west of Ireland, and in the north Protestants became increasingly introverted, conservative and anti-Catholic. Despite some successes, a movement which changed the cultural scene in Scotland was dissipated in Ireland amid political and sectarian strife. In the 19th century the Catholic Church perceived the Irish language to be an impediment to the temporal advancement of its congregation; the hostility of the church to the language rendered Protestant proselytism in Irish a futile endeavour.

However, at the end of the 19th century Catholic clerics became involved in the Gaelic League, perceiving the Irish language to be a vehicle of Catholic thought and a bulwark against Protestantism and secularism, an approach which is now regarded as obsolete (Mac Póilin 1994). The second Vatican Council, with its emphasis on a vernacular liturgy, brought a fresh emphasis on Irish. The church attempted to provide Irish-speaking clergy for districts in which the language was spoken, although at the close of the 20th century this policy became difficult to implement, owing to the dwindling number of suitable candidates.

In Scotland, the Protestant missionary campaign was more successful in its aims. Missionaries experienced considerable difficulty in introducing English-language texts to Gaelic-speaking children; the works consisted almost entirely of bibles, confessions of faith, and works of Calvinist theology, which the children learned to read without comprehension (Durkacz 1996: 61–3). When the threat of Jacobitism (equated by Lowlanders with the Gaelic language) subsided in the mid 18th century, the urge to save souls led to a tradition of teaching in Gaelic, as well as publishing religious and secular works in that language. In the 18th century, the Society in Scotland for Propagating Christian Knowledge (SSPCK) provided translations only of orthodox works, consisting of Puritan and Calvinist homilies of the previous century (MacKinnon 1991: 61–2). In doing so, the society reconciled the Reformation with the Gaelic language. The organisation's legacy was a high degree of religious orthodoxy and literacy in Gaelic among Highland

Presbyterians, who developed a strong tradition of studying the bible in private. In the Highlands, Gaelic was transformed from the language of 'barbarians' to that of spiritual purity and religious revival (Meek 1996a: 32). Some Highland Presbyterians came to believe that the distinctive Gaelic church was a bulwark against outside irreligious liberalism. At the same time certain evangelicals rejected aspects of secular Gaelic culture, such as storytelling, which smacked of 'pagan' influences; the most abiding image of this time was of the destruction of fiddles and bagpipes (Meek 1996a: 45).

Protestant missionaries were less successful in some isolated Gaelic communities, where the Counter-Reformation combined with local clan loyalties to maintain Catholicism. The legacies of these religious struggles in the Western Isles are the Presbyterian islands of Lewis, Harris and North Uist, and the Catholic islands of Barra, Eriskay, South Uist and Southern Benbecula. Despite occasional tensions, the relationship between these communities has been mostly positive, reflecting a collective hebridian identity which overcame religious divisions. In Scotland, religious and linguistic fault lines were often traversed and did not reinforce each other. Scotland, therefore, did not experience the common Irish division between Gaelic-speaking Catholics and English-speaking Protestants.

## Education

The 17th- and 18th-century Age of Enlightenment, with its emphasis on the development of scientific, technological, and bureaucratic progress, was typified by a contempt for less 'rational' cultures; subordinate groups who spoke other languages were 'not engaged in the discussion of ideas, or rather what are thought, by the culture, to be ideas' (Grillo 1989: 220). For Anglocentric 'improvers', speakers of Gaelic languages should be encouraged to abandon them for their own good. Many educational schemes were pioneered by Protestant religious organisations which believed that everyone should be capable of reading the scriptures in their own tongue; to John Knox, the aim of all educational was evangelical (Durkacz 1996: 154).

National systems of education replaced the variety of private, church and charity schools in Ireland in 1831 and Scotland in 1872. Under the new regime, the use of Irish and Scottish Gaelic was actively discouraged. In Ireland the use of Irish in national (primary) schools was completely forbidden, even as a means of teaching English to pupils who could speak no English. However, the languages were ultimately incorporated into the national school curriculum. In 1878 Irish was permitted as an extra subject in national schools, outside school hours. By 1904, schools in which the majority of children were Irish-speakers could opt into a bilingual programme, in which part of the curriculum was taught through the medium of Irish. Teaching Irish had never been forbidden at secondary level, but was not recognised as a subject, and was rarely taught. In 1899, Irish was given equal status with all other subjects in the secondary school curriculum, and by 1908 about half the students in Ireland were taking Irish as a subject for examination (Ó Huallacháin 1994: 55–6).

In Scotland the Free Church had pleaded in vain for Gaelic to be used as a medium of religious instruction, which was the policy of the church's Sabbath schools (Durkacz 1996: 117–18). Scottish Gaelic (Celtic) became a secondary-school examination subject in 1915, with the medium of instruction being English. The Education (Scotland) Act of 1918 required local authorities to provide adequate provision for teaching Gaelic in Gaelic-speaking areas; yet this was a 'paper victory' (Durkacz 1996: 180). Gaelic was taught even to Gaelic-speaking children in English, a situation which persisted throughout the 20th century in Scottish secondary schools. Gaelic was the medium of instruction in some primary schools in the Western Isles in the 1950s and 1960s, although systematic efforts to introduce a bilingual education project did not occur until 1975 (MacKinnon 1991: 97, 105, 142).

A dramatic shift occurred in the educational status of Irish following the partition of the island in 1922. In the independent Irish state a qualification in Irish was required for all secondary-school leaving certificates; this requirement was dropped in 1973, but the language remained a core-subject at primary and secondary level. Children in Irish-speaking districts were taught through the medium of the language, and until the 1960s they were encouraged to become teachers in English-language areas. Indeed, the main burden of the revival fell on the education system, which failed to revive Irish as a community language in English-speaking areas. Nevertheless, the policy led to generations of young people acquiring an acquaintance with the language. 'Compulsory Irish', as the state's policy was called, led to two contrasting images of the language: as a dreary, irrelevant subject forced upon reluctant schoolchildren; or as a proud symbol of Irish nationhood, which left existing patterns of communication in English unaltered.

## Economy

In the early years of the 19th century there were as many as 4 million Irish speakers in Ireland (Ó Murchú, M 1985: 26). Most of them had little political or economic power, and many wished to learn English to improve their lot in the world. This process of language shift was hastened during the 1846–49 famine, which killed as many as 1 million people and forced 1.5 million to emigrate. In particular, the ravages of the famine were felt by Irish speakers, as they lived in the poorer areas of the country. Many Irish speakers learned English to prepare for emigration to England and America, a tradition which was maintained throughout the 20th century. In the late 19th and early 20th centuries an increase of urbanisation and industrialisation led to the greater social mobility of Catholics, which contributed to their rejection of the Irish language (Crowley 1996: 109).

The economic privations of the Irish had their parallels elsewhere; the potato crop failures caused massive suffering in Scotland as well as Ireland. In the late 18th century the Highlands were opened up for commercial exploitation; sheep farming became a lucrative source of income for landowners, who were enthusiastic to clear the land of their tenants and settlements, to enable leases to be made available to Lowland graziers. The resulting evictions continued until local resistance and public opinion brought an end to large-scale clearances in the 1850s; the Crofters Acts of 1886 and 1892 secured Highlanders in their tenure. The combined effect of voluntary and compulsory migration of Highlanders reduced whole areas to uninhabited moorland, and confined the Gaelic language to the north-west of the country. The clearances comprise a key element of the historical memory of Scottish Gaelic speakers, evoking a class struggle with cultural and nationalist overtones – poor tenant farmers pitted against rich, pitiless, anglicised landlords and their henchmen. During the clearances some of the most distinctive institutions of the Highlands were formed, including crofting and the Highland Presbyterian churches; Gaelic communities embraced an evangelical Presbyterianism, fuelled by itinerant preachers, which satisfied a need for security during unsettled times (Durkacz 1996: 102, 122).

The clearances and commercial estate management hastened migration to the cities and overseas; in the 1690s and early 18th century large numbers of Scots emigrated from Argyllshire to Ulster.[7] From the 1740s onwards, Gaelic speakers emigrated to North America in significant numbers, initially to the Carolinas and then to Cape Breton, Nova Scotia, Ontario and Prince Edward Island. Others Gaelic speakers were drawn southwards by the rapid expansion of the industrial centres of the Lowlands. By the first quarter of the 19th century, large numbers of former Highlanders had become well accustomed to an urban way of life conducted through the medium of English.

In the late 1980s and 1990s a new phenomenon appeared in some Gaelic-speaking districts in Ireland and Scotland; businesses with full-time employ-

---

7. Some Scottish settlers in Ulster spoke Gaelic, although we cannot be sure how many. The Gaelic-speaking element of Scottish settlements in Ulster has been the cause of much debate, with various commentators maximising and minimising their number and influence; see Ó Snodaigh (1973), British and Irish Communist Organisation (1973), and Blaney (1996) for some very different positions on the subject.

ees involved in language revivalism. In both countries this economy was weakened by the expansion of Gaelic language broadcasting, and to a lesser extent educational projects. It remains to be seen whether these initiatives can stem the tide of emigration, or halt the decline of the Gaelic languages in their traditional strongholds.

## Revivalism

The rise of European nationalist ideologies in the 19th century transformed the attitudes of cosmopolitan elites to 'peasant' languages. Nationalists highlighted the role of language in the cultural distinctiveness of nations. German romantic nationalism popularised the concept of linguistic determinism, the view that a language expresses and creates a distinct and autonomous system of thought. Herder argued that if a man spoke a foreign language, he would lead a debilitating and artificial life, estranged from the intuitive sources of his personality (Kedourie 1994: 58). German romanticists believed that language was not only a guarantor of nationality but the repository of national identity (Crowley 1996: 125). Other processes, including the rise of print capitalism, contributed to a model of identity in which language was regarded as a proper basis for nationhood (Macdonald 1997: 51).

However, political and cultural nationalists did not agree on the importance of the state in protecting and reproducing national cultures. Hutchinson (1987) claims that cultural nationalists perceived the essence of nations to lie in their distinctive civilisations, rather than their distinctive politics; for some, cherishing a native culture and language became a moral end in itself. On the other hand, political nationalists used the distinctiveness of native culture to legitimise secessionism and independent statehood. Civic nationalists conceived of the nation as a community of laws and institutions with a single political will; emphasis was laid on the equality and equal access of all members of the nation, irrespective of ethnic origins or cultural allegiances (Smith 1991: 117).

In Ireland, Irish became an important element in the symbolic inventory of nationalists, whereas Scottish nationalism did not utilise Gaelic to the same extent. Gaelic language revivalism began in the late 19th century, with the founding of An Comunn Gàidhealach (The Highland Association) in 1891 and Conradh na Gaeilge (the Gaelic League) in 1893. In Ireland, the early years of the Gaelic League were preoccupied with cultural regeneration, the core of which was perceived to be the Irish language. The organisation became drawn into the wider political arena, as many members believed that the creation of an independent state was necessary to protect the language. For many language enthusiasts, the convergence of political and cultural

nationalism was inevitable; other disgruntled Leaguers, including the organisation's first president, resigned office or left Conradh na Gaeilge, believing it
to have been taken over by republicans.

The adoption of Gaelic revivalism by Irish nationalism suggested that
Ireland would be partitioned linguistically as well as politically. By the time the
British agreed to a form of self-government in Ireland in 1920 it was certain
that Gaelic revivalism would become part of the official ideology of the new
state. The Irish state embarked on an ambitious programme to conserve and
encourage the use of the Irish language. The general consensus is that these
measures failed to revive the language, while they served to delay its decline.
In everyday life in the Republic, the government Irish language policy was
manifested in a symbolic fashion; the language appeared on postage stamps
and coins, bilingual stationary, and dual language public signs. Official goodwill towards Irish was reflected by the general population, which was
favourable towards the language but made little personal commitment to
learning it. However, the 1996 launch of an Irish language television station,
Teilifís na Gaeilge (later re-named TG4), was a major boost for revivalists.
Furthermore, there was a steady growth in Irish-medium education, involving
22,000 children outside the Gaeltacht (O Murchú, H 1999: 22).

## Northern Ireland

Following partition, Unionist opinion in Northern Ireland was that Irish language revivalism increased the impoverishment of the near-bankrupt southern state, and was evidence of its essentially autocratic nature (Kennedy 1988:
182). During fifty years of Ulster Unionist Party hegemony, Irish was to have
no part in public life, a principle which was enacted in legislation in 1949,
when street signs in languages other than English were banned.[8] The Irish
language became the preserve of Catholic schools and a small voluntary
movement, consisting mostly of educated Catholics, including many clergy-
men and schoolteachers. In 1969 a small group of language activists established a small Irish-speaking community in the Shaw's Road district of West
Belfast. In 1971, they opened a *bunscoil* (Irish-medium primary school) for
their children, which expanded its intake by admitting children from English-
speaking homes in 1978. These developments were concurrent with the
growth of republicanism, which tended to view interest in the Irish language
as a distraction from armed insurrection.

This view changed dramatically in 1981, when some republican prisoners
went on hunger strike as a protest to achieve political (prisoner of war) status;

---

8. This legislation was revoked by the British government in 1995.

the British government regarded paramilitary prisoners as common criminals. The hunger strikes focused nationalist attention on the prisoners, many of whom had learned Irish despite official disapproval.[9] The language became a symbol of cultural resistance in the prisons and beyond, as released prisoners de-mystified Irish for working-class nationalists, for whom learning Irish had previously represented a middle-class intellectual activity. This potent mixture of language and politics had a wide appeal in republican areas and the demand for Irish classes mushroomed. Sinn Féin and language activists transformed what had been a private-domain activity into a public one, thereby mirroring the increased self-confidence and assertiveness of northern nationalism. The promotion of Irish by Sinn Féin incurred widespread unionist hostility to the language.

As the 1980s progressed, interest in Irish spread beyond the earlier move-ment and those influenced by the ideology of Sinn Féin. The success of the Shaw's Road *bunscoil* provided a prototype for the development of other Irish-medium primary schools in Northern Ireland, which surpassed appeals to learn Irish based on the nationalist/republican tradition (Maguire 1991: 100). Parents were inspired to learn Irish by their children and they in turn aroused an interest in their friends and relatives (Maguire 1991: 143). The revival expanded to include social activities and entertainment, as well as Irish-lan-guage media, including a newspaper, drama company, and pirate radio station. Some of these activities were funded by the British government, which devel-oped a funding strategy for Irish language initiatives at the end of the 1980s; a process many Irish speakers felt was begrudging and long overdue, causing hardship for many revivalists in the interim period.

Irish achieved a modest place in broadcasting, and the language movement made great strides in Irish-medium education. This focused on the creation of free-standing schools, rather than Scottish-style units in English-medium schools. In 1999 there were 1500 children enrolled in Irish-medium educa-tion. In 1990 a British government department provided seed-funding for the ULTACH Trust. The Trust's approach of establishing a consensual relation-ship with the government raised suspicions among some Irish language groups, which accused the organisation of being co-opted to government policy. For its part, the Trust considered itself to be part of the Irish language movement, and largely independent of government control.

As the revival grew, funding for Irish language initiatives was forthcoming from central government and from employment schemes, which provided

---

9. The prisoners were not allowed learning materials in Irish, and collaborated to construct 'Jailic', their own distinctive dialect of Irish. In the late 1980s 'Jailic' became extinct as Irish classes were introduced to the prisons. The Irish-speaking parts of the prisons in Northern Ireland were nicknamed 'the Jailtacht'.

financial help for community organisations and small businesses in poorer areas of Northern Ireland. In 1994 the IRA and the Protestant paramilitaries called a cease-fire, and negotiations to bring about a settlement to the conflict intensified. The UK government undertook to promote the Irish language in the Belfast Agreement of 1998; in March 2000 the government signed the European Charter for Regional or Minority Languages, which aims to promote and protect linguistic minorities as an essential part of Europe's cultural heritage. Furthermore, language projects were funded by European grants aimed at securing the peace and improving training and job prospects in deprived areas. In December 1999 six cross-border implementation bodies were set up to co-operate on areas of interest on an all-Ireland basis. Among these was an all-Ireland language body (a reconstituted Bord na Gaeilge, the Republic's Irish language promotional agency) which assumed responsibility for the promotion of the Irish language outside the Gaeltacht in both jurisdictions in Ireland.

In all, the Irish language movement in Northern Ireland was undergoing a transformation from a private-domain voluntary counterculture to full-time professional involvement in a revival which had an increasingly high profile in the region. The language issue continued to divide its supporters and detractors on political fault lines; most nationalists supported the revival, and most unionists opposed it.

## Scotland

For most of the 20th century, Gaelic enthusiasm focused upon the activities of An Comunn Gàidhealach and its annual cultural showpiece, the Mòd, which acquired royal patronage in the 1960s. This voluntary movement concentrated on educational and cultural issues, avoiding overtly political ones. By eschewing party sponsorship and operating as a lobby group, the organisation attracted positive responses from all four Scottish political parties, as well as some modest gains from public bodies. Furthermore, successive British governments were favourable to the Gaelic lobby, which preferred to woo influential patrons rather than alienate them with belligerent campaigns (McKee 1997: 67). Indeed, Gaelic revivalism in Scotland was relatively low-key and tended to operate within existing frameworks compared to language movements in Ireland, Wales, or the Basque country; there was no widespread withholding of television licence-fees, no organised violence against outsiders, and few demonstrations (Macdonald 1997: 56–60).

An Comunn Gàidhealach was inspired by the culture and lifestyle of the Highlands and Islands. Yet this image resulted in a complex relationship between Scottish Gaelic revivalism and nationalism. Because the overwhelming number of Scots were Lowland in language and culture, Gaelic enthusiasts encountered great difficulty in making their language relevant for most of the Scottish population, let alone promoting Gaelic as the national language of the country; at best Gaelic could only become only *a* national language, if it were to overcome its minority status. The most prevalent forms of Scottish identification, with their emphasis on separate laws, church, educational provisions, and mint, were more reminiscent of civic than cultural nationalism.

Some Gaelic enthusiasts, claiming that the language conferred a distinctive identity upon the country, advocated militant campaigning and secessionism. Their beliefs never achieved common currency among Gaelic speakers; nor did Scottish nationalist groups often return the favour. Nationalist political parties were reluctant to risk alienating urban voters in the Lowland towns and cities by embracing the peripheral Highlands image of Gaelic culture. Although some nationalists have adopted a more favourable policy to Gaelic, the popular concept of Scottish national identity remained focused on an allegiance to a set of distinct institutions rather than cultural practices. Many Lowlanders considered aspects of Highland material culture, notably bagpipes and Highland dress, to be part of their symbolic cultural repertoire, but they remained indifferent or hostile to the Gaelic language.

The course of the Scottish Gaelic renaissance will be charted in the following chapters, and the details do not concern us here. One important aspect of the Scottish revival, hinted at in the following chapters, is the tension between professionals involved in the Gaelic 'industry', and those who consider themselves to be 'on the ground', accusing the former of being self-seeking and out-of-touch. Despite great achievements, some Scottish revivalists became concerned about the ability of certain initiatives to save traditional Gaelic-speaking communities, or the likelihood of the creation of new communities elsewhere. They suspected the revival of having more shadow than substance, as it appeared to lack grass-roots activities which would secure the survival of the language. During the conference Kenneth MacKinnon warned:

> We may have the media, we may have the arts, we may have broadcasting, we may have education going forward and developing, we may even have secure [legal] status. But if there is not an actual community of speakers, and if there is not an oncoming generation, this will be merely an overcoat around an invisible man. There will be a lot of quite impressive outer garments and if they are revealed, nothing inside.

Opponents of this view are proud to have created a professional and modern revival which will attract more interest in Scottish Gaelic. Few will wish to become involved in 'grass roots' activism, they maintain, if Gaelic is not made attractive and relevant to the younger generations. Echoes of this tension are found in the Republic of Ireland, where voluntary organisations accuse professional revivalists in state employ of being more interested in their own wage packets than the survival of the language. The relative importance of activism 'on the ground' vis-à-vis initiatives with a wider and more symbolic focus is one which will occupy language revivalists in Britain and Ireland for many years to come.

## The Gàidhealtachd and the Gaeltacht

The traditional Gaelic heartlands are referred to as the Scottish Gàidhealtachd and the Irish Gaeltacht. In Ireland, the term can be used collectively, referring to all the Irish-speaking districts, or references are made to the Connaught, Munster and Ulster Gaeltachts (*Gaeltachtaí* in Irish).[10] Areas in which Irish is particularly strong are referred to as *fíor-Ghaeltachtaí* (literally 'true Gaeltachts'), whereas weaker Irish-language districts are called *breac-Ghaeltachtaí* (literally 'speckled Gaeltachts'). In Scotland, many people refer to the Highlands and Islands as the Gàidhealtachd, whether this encompasses Gaelic-speaking areas or not; the term 'Gael' can refer to a Highlander, Gaelic-speaking or otherwise (Macdonald 1997: 36).

In Ireland, despite attempts to develop an economic base in Irish language districts following independence, the outflow of Irish speakers to the English-speaking world continued. The Gaeltacht was, and is, heavily subsidised by the Irish state. Parents who raise their children with Irish in the Gaeltacht, for example, receive a grant, which at the time of writing amounts to £200 per year for full fluency and £100 for children acquiring fluency (in, for example 'mixed language' homes). Furthermore, recipients of this allowance qualify for a grant of £4000 to build a new house, as well as a number of smaller improvement grants. A special Gaeltacht authority, Údarás na Gaeltachta, was established to promote industrial development in the region. The companies concerned had to be willing to implement Irish as the first language in their factories and businesses. This scheme had a modest success, but in the long term became an anglicising factor. Very often the demand for workers could not be met locally, and therefore English speakers had to be recruited. In times of economic revival, migrants returned, bringing with them their English-speaking families, who contributed to the spread of English in the Gaeltacht.

---

10. The English-majority area is referred to as the Galldachd and Galltacht in Scots and Irish Gaelic respectively.

By the late 1960s, there were virtually no monoglot Gaelic speakers in Scotland or Ireland, and the language had a variety of roles in small isolated communities: in worship, in entertainment, in social life, and communal events. In Scotland, Gaelic was used predominantly for such activities as speaking with family and relations, certain work domains, township meetings, personal prayer and conversations with church elders. The language symbolised local community identities, with refusal to use Gaelic being attributed to snobbishness (Macdonald 1997). In the Scottish and Irish Gaeltachts, Gaelic was the unselfconscious language of home and community, and English was used with outsiders. Revivalists (often referred to as *Gaeilgeoirí* in Ireland) conceptualised the languages in terms of ideologies which were often invested with nationalist sentiments. Yet there was a degree of overlap between the two groups of Gaelic speakers. In the Republic of Ireland, some native speakers of Irish gained employment in the state-led project of language restoration. Irish speakers from Northern Ireland have noted the high proportion of native speakers of Gaelic involved in the Scottish renaissance, a phenomenon which did not pertain in their own region.

## The papers

The papers in this volume will enable the reader to develop an informed understanding of historical and contemporary issues involving Scottish Gaelic. They consider the changing nature of Gaelic identity in terms of religion, politics and culture. Manx and Irish respondents compare the Scottish material with the experiences of other parts of the Gaelic world. The final paper considers the survival of Scottish Gaelic and the Irish language in Northern Ireland.

Máire Herbert's paper touches on both historical and contemporary themes in her examination of how both Christianity and Gaelic culture transgressed ethnic lines. She describes Colm Cille's creation of a monastic federation which encompassed various polities of Gaels, Picts, Saxons and Britons on both sides of the Irish Sea. This multi-ethnic Columban community strengthened ecclesiastical, political and cultural links between Scotland and Ireland, and facilitated the spread of the Gaelic language throughout northern Britain. Conference attendees were particularly surprised to discover that Gaelic was used as a trans-ethnic lingua franca, considering latter perspectives which equated varieties of Gaelic with boundary maintenance between groups.

Donald Meek continues the theme of Christianity and the Gaelic language, setting this relationship within the wider context of Christianity's differing approaches to culture. Calvin, Meek attests, wished to reshape culture to serve the cause of Christianity, a concept later realised in the use of Gaelic as a vigorous preaching and publishing medium. Nevertheless, the Catholic Church harmonises the sacred and secular in a manner less common in Highland Presbyterianism. Meek finds the more conservative Protestant denominations, formerly characterised by their use of Gaelic as a mode of worship, moving towards a fatalistic rejection of Gaelic culture, a process he finds regrettable.

Alwyn Thomson, the evangelical respondent from Northern Ireland, declares that his fellow Protestants, evangelicals included, see no purpose in appropriating Irish Gaelic culture; indeed they consider it alien, even hostile, to their vision of the world. Thomson's paper considers Gaelic culture in Ireland in terms of both theological and secular perspectives. While he advocates that evangelicals should support cultural pluralism, he suspects that 'evangelical' Irish speakers are less tolerant of contemporary Protestant culture. It is apparent that some Highland Presbyterians and many of their co-religionists in Northern Ireland have no time for Gaelic culture, but their reasons differ considerably.

The divergence of Scottish and Irish Protestant religious attitudes to Gaelic culture hints at differing political approaches to the language. Tormod Caimbeul provides a detached account of the events which led to the creation of a professional organisation at the interface of the Gaelic-speaking community and the state. Caimbeul recounts the professional lobbying, co-option of politicians onto Gaelic organisations, and the use of Thatcherite economism to advance the Gaelic cause. Yet both Caimbeul and Robert Dunbar, a Canadian Gaelic speaker who also contributes to this theme, warn against the complacency of leaving the revival to the growing Gaelic bureaucracy and uncommitted Gaelic speakers, who only perceive the language to be a passport to self-advancement. Dunbar takes a more prescriptive approach, promoting legal recognition for Gaelic in order to protect language projects from the vagaries of government officials and 'the roulette wheel of political lobbying'.

Dunbar notes how, given the appeasing platitudes of all the major parties in Scotland towards Gaelic, the language cannot be considered to be a 'political issue'. This, of course, differs very widely from the Northern Irish experience, where the language issue divides nationalist and unionists into pro- and anti-Gaelic camps. According to Aodán Mac Póilin, the director of the ULTACH Trust, those who adopted a consensual approach to the British government could be represented as traitors to the cause of the language, yet they were involved in a creative tension with those who adopted a more radical approach. Mac Póilin's account of vitriolic Protestant hostility towards the Irish language surprised many of the Scottish guests at the conference.

A central question of any cultural revival involves the determination of exactly what is to be maintained and promoted, given that many aspects of traditional rural lifestyles seem irrelevant to language enthusiasts in the cities. Through her involvement in Gaelic-medium education, Anne Lorne Gillies is acutely aware of the need to balance the folly of recreating 'times long gone' with the mistake of creating a modernised culture that is not recognisable to many Gaelic speakers in the Gàidhealtachd. The most ironic part of her personal quest is a return journey to Tiree, where she had learned Gaelic as a child, to lecture an audience of monoglot English speakers on the benefits of Gaelic-medium education.

Malcolm MacLean continues on the cultural theme, citing modern Gaelic music as an example of how Gaelic culture can be simultaneously commercial and authentic. MacLean charts the transformation of Gaelic culture from ceilidhs to cartoons, contemporary theatre, and performances at the Edinburgh International Festival. He emphasises the need to develop a Gaelic arts infrastructure; thus children in Gaelic-medium education are encouraged to produce plays based upon their schoolbooks, and television companies sponsor dramatic training in order to improve the standard of Gaelic broadcasts. Gaelic arts organisations, in collaboration with other bodies, have created a contemporary Gaelic culture which challenges stereotypes about the language and increases the confidence of Gàidhealtachd communities.

The promotion of Gaelic as a national language in Scotland is a common theme of the conference papers. Yet, Peadar Morgan finds learners, and the organisation that represents them, to be the poor relation of the Gaelic renaissance. Indeed, the terms 'learner' and 'native speaker', often used in conceptual opposition, can misinform and denigrate the former type of Gaelic speaker, considering that a learner may become more fluent in Gaelic than someone raised with the language. In some ways, Morgan concludes, this lack of contact between urban enthusiasts and rural Gaelic speakers is not very important, as one could live in the Highlands without hearing much Gaelic; the 'nouveau Gaels' are creating their own mini-Gàidhealtachd around them, at a time when the traditional Scottish Gael is 'on his last legs'.

Lars Kabel continues on this theme, noting that the term 'native speaker' is not so 'loaded' in Ireland. He finds the same divisions between urban language enthusiasts and rural Irish speakers, although in some ways their lifestyles are converging. Native speakers do not want to perpetuate the antiquated, romantic of a thoroughly Irish-speaking Gaeltacht, immersed in an authentic Irish culture. For their part, some urban enthusiasts find themselves having more in common with each other than with the people of the

Gaeltacht, the traditional wellspring of the Irish language. Other enthusiasts regret the language barrier between themselves and native speakers, but find cultural differences render communication difficult.

Philip Gawne's thumbnail sketch of the language scene on the Isle of Man indicates some of the issues that may arise if the traditional Gaelic heartlands of Ireland and Scotland vanish. Manx enthusiasts were unsure whether they should revive 'biblical Gaelic' or the taped speech of the last native speakers. Having reached a compromise on that issue, they find they must compete against the anglicisation of Manx, the loss of native idiom, and even the loss of the Manx accent in Gaelic. The Irish and Scottish revivals are important to Manx language enthusiasts, who are inspired by the knowledge that they are not alone in their struggle to keep Gaelic alive.

All of the authors express a deep concern for the future of the varieties of Gaelic. Kenneth MacKinnon's analysis of census and other survey data has grave implications for Scottish revivalists, as he describes the demographic collapse of Scottish Gaelic. The present death rate of speakers of the language far outstrips the number of children being educated though the medium of Gaelic. In economic terms, he notes the bias of Scottish Gaelic speakers towards professional and managerial occupational groups, and the semi-unskilled crofters of the Highlands and Islands. By contrast, the Northern Irish revival appears to be led by youthful middle-class intellectuals, although there is a high interest in Irish among long-term unemployed, an indicator of the root of the present revival in impoverished Catholic districts. MacKinnon notes the global trend of 'third generational return' to language activism and the re-ethnicisation of minority lesser-used languages, but warns that the demographic trend in Scotland could overcome the successes of the revival.

At the dawn of the third millennium the fortunes of the Gaelic languages are mixed, and revivalists sometimes find themselves with more questions than answers. It is our hope that greater awareness of the various challenges and directions of the Manx, Irish and Scottish Gaelic revivals can, in some small way, contribute to the achievement of their goals.

# Ireland and Scotland:
# The Foundations of a Relationship

Máire Herbert

My purpose here is to examine the early histories of Ireland and of Scotland, and to trace secular and ecclesiastical contacts up to the end of the first millennium. The earliest phase of our shared past, the settlement of coastal areas of western Scotland by migrants from north-east Ulster, belongs to the era before recorded history. Therefore, all our inferences about the beginnings of the Irish presence in north Britain are necessarily tentative. It has been suggested that pressure on peoples east of the Bann due to expansion of Uí Néill power may have led to a quest for alternative lands. Whatever the reasons, however, it seems highly unlikely that there was a single, large-scale migration. Rather, it would seem that there was a gradual build-up of population establishing itself on facing coastlands across the sea from about the early 6th century.

Surviving written evidence concerning the Irish colony begins about the late 6th century. The name, Dál Riata transfers with the settlers, and it has been assumed by many historians that Dál Riata in Scotland was under joint rule with the home kingdom in present-day County Antrim. Yet there is no evidence of political control from Ireland over the affairs of the settlers. Instead, our historical data from the latter part of the 6th century indicates that the overseas kingdom was ruled by a king who operated within the political framework of northern Britain rather than that of northern Ireland. Moreover, the organisation of the overseas settlement as a kingdom seems to coincide with a decline in the position of the home kingdom of Dál Riata. The neighbouring kingdoms of Dál nAraide and Dál Fiatach take over the Ulster over-kingship from about the late 6th century, and Dál Riata no longer counts as a significant political player in the north-east of Ireland. Therefore, instead of assuming authority over the overseas settlement by a ruling Dál Riata dynasty in Ireland, it seems legitimate to wonder whether the royal dynasty and rulers of the Irish kingdom of Dál Riata had actually transferred across the sea in the 6th century. Certainly, the earliest texts depict Scottish Dál Riata as a fully-functioning kingship, not as a colony looking to external authority.

The arrival from Ireland of the monk, Columba (*Colum Cille*) in the year 563 initiates the next important transinsular link. Unlike the Irish pilgrims, reported in the Anglo-Saxon Chronicle as having journeyed in a boat without oars, Columba seems to have directed his overseas voyage specifically towards the Irish kingdom in Britain. The saint belonged to the royal family of Uí Néill, Ireland's foremost rulers, and his establishment in Dál Riata is likely to have been facilitated by some prior contact between his royal kin and the Dál Riata leadership.

Our earliest sources about Columba's career are the *Amra*, a praise-poem composed around the time of his death in the year 597, and a Latin *Life of Columba* by his successor, Adomnán, compiled about a century later on the basis of almost equally early testimony. Both sources agree that the practice of monasticism was the central aim of Columba's pilgrimage from Ireland, and they identify asceticism and learning as twin pillars of that monasticism. Yet, while Columba's aim may have been to separate himself from his home-land in order to devote himself more fully to these monastic ideals, he did not succeed in remaining anonymous in a remote island hermitage. Instead, his monastery on Iona soon began to attract pilgrims, penitents, and visiting dig-nitaries from Ireland and from north Britain. Moreover, further monasteries were founded from Iona throughout Dál Riata to form the nucleus of a monastic federation which would span the Irish Sea.

The founder's own status and charisma no doubt were significant factors in this phenomenon. Famed for his abandonment of the privileges of royal-ty for the privations of monasticism, the enduring success of his monastic enterprise was probably due in no small measure also to his organisational acumen. Monasteries associated with his name both in Dál Riata and in Ireland were joined in federation under the ultimate headship of Iona. Columba thereby followed the model of Irish secular overlordship practised by his royal kinsmen. The durability of this monastic organisation was ensured, moreover, by the assignation of positions of leadership within the community to monks of the founder's own Uí Néill kin. Thus, Columba's abbots and future successors would share the same influential social and political networks, as well as the same monastic vocation.

The foundation of a vibrant ecclesiastical institution which linked com-munities on both sides of the Irish Sea was not the sole achievement of Columba's career, for his influence extended also to the realms of culture and politics. The institutional links which he created between churches in Dál

Riata and those in Ireland reinforced the status and culture of the kingdom of Dál Riata itself. Without the close and continuous contact with Ireland maintained through Iona, the colony might have found it difficult to maintain itself, and might have been drawn before long into the orbit of its neighbours in Pictland or Strathclyde. Therefore, ecclesiastical associations with Ireland were a significant reinforcement of the Gaelic language and identity of the overseas kingdom. Moreover, Columba also strengthened political links between Dál Riata and Ireland. He returned to Ireland in the latter part of the 6th century to preside over a 'conference of kings' between his royal cousin in Ireland, the Uí Néill king, and his current royal patron, the king of Dál Riata. His initiative seems to have been designed to formalise an alliance between the kingdoms, a move which both secured the position of his monastic institution, and brought Dál Riata secular authority into association with a powerful kingship in Ireland.

The Columban monastic community thus was influential in strengthening ecclesiastical, cultural and political connections across the Irish Sea. Moreover, while institutionally based in societies which were ethnically and culturally Irish, the Columban community was not exclusively Irish either in personnel or in orientation. Indeed, our sources reveal that by the 7th century all four peoples of North Britain; Picts, Britons, Saxons, and Gaels, were represented among the membership of the monastic community. Columba himself was a friend of the king of the British kingdom of Strathclyde. He travelled in still-pagan Pictland and negotiated with its king. In effect, the Columban community was an active participant in the same North British world as was the kingdom of Dál Riata. Iona became a pivotal point of transinsular contact for clerics and laity throughout the Irish Sea regions. Our earliest contemporary historical documentation in the Irish annals was recorded on the island, and these monastic notes of ecclesiastical and secular events throughout Ireland and North Britain reflect the diverse places of origin of Iona's sources of news.

In the 7th century Columban monastic associations became even more inclusive of different ethnicities and languages, as foundations were established among the Picts and the Anglo-Saxons. While contacts with Pictland dated back to Columba's time, the invitation to preach to the Anglo-Saxons had come in the 630s, from the Northumbrian king, Oswald. On regaining power after a period of exile spent among the Irish, the king requested Iona monks to preach Christianity in his kingdom. Thus, from the resulting foundation at Lindisfarne, a Christian network radiated throughout Northumbria. Some thirty years later, however, the Northumbrian venture ended as a result of controversy in the kingdom over the date of Easter. The Columban community wished to maintain its own Easter custom in the face of those who vigorously advocated the need for all of Christendom to be united in observance. This dispute, which ranged local particularism against universal custom, had already been aired in Ireland in the 630s. The Columban community clearly prided itself in its intellectual tradition and, secure in its own diversity, it was apparently unmoved by arguments in favour of universal conformity in ecclesiastical practice. Yet defying the consensus of Christendom in the matter of Easter was not ultimately a tenable position. Fortunately, before the end of the 7th century one of Iona's ablest abbots ensured that the distinctive transinsular and transcultural unity of his community would find a more positive expression.

Adomnán, Columba's biographer, as well as his successor as Iona abbot, was the inspirational figure of the late 7th century. In 697, the centenary of Columba's death, he oversaw the proclamation of a legal measure to secure the protection of non-combatants, women, children, and clerics, in time of conflict. Called 'The Law of the Innocents' in contemporary annals, and subsequently named for its instigator *Cáin Adomnáin*, 'The Law of Adomnán', its provisions, and a list of guarantors, are still extant. The list of guarantors reveals that Adomnán secured the backing of his kinsman, Ireland's most powerful Uí Néill king, as well as from about ninety other secular and ecclesiastical leaders from Ireland, Dál Riata and Pictland. The law was an imaginative innovation, both as a joint church–state measure for the betterment of social conditions, and as a public act which united rulers and peoples across the Irish Sea. To ensure protection for the vulnerable in society, Adomnán had created an association of Christian leaders which transcended boundaries of secular and ecclesiastical jurisdictions. Moreover, by uniting the Picts with the Gaelic world in assent to his law, Adomnán had reinforced links across the divides of ethnicity and language.

The Iona abbot's ideal of kingdoms and peoples on both sides of the Irish Sea joining together in acceptance of common Christian laws might have flourished further had the stable circumstances of the 8th century persisted. However, the final years of the century saw the first Viking raids and the beginning of the fracture of political and ecclesiastical institutions. The perception of a Christian identity which superseded ethnicity may still be discerned in monastic annalists' initial characterisation of Viking raiders simply as *genti*, 'pagans'. These intruders, however, were not just the destroyers of Christian churches. Rather, they were to be catalysts of change on both sides of the Irish Sea.

Plundering attacks on vulnerable island and coastal monasteries marked the first phase of Viking activity. Early in the 9th century the monastery of

Kells in the Irish midlands was founded by the Columban community, probably as a refuge for personnel and precious objects from beleaguered Iona. Though the island monastery was not deserted despite several destructive raids, Vikings had begun to settle in the Western Isles, and, in the course of the 9th century, the sea which had linked churches and peoples became a hostile environment dominated by Viking fleets and coastal settlements. The monastic communication necessary for Iona's governance of its far-flung federation of monasteries was disrupted. A fissure between east and west was opening up.

Political life was changing also. What historians termed 'the passing of the old order' tended to be attributed solely to upheaval caused by the Vikings. Yet in Ireland it would seem that the Viking presence did not so much overturn the past as accelerate changes already in train, especially in the nature of royal power. The greater Irish provincial kingships had already strengthened at the expense of smaller political units during the 8th century, and around the mid 9th century, in the wake of the establishment of Viking settlements, Ireland's premier dynasty, the Uí Néill, actively began to shape a coalition of the country's major kingdoms against the Vikings. A 'kingship of Ireland' was thereby claimed for the Uí Néill king, though its basis was constituted more by personal alliances than by any institutional structures.

Across the Irish Sea there was a more complex picture of continuity and change. There had been warfare between Dál Riata and the Picts in the 8th century, with the latter in the ascendant initially, but Dál Riata dominant in the latter part of the century. Whether Dál Riata actually annexed lands in Pictish territory is uncertain, but after Vikings began to settle in the Western Isles there seems have been some movement eastward by inhabitants of Dál Riata. Given the fraught nature of sea-contact with Ireland, it is hardly surprising that the Irish annals, our sole contemporary source, contain only meagre information from outside Ireland from this period. Columban monasteries, precariously maintaining contact with fellow-monasteries to the west, may have been the channels of transmission for the surviving data.

This data indicates that records of kings styled *rex Fortrenn* seem to coincide with cessation of records referring to *rex Dál Riata* in the early part of the 9th century. Could this mean that Dál Riata kingship had transferred from its western homeland, establishing itself, as the title rex Fortrenn indicates, in a territory synonymous with southern Pictland? Such a move might recall an original transfer of royal authority from Antrim to Argyll in the unverifiable 6th century past. Did the Dál Riata leadership set out to re-invent its kingdom in a new location as a result of Viking pressure on the west? Lack of evidence prohibits firm conclusions at this point.

The annals do attest, however, that the territory ruled over by *rex Fortrenn* itself became a Viking target. A devastating attack on southern Pictland in the year 839 resulted in the killing of many nobles of the kingdom. In the aftermath of these events, the next ruler whom the annals title 'king of the Picts' is Cináed mac Ailpín, whom genealogies identify as a descendant of early Dál Riata kings. Significantly, it is Cináed who is retrospectively nominated in sources of the following century as the first Gaelic ruler from the west to establish his kingship in Pictland. Cináed's achievement may well have built on previous movement from west to east. Yet the history of his assumption of power matters less than the *fait accompli*. Indeed, more important still is the fact that the kingship gained by Cináed was retained by successive generations of his family. Dynastic rule by a Gaelic royal line became established over peoples and territories which were originally Pictish. The seeds of a new kingship were being sown.

While their new domain in Pictland set the Gaelic kingship of Cináed at a greater geographical remove from Ireland, nevertheless the ruler's Irish heritage was initially influential. On attaining power, Cináed renewed the close alliance which had existed in the west since Columba's time between Dál Riata rulers and the Columban community headed by Iona. The island now lay in Viking-dominated territory, but Cináed is reported to have brought relics of Columba from Iona to a church which he had founded in his new realm, probably at Dunkeld. Thus, he re-enlisted Columban prestige and patronage in support of the kingship which he had established. Moreover, the network of Columban monasteries which had been founded among the Picts from the 7th century must have played a significant role in the 9th century developments. While the Columban community was multi-ethnic in composition, its leadership's close association with the Irish world was epitomised by its continuing genealogical connection with the Uí Néill dynasty from Columba's day. Thus, the Columban presence in Pictland had the potential to be a significant support system for the advancement of Gaelic kingship and Gaelic culture among the Picts.

The family of Cináed evidently recognised the benefit, not only of Irish ecclesiastical connections, but also of Irish political connections. Around 870, when Cináed's son, Cusantin, was reigning, a daughter of Cináed, Mael Muire, was married to an Irish king, Áed Finnliath of the northern Uí Néill. The emergent dynasty had an evident interest in acquiring prestige and support through an Irish alliance, but the Irish side may well have had equal interest in securing overseas allies against Viking power on the Irish Sea. After the death of Áed Finnliath in the year 879, Mael Muire was married to an even more powerful Uí Néill king, Flann Sinna. This marriage apparently was significant as a strategic and symbolic assertion of Flann's position over his predecessor's kingdom rather than as an alliance with Mael Muire's dynasty. Yet, though not primarily designed to enhance the position of her royal relations, Mael Muire's marriage to Flann Sinna was at least indirectly instrumental in so doing.

Flann Sinna's father, Máel Sechnaill, had been the first Irish ruler to have been titled *rí Érenn,* 'king of Ireland', and Flann followed in his father's footsteps. Indeed, Flann's title of *rí Érenn* is prominently engraved on Irish artistic works made under his patronage, such as the Cross of the Scriptures at Clonmacnoise. The achievement of father and son lay in their rule over 'the men of Ireland', a designation which signified that their followers included, not only their own people, but those from other major kingdoms as well. It was this dimension of Uí Néill kingship which seems to have set a headline for their in-laws across the sea.

In the contemporary annal-notice of the death of Cináed's grandson in the year 900, he is not given the title of 'king of the Picts' held by his father, uncle, and grandfather. Rather, he is styled *rí Alban*, 'king of Alba', a new title which follows the Irish model. Just as his contemporary Flann Sinna could designate himself king over 'the men of Ireland' as a result of his obtaining allegiance from the various provinces, in the same way, rulership over Gaels and Picts, hitherto not explicit in the title 'king of the Picts', could be envisaged and expressed in a new way. Thus, in accordance with Irish practice, the island-name was adopted as a harmonising marker of identity for the diverse membership of a political collective. Rule over Gaels and Picts was redefined as rule over 'the men of Alba' and their king was thereby called *rí Alban*.

This new departure had far-reaching consequences. Gaels and Picts had been assigned a common denomination to which both could give assent. A change of name had evident psychological benefit as marking a departure from the past. While Pict and Gael had separate histories, collectively as 'the men of Alba' they could look forward to shaping a single future. The concept of a kingship of Alba provided an allegiance which looked to the future rather than to the past. It was to prove to have enduring force, so that inhabitants of the kingdom within a comparatively short space of time were identifying with, and being identified by, their new description as *Albanaig*, a designation which came to mean 'Scots'.

In fact, though the kingship initiated by Cináed owed much to Irish and Dál Riatan affiliations, in its redefined identity as the kingship of Alba, it began to chart an independent political course. Its new status was not unproblematic for men of learning and political theoreticians in Ireland. These sought to integrate past and present by constructing a view of 'the men of Alba' as lineal descendants of the settlers of Dál Riata. Thus, the people of the new kingdom could still be reckoned as belonging to the genealogically-defined kindred of the Irish. Indeed, up to the 11th century *fir Alban*, 'men of Alba' were theoretically counted as part of the Irish political cosmos, and as potential subjects of an Irish over-king. The reality, however, was that Alba had begun to regard itself as a separate political entity, and people who had divergent loyalties as Picts or Gaels now gave allegiance to a common kingship of Alba.

Yet political identity was not exclusive of other identities. Those who were politically *Albanaig* or Scots might still identify themselves culturally or linguistically as *Gaeil*. In fact, one of the striking features of the close of the first millennium is the manner in which the Gaelic language became a medium which linked peoples across the divides of ethnicity and political affiliation. It was not solely a cultural bond between those of Irish descent overseas and their kin in the homeland. Rather, as it became accepted as the common language of the new kingdom of Alba, it linked Pict and Gaeil across the divide of ethnicity. Furthermore, as it had been adopted as the language of the Viking settlers of the Western Isles, Gaelic became the medium of their integration with their neighbours on either side of the Irish Sea.

The language was not just a medium of practical communication between peoples of different origins and affiliations, it was also a medium for the transmission of a vibrant literature. This is probably best epitomised in the depiction around 1200 of the story-world of the heroes of the Fianna in the text known as *Acallam na Senórach*. These heroes are portrayed as equally at home in Ireland and in Alba. Warriors from the Hebrides are included in their companies. The verses of visiting Irish poets are intelligible to the king of Alba's Viking wife. The sub-text of such literary depictions is that the cultural world of hero-tales and poetry extended to all who shared a common language, whatever their affiliations. Poets and literary men had open access across political and ethnic boundaries, so that they created cultural bonds 'from Cape Clear to Caithness'.

Looking back over the history of the period leading up to the first millennium, therefore, it is evident that relationships across the Irish Sea had gone through many vicissitudes. Ultimately, the enduring connections were those of Christianity and of culture. In those areas, relationships were defined by inclusiveness and by the transcendence of boundaries. In the wake of the Viking era, Ireland and Scotland had developed politically separate kingdoms. The Columban monastic federation, which had linked communities in Dál Riata, Pictland and Ireland from the 6th century had lost most of its institutional transinsular dimension by this time also. Yet veneration of Columba and of Iona remained a common bond between Christians throughout the regions. Indeed, the holy island of Iona, a place of pilgrimage or burial for rulers from Ireland and Alba, was also the place of religious retirement for the Viking king of Dublin in the year 978. Thus, common Christianity offered the possibility of a shared heritage, while a common language and literature also provided a unifying cultural space for diverse peoples. The beginnings of Irish-Scottish history laid down important foundations for the future.

## Note

This article draws on my previous published work:

*Iona, Kells, and Derry: The history and hagiography of the monastic familia of Columba* (Oxford, 1988, repr. Dublin, 1996).

'The legacy of Columba', in TM Devine and JF McMillan (eds) *Celebrating Columba* (Edinburgh, 1999).

'Sea-divided Gaels: Constructing relationships between Irish and Scots c.800–1169', in B Smith (ed) *Britain and Ireland 900–1300* (Cambridge, 1999).

'*Rí Érenn, Rí Alban*: Kingship and identity in the ninth and tenth centuries', in Simon Taylor (ed) *Kings, Clerics and Chronicles in Scotland, 500–1297* (Dublin 2000).

# God and Gaelic:
# The Highland Churches
# and Gaelic Cultural Identity

Donald E Meek

This paper continues a process of reflection which was initially forced upon me in the late 1980s and the early 1990s.[1] The 'force' was supplied by invitations from different bodies to give papers on the theme of the relationship between Gospel and culture in the Scottish Highlands. Through the kindness of these bodies (which I am sure are not indulging in any form of conspiracy) I have been provoked into putting my thoughts into the public arena, and (more frighteningly) exposing my views on this sensitive subject to the scrutiny of the churches whose attitudes to Gaelic language and culture I have been encouraged to assess. The story of Daniel in the lions' den comes readily to mind whenever I embark on a paper on this theme. The Daniels are few, but the lions are many, and their mouths are hard to shut!

## Introducing the Highland churches

All the main Scottish churches have Highland wings, which, for the most part, have used the Gaelic language as a means of communicating their message. The Roman Catholic Church, once very strong in the Highlands, was progressively displaced, particularly during the course of the 18th century, and became a minority. Today the Roman Catholic Church is strongest in Barra, Eriskay, South Uist, the Small Isles (Rum, Eigg and Muck), and on the western edges of the Highland mainland. Protestant Presbyterianism became the dominant religious power in the area after 1690, and is represented today by the Church of Scotland, the Free Church of Scotland (formed by the Disruption of 1843), the Free Presbyterian Church of Scotland (formed by a secession from the Free Church in 1893), and the Associated Presbyterian

---

1. See Meek (1996a). For a list of my various articles, etc on this theme, see Douglas Ansdell (1998: 227–8).

Churches (formed in 1989, as a result of a split in the Free Presbyterian Church, precipitated by the suspension of one of its members, Lord Mackay of Clashfern, for attending a requiem mass). From 1900 the Highlands and Islands also accommodated congregations of the United Free Church of Scotland (formed by a union of the majority of the Free Church of Scotland with the United Presbyterians), but these have all vanished from the rural areas. The present Free Church of Scotland is the descendant of the minority which refused to enter the 1900 union.[2] In addition to accommodating various branches of Presbyterianism, the Highlands and Islands have also been home to several non-Presbyterian bodies: the Scottish Episcopal Church is still active in mainland Perthshire and Argyllshire, with some congregations in the Hebrides, while the Inner Hebridean islands of Colonsay, Islay, Mull and Tiree contain small Baptist churches, planted as a result of vigorous itinerant missionary endeavour in the first half of the 19th century (Bebbington 1988). I myself was brought up in the Baptist Church in Tiree, where my father was minister until 1965 (Meek 1988a). In the 1950s and early 1960s, my father preached predominantly in Gaelic; thus I heard 'pulpit Gaelic' on Sundays, and spoke 'ordinary Gaelic' for the rest of the week. At that time, Gaelic-speaking Baptists had a form of service very similar to that of evangelical Presbyterians. In part, my interest in the theme of the churches and culture stems from my very deep awareness that the 'Gaelic Baptists' of the Inner Hebrides were, in their hey-day, quite distinct from the majority of Lowland-based Scottish Baptists. Their profile was formed by their interaction with Gaelic language and culture.[3]

## Confronting complexity

If the profusion of churches in the Highlands is complex, the theme of Christianity and Gaelic culture is no less so. It becomes all the more challenging when it is set in the context of national or regional identity – the issue we are exploring in this book. In my own very limited experience, I have learned that it is very dangerous to generalise or to make assumptions.

---

2. Ansdell (1998) provides a very useful general account of the Highland churches. The classic account for the period 1688–1800 is John MacInnes (1951).

3. Since leaving Tiree in 1965, I have found it difficult to settle happily in any Lowland Baptist church. I would now define myself as an independent evangelical, as I am not currently in membership of any church or denomination, though my natural affiliation is with Baptists. I suspect that my unease may be due in part to the distinctively Gaelic flavour of Tiree Baptist Church as I knew it in my formative years. No Baptist church in the Hebrides (or elsewhere) now uses Gaelic in regular worship; I am, in effect, a relic of a bygone era! Lowland Baptist churches have their own distinctive cultural forms, though Lowlanders are not always aware of that, and tend to regard their 'way of doing things' as normal. (Therein lies another paper.)

The first issue in the complexity is to define 'culture'.[4] It is a slippery, all-embracing term, but perhaps those of us who are Gaelic speakers (and here I include Irish!) do have the advantage of being in minority cultures which are different from English mass culture, and are underpinned by a distinctive language. Language provides a particularly conspicuous marker which acts as an indicator of the way in which religious expression is seen to interact with the cultural context. A distinctive language can be either accepted or rejected, or perhaps merely tolerated, by a form of religion (in this case Christianity) which normally uses a majority language (in this case English). My main concern in this paper will be with the Gaelic language, but I will also touch briefly on those dimensions of Gaelic culture which cannot exist without the language – the songs, tales and forms of expression used and enjoyed by Gaelic people. It is possible for churches to embrace language while accepting selectively, or rejecting outright, certain other aspects of the associated culture.

The second issue in the complex weave of Christianity and culture is to assess how far Christianity interacts with culture in such a way as to create a distinctive brand of Christianity which may be 'Scottish', 'Highland', 'Gaelic' or whatever. Christianity, as represented in different churches and denominations, can never be wholly identified with a single culture. If it is totally identified with the whole of a culture, Christianity will cease to be distinctive. Christianity reserves the right to challenge culture. Even so, Christianity is born into different cultures, it responds to these cultures, and it takes much of its form from the conventions of these cultures. It also provokes responses from, and to, the cultures. These responses can vary with the nature of the individual culture, and also with time, place and denomination.[5]

Responses to culture can also vary within denominations or churches. All denominations known to me have their 'liberal' and 'conservative' wings, and approaches to culture vary accordingly. In the final analysis, denominations consist of individuals, and individuals may hold different views from the spokespersons of their denominations. What 'the minister' says may not be compatible with the view of 'the person in the pew'. Such distinctions can be multiplied. For this reason, 'the church's' view of culture may be open to question as a valid generalisation. When we speak about 'what the church did for Gaelic', we often mean 'what enthusiastic individuals within the church' did for Gaelic. Achievements such as monumental translations of the Bible into Gaelic (and Irish too) reflect the commitment of such individuals, who have sometimes gone against the flow of institutional policy, and have there-

---

4 See Lesslie Newbigin's definition at the end of this paper.

5. A very important set of papers on churches and culture across the globe can be found in John Stott and Robert T Coote (1979). (I am very grateful to my colleague, Professor Howard Marshall, for allowing me to consult his copy of this important volume.)

by preserved the honour of the institution in particular cultural contexts.[6] How we see their achievements and how we view the church(es) may also depend on our own relationship to the church(es) concerned. Few of us will be neutral, and our impressions will have been created primarily by the segment of the church(es) with which we are most familiar. There are few subjects on earth that can be more at the mercy of personal biases.

Despite these problems, it is with 'broader' Christian responses to Gaelic culture, including language, that I will be concerned primarily in this paper. I will reflect on how, and at what levels, Christianity has approached, and shaped, the Gaelic culture of the Highlands and Islands, and how Gaelic culture has shaped the kind of Christianity one finds in the Highlands. I will refer occasionally to similarities to, and differences from, the circumstances pertaining in Ireland. To aid my study, I propose to refer to the work of several theologians of culture, particularly Richard Niebuhr, whose book, *Christ and Culture* (published in Britain in 1952), remains fundamentally important to the debate. Niebuhr's book is a remarkable piece of scholarship, and, while global in its overall approach, is relevant to any attempt to assess Christian approaches to culture in these islands. It is curious (and doubtless a reflection of the impoverished nature of the debate) that Niebuhr's perspectives have not been applied to the Gaelic cultural context until now.[7] I will also draw on the writings of the late Bishop Lesslie Newbigin, whose books on many aspects of missionary strategy and indigenous culture are relevant to the discussion.[8]

## The Roman Catholic/Protestant divide

Let me begin with the Roman Catholic/Protestant divide which is known in both Ireland and Scotland, but is much less marked in the Scottish Highlands, at least in cultural terms, largely because Scottish Gaelic crosses religious and political divisions, and gives cultural cohesion to Protestants and Roman

---

6. Here I think particularly of William Bedell in Ireland and James and John Stuart in Scotland.

7. For a recent response to, and critique of, Niebuhr, see Glenn H Stassen et al (1996). (I am grateful to Maolcholaim Scott for drawing this book to my attention.) It is not my purpose in this paper to offer observations on Niebuhr's approach; I accept his main categories as broad working definitions. Nevertheless, I am somewhat uneasy with his use of the name of Christ to represent a particular view, since the positions relative to culture outlined by Niebuhr are not necessarily those of Christ himself; rather they are those which have been elaborated by Christ's followers in the course of the centuries. Some of these positions derive their essence from the scriptures, but others are conditioned by cultures and circumstances not consistent with those of the New Testament. This point is discussed effectively by Yoder (Stassen et al 1996: 58–61). As can be seen in the latter book, later critics have exposed some of Niebuhr's weaknesses, but it would be difficult to dislodge the general relevance of his categories. Of course, one can readily supplement these categories by others. Niebuhr's models may also need to be fine-tuned to suit different cultures.

8. In particular, I have benefited from Newbigin (1995).

Catholics. Sometimes people imagine that, in the Highlands, there is a clear line between Roman Catholics and Protestants when it comes to cultural identity. The post-Reformation dichotomy between Protestants and Roman Catholics is often seen as a dividing line between different attitudes to culture. The usual argument is that Protestants have been, and still are, far less tolerant of secular culture than Catholics; and that Gaelic tradition has been better preserved by Catholics than by Protestants.[9] Protestants, on the other hand, can take some pride in a long period of fairly active involvement in Gaelic culture; they stress, rightly, that Protestantism has been bolstered by the printing press, and that the printing press, applied in the Gaelic context, has contributed greatly to the maintenance of Gaelic, from the time that the first Gaelic book was published in 1567. That book was John Carswell's translation of John Knox's *Book of Common Order* (see Thomson 1970). Again, Protestants can point to the empowerment of Gaelic through preaching and praying, and to the literary activities of ministers (both moderates and evangelicals) who rescued much Gaelic song and story from oblivion.[10]

It is, however, arguable that Roman Catholicism and Protestantism have more in common in their approaches to culture, and specifically Gaelic culture, than we may think. It is true that certain forms of Protestantism in the Highlands have turned their backs on Gaelic culture because of its pagan taint, but it is also evident that Roman Catholicism in the Highlands has not been as supportive of Gaelic, per se, as it could have been. No denomination represented in the Highlands, Protestant or Catholic, has ever had an official policy supporting Gaelic (though the Free Church Presbytery of Lewis constructed a local policy in 1997).[11] If we look at Ireland, we find that Roman Catholicism has, at times, acted in ways that resemble evangelical Protestantism in the Highlands, and has turned its back on Irish and Irish culture (Wall 1969: 84–5). The 'flight from Irish' in Ireland had to be counteracted in the first half of the 19th century by the protestations of Scottish evangelical Protestants such as the Rev Christopher Anderson, the founder of the Edinburgh Society for the Support of Gaelic Schools.[12]

It will be useful here to introduce the work of Richard Niebuhr to define Christian approaches to culture. The first of Niebuhr's models in *Christ and Culture* is the position which he calls 'Christ against culture', in which Christians reject secular culture because of its pagan associations (1952:

9. This is the generally accepted position; see, for example, MacDonald (1968: 181).
10. Pending a fuller study of this theme, see Meek (1996a: 42–3).
11. It remains to be seen whether the policy formulated by the Free Church Presbytery of Lewis will be more than a dead letter.
12. See Christopher Anderson's remarkable book (1828), packed with relevant detail and arguments for the maintenance of the Irish language. For an overview of Anderson, see Meek 1992 (ed), especially pp 17–24.

58–92). Antipathy to pagan culture is found in some early church fathers, notably Tertullian (c160–c225 AD), whose question, 'What has Athens to do with Jerusalem?', has echoed down the centuries in different forms (MacMullen 1997: 87–8). This attitude is well attested in the Scottish Highlands, from the time of John Carswell to the present day. Yet it is by no means a solely Protestant response. Pre-Reformation and Roman Catholic believers have also built walls (sometimes literally) between themselves and the paganism of secular culture. There have been, and still are, monasteries in the Highlands, whose occupants have taken nothing whatsoever to do with Gaelic culture.[13] The severely devotional medieval Valliscaulian monastery at Beauly, for example, contributed nothing (as far as we know) to Gaelic culture. Christian devotion in any context, and in any denomination, demands a differentiated lifestyle in order to bear witness to the transforming power of the Gospel. This may lead to separation from the world and from those things that would destroy the Christian's single-minded contemplation of Christ. On the other hand, Christians both before and after the Reformation achieved working compromises with secular culture.[14] We cannot assume that a line can be drawn between Catholic and Protestant attitudes to culture in the Scottish Highlands.

## 'Calvinism' and culture

It is no safer to assume that the urge to reject secular culture is the peculiar trait of a 'Calvinistic' strand within the Protestant family or that it occurs solely in the Highlands of Scotland. It is shared by several Protestant bodies, including those who would not pay even as much as lip service to the name of John Calvin. As I have already indicated, I was brought up in a strongly evangelical Baptist family in the Inner Hebridean island of Tiree, and I was well aware that certain aspects of secular culture (eg, consumption of alcohol and social occasions which encouraged such behaviour) were simply unacceptable. John Calvin was never mentioned, but the Bible was well known and its principles were followed. My parents nevertheless fostered my interest in Gaelic language, song and story. In other contexts, too, 'vain' or 'pagan' aspects of culture can be rejected in a manner which may be seen superficially as the consequence of 'Calvinism'. For instance, in a report on missionary work in a very different island, Papua New Guinea, in 1996, it is stated that 'it is unfortunate that some Pentecostal groups denounce all pre-Christian cul-

---

13. I have chosen this example almost at random, but it is perhaps worth noting that, even in the Middle Ages, the Highlands tended to attract strictly regulated forms of Christianity. In addition to their house at Beauly, Valliscaulians established themselves at Ardchattan, Argyll.

14. This is particularly evident in the early Irish context, notably in the recording and composition of early Irish tales and sagas within an ecclesiastical (and commonly monastic) milieu.

ture as worthy only of obliteration'[15] – and Calvin has nothing to do with Pentecostalism. You will be aware, of course, that in Scotland John Calvin and the baneful blight of 'Calvinism' are popularly believed to be among the primary sources of the country's many ills. The 'dour Scot' is 'dour' either because of the weather or the theology; in addition to the likelihood of being frequently soaked by the rain, he or she runs the risk of imbibing (with the mother's milk) the vicious, soul-destroying doctrines of Geneva. A version of this paradigm is found in the Highlands and in works dealing with 'Highland Christianity'. It claims that the 'Calvinist church' banished joy and happiness and songs and cèilidhs from the Highlands. This stereotype – an intellectual short-cut which is sometimes driven by an emotional sense of exclusion from the spiritual community – flourishes in literature, in Gaelic and English (Meek 1996a: 58–61).[16]

Calvin, by this understanding, is the epitome of Niebuhr's 'Christ against culture'. Yet, when we read Niebuhr's book, and come to his fifth model, 'Christ the transformer of culture', we discover (somewhat to our surprise) that Calvin's view of culture is predominantly one of transformation (1952: 192–218). Thus it follows that Calvinism which is true to its founder (rather than to later reformulators, like Calvin's successor, Theodore Beza, who reacted very strongly against his own youthful poetic indiscretions and imparted a very hard theological and cultural shape to post-Calvin 'Calvinism') seeks to remould and reshape culture to serve the cause of Christ, and hopes to achieve the cleansing and reutilisation of secular culture, rather than its destruction.[17] Calvin was much more tolerant of benighted

---

15. Brenda Worton, 'Mission in Melanesia', *New Christian Herald*, 17 August 1996, pp 10–11. This should not be taken as a comment on the approaches of all missionary work in Papua New Guinea; this would be to commit the same error with 'Pentecostalism' as is commonly committed with 'Calvinism'. The paragraph from which this observation is taken reads as follows: 'Most Christian workers seek to remove only the negative and harmful tribal practices. All the "mainstream" denominations are anxious to uphold a culture fascinating in its diversity. Tribal music and dance have been integrated into Christian worship. It is unfortunate that some Pentecostal groups denounce all pre-Christian culture as worthy only of obliteration.' The role of many (though not all) modern missionaries in seeking to preserve indigenous customs and practices in the face of intense westernisation in such regions as Melanesia deserves notice, since the popular (mis)conception of missionaries (as of Highland 'Calvinist' ministers) equates them with cultural destruction. Stereotyping of ministers and missionaries is a global pastime.
16. Most recently, Ronald I Black refers to Highlanders' experience of 'a ghastly 200-year cycle of Macpherson's Ossian, Calvinism, landlordism, emigration, clearance, famine, cannon-fodder, balmorality, land struggle, educational deracination and population drift'(1998: 3). One must be grateful for the small mercy that 'Calvinism' is seen as part of this 'cycle', rather than its sole cause and effect.
17. Niebuhr concludes that Calvin's emphases 'lead to the thought that what the gospel promises and makes possible, as divine (not human) possibility, is the transformation of mankind in all its nature and culture into a kingdom of God in which the laws of the kingdom have been written upon the inward parts' (1952: 217). Thus, according to Niebuhr's interpretation of Calvin, Calvin believed that human nature and culture could be reclaimed ultimately for Christ.

pagans than his successors have generally been.[18] Therefore, not only do we have to be careful that we do not blame Calvin for all our cultural disasters, we also have to ask why it is that, when certain parts (at least) of the Highland churches do turn their backs on secular culture, they are conforming to what is widely recognised to be a world-eschewing model which is more typical of 16th century Anabaptists and later English Puritans than of John Calvin. That is a question which I will seek to answer in this paper.

When we look closely at Christianity in the Highlands, and especially the Protestant representations of Christianity, we certainly find evidence for 'Christ against culture', but we also find evidence for 'Christ the transformer of culture'. The transformation of Scottish Gaelic culture can be seen to a large degree in the use of Gaelic in worship, the adaptation of secular tunes for Gaelic hymns and the general influence of the Gospel in society. There has been a beneficial element of transformation alongside a more conspicuous element of rejection. It is also true to say that, just as Christianity has transformed parts of Gaelic culture, that same process of transformation has worked in the other direction and has imparted a distinctive flavour to what is sometimes called 'Highland religion'. Dr Jane Dawson has recently argued the case for the existence of 'Highland Calvinism' with a distinctively Gaelic cultural 'wrap' in the 17th century. Thus a form of Christian expression which owed much to Geneva and (after 1647) to Westminster wore Highland dress (Dawson 1994).

One of the reasons for the acceptance or rejection of certain parts of Gaelic culture has little to do with Calvin, but a lot to do with the ways in which the Protestant church approached the task of evangelising the Scottish Highlands. It had to find a way into the culture. The church therefore established a *modus vivendi* with Gaelic secular culture in the 16th and 17th centuries. As a consequence of the church's accommodational approach at this stage, the foundation of a Gaelic Protestant religious culture was laid in the Highlands. It was, of course, a carefully built foundation; it aimed to preserve spiritual purity, and for that reason it did not draw its sustenance from all aspects of Gaelic secular culture.[19] Ireland could have followed the same path, and did so to a certain extent, but Scotland's Protestant Gaelic culture became distinctive from the immediate post-Reformation period. The Highland Protestant church assumed an identity which was strongly influenced by

---

18. For a stimulating discussion of this theme and wider issues, see MacFhionnlaigh (1996: 37–50, especially pp 42–3).
19. For some preliminary perspectives on this complex theme, see Meek (1996a), and Dawson (1994). See also the very important article by TP McCaughey (1989).

Gaelic – despite the fact that the overarching political strategy of central government, from at least the early 17th century, was to eradicate Gaelic.[20]

## The transformation of classical culture

It may be useful to bring Ireland and Scotland together at this point to show the degree of common ground which they held at an early stage, though they went their different ways in a later period. It is well known that Ireland and Gaelic Scotland shared a common cultural tradition in the Middle Ages; the two countries had a common high culture, a Roman Catholic culture which was given shape by a classical literary language, schools of poetry, law and other institutions. The Protestant church in both Ireland and Scotland found its way into the Gaelic world by employing the high culture of the late Middle Ages. It was the classical literary language, perfected by the poets, which was used by John Carswell to translate Knox's *Book of Common Order* (Thomson 1970: 13–14). It was the classical language too which was employed in Ireland in the bible translations of William Ó Domhnaill and William Bedell in the 17th century (Meek 1988b). In the 18th century, a modified form of this classical language (Early Modern Scottish Gaelic) was employed in Scotland by the 'translators' of the Scottish Gaelic New Testament (1767) and the Old Testament (1801); modified, that is, to come closer to the vernacular language of Gaelic Scotland (ibid: 15–18). This Scottish form of modified classical Gaelic came to be the language of the church, in psalmody, sermons and prayer. This style still underpins the form of Gaelic used in the Protestant churches of the Highlands (Meek 1996a: 38–42).

'Christ the transformer of culture' is therefore attested in the Highlands, and to some extent in Ireland, in the 16th and 17th centuries. In Gaelic Scotland, as in Ireland, it is certainly the case that the Protestant church absorbed Gaelic classical culture and transformed parts of it for its own use. The process in Scotland was, however, much more thorough-going. The church in the Highlands came to have control of the high culture of Gaelic, and a fairly high-brow form of Gaelic Protestantism emerged.[21] Thereafter, in the 18th and 19th centuries, we find that some aspects of secular Scottish Gaelic culture were transformed and reclaimed by the Protestant church. But there was a limit to such reclamation. Why did the Protestant church in the Highlands fail to reclaim the whole of Gaelic culture for religious purposes?

---

20. The church's general approach, taking its colour from that of government, is discussed in some detail (and perhaps a little glee) by John Lorne Campbell (1945).

21. Contemporary Scottish Gaelic lacks a well developed high culture. One reason for this must be that high culture became the domain of the Protestant church, which seriously constricted its range. It failed to grow beyond the point reached c1690; the connection between ecclesiastical culture and the earlier creative arts of the Middle Ages was largely forgotten.

# The rejection of popular culture

The failure of the Protestant church to reclaim the whole of Gaelic culture reflects not only its understanding of culture, but also its practical inability to conquer the entire land. It battled constantly to assert its supremacy over popular culture, but did not succeed to the same degree as with high culture, partly because it never had enough personnel to evangelise the whole Highland area. It had barely enough men to maintain the high culture position. After 1690, following the restoration of Presbyterianism in Scotland, the Protestant church in the Highlands got into 'missionary mode'. Its efforts were supplemented pre-eminently by the Society in Scotland for Propagating Christian Knowledge (SSPCK), which assumed a strongly anti-Gaelic stance until the middle of the 18th century, and aimed to eradicate both Gaelic and Popery. Other missionary societies joined the fray after 1800 (Meek 1997).

As a result of the crusading spirit of successive Protestant missions to the region, an 'external', antipathetic view of Gaelic culture gained ground. This was rather different from the internal perspectives which informed the use of the classical language in the 16th and 17th centuries. The Protestant church tended to internalise the 'external' perspective. Indeed, some would claim that it was the chief promoter of that perspective (Meek 1997). Its ancillary agencies (like the SSPCK) came to see popular culture, including the Gaelic language, as inimical to the Gospel. This view prevailed for much of the 18th century. Post-1800 missionaries were kinder to the language. Nevertheless, raw popular culture was generally perceived to contain superstition, immorality, intemperance and other vices, including (pre-eminently) Popery, which issued in rebellion and insurrection.[22] In the midst of such godlessness, the Protestant church in the Highlands, increasingly influenced by Puritan paradigms (eg, Bunyan), developed an 'inner circle' of men and women who formed a 'godly community', distinct from the world around them (rather like Anabaptists).[23] The role of missionary endeavour (some of it very much Baptist) in helping to create this 'inner circle' and in condemning 'the world' is apparent in the fact that ministers who served as front-line, itinerant missionaries among Gaelic-speaking Highlanders were often the ones who indulged in the strongest condemnations of popular culture. James

---

22. Popery and insurrection were major concerns of eighteenth century bodies like the SSPCK. They were less prominent after 1800, but 'popish scares' were by no means unknown, since they helped to boost Protestant missionary activity.
23. Much Puritan literature was translated into Gaelic after 1750. It is beyond doubt that this encouraged the emergence of a deeply introspective and at times almost mystical form of spirituality; cf MacFhionnlaigh (1996: 40–1).

MacGregor (1759–1830), a native of St Fillans, Perthshire, who became a missionary minister in Nova Scotia, articulated his Gaelic version of 'Christ against culture' with a precision which shows how well he himself knew the old, 'unconverted' culture of the Highlands:

Cha noimheachd air Oisean nam Fionn
No gaisgeach bha riamh am feachd;
Cha noimheachd air creachadh nan Gall
Le ceathairn nan gleann 's nan srachd,
No idir air siubhal nan gleann
An éideadh nach ceangladh glùn;
Cha noimheachd air fineachan treun
A chogadh 's nach géilleadh beò,
Clann Ghriogair bha aineolach, gleusd',
Clann Domhnuill le'm b' aiteas làmh dhearg,
Clann Chamshroin bha calma gun chéill,
Ach noimheachd air soisgeul nan gràs,
Bhi sgaoileadh 's gach àird mun cuairt (MacInnes 1969–70: 336).

It is not a story of Oisean of the Fians
or of a hero who was ever in a troop;
nor yet a story of the plundering of the Goill
by the strong men of the glens and straths,
nor does it have to do with traversing the glens
in an attire that would not impede a knee;
it is not a story about brave clans
who would fight and not yield while alive,
Clan Gregor who were ignorant, though skilled,
Clan Donald who rejoiced in the Red Hand,
Clan Cameron who were brave but senseless -
rather it is a story of the Gospel of grace
spreading around in every direction.

'Clan culture' and its associated wildness thus bore the brunt of the missionary attack; 'Christ against culture' became the implicit approach among the converted and their leaders. This is nowadays seen by many as the typical Presbyterian 'slant' on culture in the Scottish Highlands.

Yet, alongside such rejection, the missionary movement continued to transform certain aspects of popular culture for its own purposes. The Gaelic language was used as a vigorous preaching medium, and it was 'sanitised' and strengthened through this role. The 'sanitising' of secular tradition too is evident in the work of no less a person than the aforesaid James MacGregor, who used the metres and tunes of popular Gaelic songs to convey his 'new' evangelical message. In fact, his enthusiasm for the secular tunes was such that, on at least one occasion, he gave some offence to the tastes of the truly ascetic evangelicals of his own day (MacInnes 1951: 274). Likewise Peter Grant (1783–1867) of Grantown on Spey, the celebrated Baptist evangelist and composer of Gaelic hymns, ostensibly rejected the old paganism of the Highlands, but used the tunes of the 'vain songs' for his hymns (Meek: forthcoming). Sometimes individual evangelical ministers, like Neil MacKenzie of St Kilda (1906), made important collections of secular Gaelic songs.[24]

The missionary movement may have failed to convert the entire Highlands, but through preaching, teaching (the latter in the Gaelic School Societies), hymnology and publication it did succeed in converting the Gaelic language and certain crucial aspects of the culture for evangelical use. In Gaelic Scotland much more was achieved than in Ireland, chiefly because Protestantism became the dominant faith in Scotland, and Protestantism was of a mind to use the serviceable parts of the indigenous Gaelic culture of the Highlands to communicate the Gospel. In Ireland, Protestants were a minority group who made fitful use of Irish to communicate the Gospel, but they lacked the power of their counterparts in Scotland to facilitate the use of Irish as a widely effective evangelistic medium. In addition to facing deeply entrenched prejudices, they had problems in finding personnel, and at times had to bring Gaelic ministers over from Scotland.[25]

Therein lies a fundamental difference between the religious and political affiliations of the Gaelic languages of Ireland and Scotland. The salvation of Gaelic in Scotland was connected to the manner in which it was taken up and used by the evangelical movement, and thus enclosed in a predominantly Protestant frame. In Ireland (and pre-eminently in Northern Ireland) Irish is identified primarily with Roman Catholicism, despite the growing Protestant interest in the north (McCoy 1997). Would the Gaelic language have survived in Scotland if it had not been brought within the Protestant, evangelical fold?

## The conversion of culture – or a culture of conversion?

Despite its tendency to reject certain aspects of Gaelic culture, the Protestant church in the Scottish Highlands pulled close to Gaelic. In assessing the ways in which the Protestant faith adapted itself to Highland culture, Niebuhr's work is again relevant. He offers three other models of interaction between Christianity and culture – 'the Christ of culture', 'Christ above culture' and

---

24. I mention MacKenzie's contribution to the preservation of Gaelic culture since it offers a counterbalance to the general view of evangelicalism as one of the main factors in the decay of St Kildan culture and society.

25. The problems faced by Protestants in Ireland are well sketched out by TC Barnard (1993). See also the excellent overview by Roger Blaney (1996).

'Christ and culture in paradox'. These have all have been attested in the Highlands at some point. Some can even be identified at the present time. We can readily find parallels for 'the Christ of culture' (Niebuhr 1952: 93–122). By this model, Christ is interpreted through culture, and is the sum and substance of the virtues of the culture; at its most extreme, this is a deistic position more typical of theological liberalism, and it is apparently espoused nowadays by some of the devotees of 'Celtic Christianity' (Meek 1996b).

Yet this position contains an important general truth, namely that Christ is perceived and interpreted through the lens of culture. In addition to being perceived through culture, He is seen to accept or reject aspects of the relevant culture. In the same way, the lifestyle of converts to evangelical Christianity is expected to conform to a certain cultural pattern. Thus the restrictions and taboos which evangelical Protestantism in the Highlands places on church members are conditioned by Gaelic culture, and consist of the abandonment of such pursuits as dancing, piping and the singing of secular songs (Meek 1996a: 45–8). Such requirements cannot be readily transferred to (let us say) Africa, where the issues for Christian believers, relative to secular culture, may be quite different. The question of playing the bagpipes for a Highland Christian may equate with playing the drums for African Christians, but very different perceptions may be evident in Africa.[26]

Although a Christian must stand apart from 'the world', a conversion model which unduly emphasises the convert's rejection of certain aspects of culture is potentially open to criticism for a number of reasons. First, it is possible to exhibit the symptoms of conversion without a genuine experience of saving faith. This outward (but misleading) conformity may extend to other aspects of evangelicalism. For example, sabbatarianism or some other cause can be espoused by people who have made no real commitment to the Christian faith. Legalism of this kind can lead to confrontations which do nothing to commend the cause of Christ.[27] Second, culture changes with time, and the dangerous aspects of culture also change. Thus, what may have been regarded as particularly inimical to faith 100 years ago may not be as dangerous in the closing years of the 20th century, partly because of the salvific power of the Gospel itself; conversely, there may be aspects of 20th-century culture which are potentially very dangerous for Christians, but which may not be recognised as such by the churches. Third, the churches' insistence on the 'sinfulness' of particularly 'small' aspects of culture may seem ridicu-

---

26. Cf the list of 'practices [which] must be given up by all those who wish to call themselves Christians' in Stephen Neill (1979: 13–17). The 'practices' rejected by evangelical believers in the Highlands seem slight by comparison, and it is evident that a fair number are cultural 'signals' rather than profoundly ethical choices; most belong to Neill's Type 4.

27. I am thinking here of the 'verbal salvoes' which are launched whenever the question of 'Sunday ferries' becomes an issue in Lewis and Harris.

lous in the context of greater concerns, including the over-riding importance of maintaining evangelism and a positive Gospel witness. Fourth, there is a very real danger that culture may be used to judge the quality of a person's spiritual life. If a convert takes to do with a 'taboo' area (eg, the singing of secular Gaelic songs in public contexts), it may be assumed that he or she may be in severe spiritual danger, in a 'compromised' position, or even 'decon-verting'. The same yardstick can be applied to churches or denominations when their members are seen (by rival denominations) to be associating them-selves with the forbidden domains of culture.[28]

The 'culture of conversion' which has developed in the Highlands may reflect another of Niebuhr's models. In 'Christ and culture in paradox', he describes a position in which Christ and culture stand in tension with one another, reflecting a dualistic conflict between the nature of God and the nature of man, not between Christianity and paganism, as happens with 'Christ against culture'. The 'paradox model', as Niebuhr reminds us, passes judgement on human nature across the board, and feels 'the sordidness of everything that is creaturely, human and earthly when it is in the presence of the holy' (1952: 158). The 'paradox model' is by no means unknown to Highlanders. I have often heard very similar sentiments (consistent with Paul's statement that 'all have sinned and come short of the glory of God') uttered in evangelical Gaelic preaching in the Highlands. In fact, it seems to me that the model of 'Christ and culture in paradox' (typical of Luther rather than Calvin) has greater sway in the Protestant Highlands than that of 'Christ against culture'. This is because the essentially dualistic 'culture of conversion' (what people must reject negatively, rather than what they ought to embrace positively) has become the core of Highland religious experience. This form of dualism helps to maintain the position of 'Christ against culture', even when 'pagan' elements of secular culture have lost their old associations.[29]

It is this dualism too which gives rise to the stereotypes which are regular-ly assaulted by contemporary poets and writers. The broader interaction of Gospel and culture, through a wide range of contact-points, is forgotten. It needs to be remembered that the Highland Presbyterian churches have only small cores of people who are full members, and who would be expected to adhere strictly to a rejectionist position with regard to culture. The majority of those associated with the churches are adherents, who do not sit at the Lord's table and partake of communion. Nevertheless, they are often included in the

---

28. The animosity between the Free Presbyterian Church and the Free Church often reveals itself in sharp comments by the former on the cultural 'compromises' of the latter. See, for example, 'FP maga-zine attacks Free Church "party" ', *West Highland Free Press*, 18 April 1997.
29. There has been little, if any, reflection within the Highland churches on the manner in which the Gospel can purify and reclaim originally 'pagan' aspects of secular culture.

total tally of members of the conservative Presbyterian churches. Thus, there have been, and continue to be, many families who have close links with the churches, but who maintain the 'vain songs' and many aspects of older Gaelic tradition. In the case of some members and even elders of churches, a delight in Gaelic secular tradition, particularly song, has not been eradicated. Dualism may be something for the sabbath, and for defining standards in the head, but it does not always hold firm in the heart or in the home (Meek 1996a: 50–2).

## Catholicism and culture

In 'Christ above culture' Niebuhr presents a model in which Christ is seen as being part of culture, but he is ultimately beyond culture; he is not simply an aggregate of all the good things in culture. He is higher and greater than all of these. As a result, humanity strives to achieve union with him, through monasticism, meditation and 'works' of various kinds. This too is a synthesist position, but it differs from 'the Christ of culture' in having an overarching concept of Christ. From the time of Thomas Aquinas, this has been the main Roman Catholic position (Niebuhr 1952: 123–53). This has allowed Roman Catholicism to bring together both sacred and secular, while preserving transcendence. The high culture of the Gaelic world in the later Middle Ages was the beneficiary of this synthetic approach; secular texts were transcribed and recorded, bardic verse was used for sacred and secular purposes, and Gaelic culture was sustained by secular patrons who acknowledged the central role of the church. In the Scottish Highlands after the Reformation, the Roman Catholic Church was displaced from the high culture of the Gaelic Middle Ages by the tactics of the Protestant church, which managed to repackage classical Gaelic as its own commodity. The result (paradoxically) was that the Roman Catholic Church, in ordinary life, drew closer to Gaelic popular culture, while employing (until Vatican II) ecclesiastical Latin for its main church offices.[30] The predominant use of Latin until a fairly late stage may also have brought an unexpected 'benefit', namely that the Roman Catholics were not compelled to adhere to an upper-register Gaelic liturgy (although they had such).[31] They could therefore interact more freely with the vernacular language. Occasionally, however, this may have made it difficult for priests to communicate across the Gaelic dialects; one of the advantages of Protestant

---

30. MacDonald (1968: 181) points out that 'Although [the Roman Catholic Church] has traditionally used Latin for the most important parts of its liturgy, in Gaelic-speaking areas a great deal of Gaelic has been used, for example in the readings of epistle and gospel, in litanies, sermons, hymns and special services, and parish priests have been expected either to have or acquire sufficient knowledge of the language to enable them to carry out their pastoral duties.'
31. MacFarlane (1834; most recent edition, Stirling, 1963) contains the Gaelic versions of Catholic prayers, missal and liturgy.

'church Gaelic' is that its supra-dialectal register provides a core of well-known theological terminology and diction.[32] Acceptance of other aspects of Gaelic culture was eased by the fact that 'conversion' to the doctrines of the Roman Catholic Church did not always demand a renunciation of 'the world'.

These factors perhaps explain the cultural complexion of the Roman Catholic faith in the islands; there is a much higher degree of active integration between the Catholic Church and Gaelic secular culture, with a more obvious degree of ecclesiastical affirmation of the latter. This can be seen in various contexts. In the community context, it is attested in the special services for the blessing of the fishing fleet. At the creative level, it is exemplifed, for instance, in the prayers, charms and incantations, *Carmina Gadelica*, gathered in the islands by Alexander Carmichael in the second half of the 19th century, and currently at the centre of the revival of 'Celtic Christianity' (Meek 1996b: 146). Again, Fr Ewen MacEachan's 19th-century translation of the New Testament admits a far higher proportion of vernacular Gaelic than one finds in the Protestant 1767 translation (Meek 1988b: 20–1). In Gaelic scholarship, it is noteworthy that priests have taken a keen interest in Gaelic lexicography, represented in the dictionary (1932) of Cyril Dieckhoff and the very valuable vocabulary list produced by Allan MacDonald of Eriskay (Campbell 1958). Priests have also contributed to major modern initiatives. The Scottish Gaelic *fèis* movement, for example, began in the early 1980s in the predominantly Roman Catholic island of Barra. It was instigated (in part) by the local priest at that time, Fr Colin MacInnes, who is currently in Ecuador. Fr MacInnes (with whom I worked on Gaelic committees) was also active in Gaelic language revivalism of other kinds, notably in broadcasting. Several priests have been strong supporters of modern Gaelic activism.[33]

## The churches and the contemporary Gaelic 'revival'

We can see that all the various models sketched by Niebuhr can be found in the Highlands at different stages, sometimes simultaneously, and even in the same person (as the example of James MacGregor indicates). Niebuhr's models are, of course, guides to attitudes, rather than definitions which belong to particular times or places, though there are phases when one model appears to hold greater sway than another. The models operate in the present as well as in the past. They are also stimulated and, at times, re-created afresh by changing ecclesiastical and cultural perspectives. When we turn to the closing years of the 20th century, with their liberalising, post-modern ethos, this last

---

32. Cf the comments on Fr Colin Grant in Alasdair Roberts, 'William McIntosh: An untypical link between east and west Highland Catholicism', *The Innes Review*, 42 (2): 140–1, and also p 142, footnote 22.
33. This was evident in the contribution of priests to Comunn na Gàidhlig in the 1980s.

point is well illustrated in the Gaelic context. It is apparent that 'Christ against culture' and 'Christ and culture in paradox' are currently very potent within Highland evangelicalism. The Protestant churches, especially those which hold conservative positions, have become increasingly embattled in their fight against the world, the flesh and the Devil. They therefore tend to oppose the bad, rather than act as facilitators of the good. The integrating strand of 'Christ the transformer of culture' has been apparent at various points, but is now wearing thin. We in Gaelic Scotland are presently at a stage when 'Christ and culture in paradox' and even 'Christ against culture' are being ever more heavily stressed by the spokespersons of the conservative Protestant denominations (whose views, it must be remembered, may not be those of all within their denominations).

One of the potential casualties of this new drive towards purity is the Gaelic language. Until recently the Gaelic language was 'above the battle', so to speak. It is not so any longer. The use of Gaelic within the churches is now under severe threat. One minister (a Free Presbyterian) subscribes to a paradigm which could be called 'God against Gaelic'. He has concluded that, since the number of Gaelic-speaking candidates for the ministry of his denomination has declined to zero, God's will is against the continuation of Gaelic.[34] This may seem logical enough, but it is a human observation, based on one particular denomination, and may not be true of others, such as Roman Catholics, who have been able to maintain a supply of Gaelic priests – with God's approval, I presume! In fact, the numerical decline of Gaelic-speaking candidates for the ministry is part of a very serious and much wider problem with ministerial recruitment which is affecting both the Free Presbyterians and the Free Church of Scotland at present.[35] This, at base, has nothing to do with language, but may have something to do with the manner in which these churches are now perceived. Recent controversies have given them unfortunate publicity, and this may have contributed to the difficulty. If the Almighty is speaking through this state of affairs, he seems to be saying less about Gaelic than about the consequences of unseemly squabbles which, in the

---

34. 'Since the Lord is not sending out Gaelic-speaking labourers to toil in His harvest, I must draw the conclusion that it is not His will that Gaelic survive as a language' (thus quoted by Ted Brocklebank in the *Daily Express*, 23 May 1996, p 9). The minister in question is anxious to stress that this was a personal observation. More recently he has made it clear that his observation applies to his own denomination: see Peter MacAulay, 'Loosening link between Gaelic and the churches', *West Highland Free Press*, 21 November 1997, p 7.

35. Several recent newspaper articles report this difficulty; see, among others, '[Free Presbyterian] Church runs out of future ministers', *Press and Journal*, 20 May 1996, and 'Free Church in secret discussions with Kirk', ibid, 14 March 1998, where it is claimed that 'Now, for the first time in living memory, there are no new student applications [for the ministry of the Free Church].'

longer term, undermine the credibility of the churches.[36]

In addition to the negative impression given by their internal wrangles, the spokespersons of the churches are in danger of creating unnecessary tension between themselves and their communities. This is reflected in their occasional comments on Gaelic culture. The minister to whom I have already alluded believes that the quality and purity of Gaelic are being undermined by secular broadcasters and those who are now fighting for the language.[37] It is evident that the latter perspective also finds a place within the Free Church of Scotland, which, from time to time, sees fit to fire at 'the Gaelic lobby', which, it claims, has 'little or no interest in the church'.[38] Precisely what is meant by 'the Gaelic lobby' or 'little or no interest in the church' is not clear; it is likely that the ecclesiastical gunners have their sights on specific individuals rather than 'the lobby' as a whole.

The churches are, of course, aware of the wider world. They know that their own role within the Gaelic world is now less prominent and less credible than it was. They are also keenly conscious that, as a culture shift takes place, English is penetrating Gaelic communities at a considerable rate. Pressure to provide more English-language services is growing, not least among young people, many of whom prefer to hear a service in English rather than Gaelic.[39] The churches' argument for the use of English is thus pragmatic. Christ is, in Niebuhr's phrase, 'above culture'. Culture must not dictate the way that the faith is proclaimed; the Gospel should not become the hostage of culture. We may accept that. However, there is room for realistic reassessment, rather than disorderly, panic-stricken retreat. There is need to develop new models of Gaelic worship to meet the rising generation of Gaelic learners, for example. It is this need that the churches are failing to address.[40] The model on which the Protestant churches have operated across the centuries has been moulded by classical Gaelic culture (as we have already seen); the main bible texts, the Gaelic metrical psalter, and the language of preaching are indebted to the classical tradition. To preserve Gaelic in the churches, it would be wiser to move to a contemporary Gaelic model of text and language which would make use of modern vernacular Gaelic to a greater extent. It is, however, improbable that the churches will have the desire or the flexibility to move to such a model. Seeing Gaelic (rather than the churches'

36. The tensions within the Free Church over the last three years have undoubtedly had an influence on recruitment, but there are other factors too, including the status of the courses offered by its college in Edinburgh. See ibid.
37. MacAulay, 'Loosening link', note 34.
38. See my letter in response to this claim in *The Monthly Record of the Free Church of Scotland*, October 1996, p 229.
39. MacAulay, 'Loosening link', note 34.
40. Attempts to assist the churches to reflect on these issues have, on the whole, met with little success.

use of Gaelic) as outmoded or sullied removes the need to think and act in a fresh and stimulating manner about the future of the language in worship. It is easier to move directly to English.

The current position of Gaelic in the churches thus gives great cause for concern. There are, admittedly, signs of hope within the Free Church; the creation of a Gaelic policy by the Presbytery of Lewis in 1997, and also the reintroduction of Gaelic services in Aberdeen and Perth in 1998, are very welcome moves. Nevertheless, policies on the training and placement of Gaelic ministers are conspicuous by their absence. Much depends on whether a minister with Gaelic can be found by the congregation, and whether the need for such a minister is upheld in the face of the current scarcity.[41]

In general, across the denominations, it appears that a considerable chasm is opening between the churches and the Gaelic enthusiasts. The churches are seen (rightly or wrongly) to be retreating 'officially' from Gaelic at the very time that many people are finding pleasure and identity in it. These people, of course, are not always conventional Highlanders, with a respect for the church. Not all members of the modern Gaelic community, far less those of 'the Gaelic lobby', are home-made, conservative evangelicals (though 'the lobby' does have a lot of support from that quarter). As a consequence, one side sees the other as a threat or an irrelevance; 'Christ against culture' becomes the watchword of both sides. Here, it seems, is one of the great Gospel opportunities of our time, and the Highland churches seem ill-prepared for it, and perhaps even unwilling to face it.

## Conclusion

Gaelic culture has influenced the churches in the Highlands in several different ways across the centuries. Their identity has been defined, at least partly, in Gaelic terms. The 'umbrella' provided by the Gaelic language and Gaelic conventions has been used, but the churches have not accepted everything that is under the 'umbrella'. Their identity has been forged by rejecting, as well as by accepting, certain aspects of Gaelic culture. Nevertheless, they do have a distinctively Gaelic identity which (in the case of the Protestant churches) was created on the basis of earlier pre-Reformation classical Gaelic culture.

41. The Gaelic policy of the Free Church Presbytery of Lewis does not prevent the introduction of ministers without Gaelic to strategic charges, but the presbytery can insist on a commitment to learn Gaelic on the part of ministers who do not have the language; see the account of the recent induction of the Rev Donald Campbell to Great Bernera, Lewis, in 'Newsline', *West Highland Free Press*, 13 February 1998. On the churches' provision for Gaelic, see MacAulay, 'Loosening link', and also his articles, 'Free Church grappling with decline in Gaelic services', ibid, 13 March 1998, and 'Church [of Scotland] lost for words on language policy', *Scotsman*, Gaelic Page, 7 January 1998. The last-named article draws attention to the imminent induction of a non-Gaelic-speaking minister to the High Church in Stornoway, 'a rock-solid Gaelic congregation since it began 90 years ago'.

At present the Protestant churches are facing an identity crisis. As Gaelic is enjoying a continuing 'roll' among enthusiasts, both native and non-native, there is an obvious door of opportunity for the churches. They need to come out of the past, and step boldly into the present to meet the needs of this new constituency. A mission field has come to the churches, but the churches (it seems to me) are looking in other directions, and are trying to find another identity for themselves. They are looking towards English as the pre-eminent medium of preaching. They are also concerned with the preservation of ecclesiastical purity; this has become very evident in the tensions which have afflicted the Highland wings of the conservative Presbyterian churches as the 20th century comes to its close. There seems to be a belief that the English language is not only the better medium for reaching the masses, but that it is also (somehow) purer, less sullied than Gaelic in its modern context. Some Highland churches appear to believe in the existence of what the late Bishop Lesslie Newbigin (in another context) has wryly called 'a culturally uncontaminated Gospel' (1995: 149). In the search for this culture-free revelation, some churches are trying to clean out the last vestiges of contamination as we begin a new millennium. The Gaelic language itself, once decontaminated and used as the primary vehicle for the evangelisation of the Highlands, is unclean once again. Come in, SSPCK!

Against this tendency, we are needing to recover and reassert the importance of 'Christ the transformer of culture'. Language is the great human bridge to that transformation, and I would wish to suggest that there is a place for Gaelic and Irish in the ancient, ongoing challenge of building that bridge. I have sustained this paper through the outstanding scholarship of Richard Niebuhr, and I now conclude with words from Lesslie Newbigin (as a tribute to his great contribution to this field):

> When we speak of culture in its broadest sense, we are speaking about the sum total of ways of living that shape (and also are shaped by) the continuing life of a group of human beings from generation to generation. We are speaking about the language that enables them to grasp, conceptualise, and communicate the reality of their world; about law, custom, and forms of social organisation, including marriage, family, and agriculture. These things shape the life of each member of society. They are also shaped, modified and developed from generation to generation by the members of the society. From the point of view of the individual member they are given as part of the tradition into which he or she is born and socialised. But they are not changeless absolutes (ibid: 142).

In the last sentence lies hope – and a mighty challenge.

# Evangelicalism, Culture and the Gaelic Tradition in Ireland

Alwyn Thomson

In the hymnbook used in my church, we have a rendition of Psalm 46, which begins, 'God is our refuge and strength, a very present help in trouble'. We sing it to the tune of 'The Dambusters' March'. In that respect we follow in the long tradition of General Booth and others who expressed their Christian convictions through the vehicle of popular culture.

This phenomenon, above all else, defines the relationship between evangelical religion and culture. In developing this I want to make three observations. The first concerns the relationship between evangelicalism and culture in general; the second, the relationship between evangelicalism and Gaelic culture in Ireland; and the third, a Christian and evangelical vision of society and the place of culture within it.

## Evangelicalism and culture

David Bebbington (1992) has come closest to providing a broadly acceptable definition of evangelicalism. Evangelicals are people for whom the bible is central, for whom the core of the bible story is the death of Jesus on the cross, and for whom the key human response to the story is repentance and faith. Evangelicals are, to use his words, 'biblicist', 'crucicentrist', and 'conversionist' (Bebbington 1992: 1–17). But, to use his fourth term, evangelicals are *activist*. Evangelicalism has a powerful missionary and proselytising impulse, for evangelicals want to tell others the story and to call for the same response. And it is that activist mentality that largely defines evangelical attitudes to culture. Evangelicals are cultural pragmatists; if it helps them to communicate the story, then they will be largely willing to use available cultural resources.

For example, William Carey, whose vision led to the creation of the Baptist Missionary Society, learned many of the languages of India and the Near East in order to preach and translate the bible for his Indian hearers.

Hudson Taylor, founder of the China Inland Mission, went to that country and adopted the form of dress and many of the cultural practices of the people to whom he was preaching. And, as I have indicated, General Booth and the Salvation Army put Christian words to popular tunes.

In that respect these evangelicals were following the example of the apostle Paul, who wrote:

> To the Jews I became like a Jew, to win the Jews. To those under the law I became like one under the law… To those not having the law, I became like one not having the law… To the weak I became weak. I have become all things to all people so that by all possible means I might save some. I do all this for the sake of the gospel. (1 Corinthians 9: 20–23)

However, this evangelical activism and pragmatism has its weaknesses, and I want to highlight two of these. The first weakness is that when there is no benefit to be had in becoming like a Gaelic speaker, for the sake of the Gaelic speaker, in order to win the Gaelic speaker for Christ, there is a tendency to slip into Niebuhr's 'Christ against culture' model. Without getting sidetracked, it does seem that evangelicalism is a religious tradition that focuses strongly on boundaries, and evangelicals often instinctively place many aspects of culture outside the boundary, beyond the pale. This instinctive response occurs when culture is being viewed as an end in itself rather than a means to an end.

This first weakness, I think, is a consequence of a second weakness. This is that, in the words of one recent lament, 'Evangelicals have failed to develop a Christian mind', failed specifically to think about the relationship between Christ and culture. While there has been a welcome increase in the depth and range of evangelical thinking, still the majority of evangelical people are driven by purely pragmatic considerations. Evangelicals in Ireland and Scotland, when they do think about Gaelic language and culture, (which, I suspect, is not often) do so largely from a pragmatic perspective.

## Evangelicalism and Gaelic culture in Ireland

As Professor Meek notes, there are certain considerations that apply in Ireland that do not apply in Scotland. It seems that in Scotland the language and the culture can rightly be seen as the common possession of long-established Highland communities, whether Catholic or Protestant. I would assume that there would be few, if any, in Scotland, holding the view that Highland culture was antithetical to their own culture, or that Highland culture was a tool of exclusivism towards them and their culture.

However, rightly or wrongly, for good reasons or bad, most Protestants in north-east Ireland perceive the Gaelic language and culture of Ireland as something that belongs to another and that excludes them. Mark, the unemployed Protestant, quoted by Aodán Mac Poilín in his paper (pp 89–90), may engender a certain amusement, but it would be unwise to dismiss the reality or the depth of that perception. Similarly, it is unwise to assume that that a little education will make it all right, because most educated Protestants are not interested in Gaelic culture and Gaelic language. In fact their culture is largely western and modern; they are part of a much bigger culture than either Ulster Protestantism or Gaelic Irish culture. Most evangelicals are part of that Protestant community and, rightly or wrongly, share that perception. It matters little if the Gospel may once have been preached in Gaelic by their Presbyterian forebears. What matters is that the Irish language is perceived to belong to one side of a divided community.

While evangelicals could, in theory, hold that identification with Irish culture might be a valid means to the end of telling the Bible's story to the wider community, few evangelicals feel an emotional or historical attachment to that culture. Evangelicals in the north of Ireland do not feel a sense of ownership or identity with the Irish language or culture because evangelicals, together with the wider Protestant community, often encounter Irish culture as a weapon. It is a weapon being wielded in a conflict in which their culture and identity, it is suggested, is inauthentic and alien.

Despite the goodwill of many in the Irish language community and their desire that it be seen as an inclusive reality, language and culture have been used as part of the conflict in Ireland. Indeed it would be incredible if they were not used in such a way. Despite all the talk about a common Gaelic heritage, there is an ethnic conflict in this community. Ethnic markers are points of division; they are boundaries, they are places of conflict. It needs to be stressed that this is not just a matter of unjustifiable perceptions that can be educated away. There are real questions for those who wish to see Irish language and culture as something unifying, and as something inclusive; questions to be addressed, not just perceptions. Aodán gives some examples of how attitudes to the Irish language have changed, contrasting the response when Queen Victoria came with what you could expect today. There is a serious question that needs to be addressed – why has it changed? What has engendered hostility on the part of folk from a Protestant tradition to Gaelic language and culture?

In the long term, if that is to change, it will require a fundamental change in our society. In the short term, I suggest two things could be of benefit in encouraging Protestants to feel more comfortable with Irish language and culture. First of all, advocates of Irish culture should, dare I say it, be less evangelistic. For people who feel their own culture is already being diminished, even the best-intentioned advocacy of Irish culture can be seen as threatening. Second, while I take on board Aodán's desire for Irish language and culture to be inclusive, that is something that is not heard. It would be good for those who see Irish culture in inclusive terms to raise their voices more clearly when that culture is used by others in our society in exclusive terms. Now it may be that people don't want to hear it; it may be also that our friends in the press don't consider it worth reporting, but nonetheless that is something I think that needs to be stressed.

## A Christian and evangelical vision of society

It seems that churches have been actively involved within the Scottish Constitutional Convention and other fora in shaping a vision for Scotland. This vision is of a pluralistic and inclusive Scotland based upon a civic rather than an ethnic understanding of nationalism. The significance of this, and the churches' involvement, should not be underestimated; it was only in 1923 that the Church of Scotland produced a report excoriating the Irish Catholic community of Scotland. And Scottish society also bears the scars of sectarianism. Now, however, as we know, the new parliament will sit for the first years of its existence in the General Assembly Hall of the Church of Scotland. Where objections have been raised to this arrangement it appears they have more to do with city rivalries than religion. I think that this envisioning of a civic society and the involvement of the churches in shaping that vision is tremendously significant.

As for its implications for Highland culture, I would like to make two comments. First, in a civic society, the language is free to be the language of all. It is no longer an ethnic marker, a determinant of authenticity. It becomes free for all the people of Scotland to own the language. The vision of civic nationalism subverts the threat from ethnic nationalism where language and culture can become instruments of conflict and division.

Second, in a civic society, because language and culture do not define national identity, they are, inevitably, in danger of increasing marginalisation. That may be their fate. However, because they have been removed from the sphere of conflict and confrontation, new possibilities may be created for the growth, development and flourishing of the culture.

Now the question arises, What kind of vision do we have for society in Ireland, north and south? I am not sure that many of us, churches, political parties or governments, have any clear vision of society. It seems to me that in both parts of Ireland, the north more so than the south, we are still tied strongly to ethnic conceptions of identity, with all the consequences that has for the use and abuse of our ethnic markers – language, music, religion, and so on. In our society these are our boundaries, and places of conflict and division.

Perhaps it is time for Ireland, north and south, or Ireland and Scotland together, to begin creating a vision for an Irish civic society, north and south. This new vision of a civic society would give a new freedom to Gaelic language and culture, and other cultural manifestations in Ireland. It would be a freedom to fade to the margins, perhaps, or freedom to be embraced more widely and to flourish.

## Conclusion

In conclusion, evangelicals believe in a God of infinite creativity and in men and women who are made in His image. It seems to me that if evangelicals can think in a more critical way about culture, their conclusion can only be 'the more, the merrier'; more languages, more music, more dances, more colours, more songs, more poems, more stories, more accents. Evangelicals should be advocates of cultural diversity and pluralism for its own sake. I would like to think, if we could envisage a civil society for Ireland, north and south, that evangelicals would be in the forefront of learning, teaching, and thinking about Gaelic culture and identity, Scottish and Irish, and all the other cultures and identities that are part of our society.

# The Politics of Gaelic Development in Scotland

TORMOD CAIMBEUL

*The following are solely my impressions of the recent dynamic in the Scottish Gaelic speech community and in no way represent the views – official or otherwise – of the BBC. Many people advised me on a no-names basis and I thank them.*

Let me ask you to guess what kind of person uttered the following words two years ago: 'Gaelic culture has been subjected for centuries to a repression unashamedly aimed at its obliteration. This cultural genocide cannot be laid at the door of the English: its initiators were Lowland Scots.'

Believe it or not that was said by the then Tory secretary of state for Scotland and ultra-orthodox Thatcherite, Michael Forsyth. He went on, in a speech on 26 April 1996 at Stirling University, to state that the Battle of Culloden was 'Gaeldom's Golgotha'.

In Scottish politics and public life Gaelic has moved from being the language of 'barbarity' according to our medieval rulers, to being – in March 1998 – on the verge of gaining some kind of secure legal status. There is a minister for Gaelic in the Scottish Office, Brian Wilson, whose own children attend a Gaelic-medium school and who earlier this month announced research into the possibility of free-standing Gaelic-medium schools in the cities. Press releases come from the new Labour government almost every week on some language-related topic or another. Things have moved a long way since the death of the last Gaelic-speaking Scottish monarch – interestingly a learner of the language – in 1513. To trace that shift would require a whole conference – what I've been asked is to analyse the more recent decades of advance.

When did the modern wave of Gaelic activism begin? There are many answers to that question, but there is no doubt that a seminal point was the restructuring of local government in Scotland in 1974–75. The Wheatley Commission's shake-up of the old county councils saw Gaelic move from being a marginal and almost-ignored phenomenon to being at the centre of at least one of the new local authorities. The Western Isles Council quickly moved to agreeing a bilingual policy which allowed use of the language in the council chamber with translation facilities for non-Gaels.

There were two crucial spin-offs. First, it fired the imagination of Gaelic activists to realise there was life beyond Gaeldom's annual music festival, the National Mòd. And second, the policy was a springboard for people like Dr Finlay Macleod of the council's education department to begin creating a bilingual *education* project. This eventually operated in all Western Isles primary schools, on paper at least. Its first phase saw twenty out of the then total of fifty-nine Western Isles schools involved. A further fourteen came on board in the years up to 1981. It concentrated on teaching children environmental and local historical topics through Gaelic.

Its supporters insist to this day that the policy was not meant to save a language, but rather to enhance the education of the child. But as we shall see, its failure to reverse language decline was a motivating factor in the growth of Gaelic-medium education. A form of bilingual education had been carried out on a very limited basis and narrow range of subjects since 1958 in some schools on the western seaboard and islands. But there is no doubt that this simply was not working, if language maintenance and use was any measuring-yard.

The Western Isles Council was also instrumental in setting up the Gaelic publishing house, Acair, in the late 1977 and by 1981 there was a definite stirring in the Gàidhealtachd. But 1981 saw perhaps the dark before the real dawn. Gaelic had enjoyed lip-service from politicians of all hues but a bill created by Scottish National Party MP Donald Stewart in that year was 'talked out' so failing to gain a second reading in the house of commons. The bill would have offered the following measures: the Western Isles, Highland Regional Council and the former counties of Argyllshire and Perthshire would have been designated as Gaelic-speaking areas, with a statutory requirement on local councils to provide education in Gaelic; anyone so wishing would have the right to use the language in legal proceedings; Gaelic versions of certain official government documents would be made available at ministerial discretion; and a broadcasting committee, taking in BBC and IBA representatives, would have been set up to promote and oversee Gaelic television and radio.

Although Donald Stewart had been careful to avoid making political capital out of the issue, and although he had support from Liberal, Labour and Conservative MPs, the bill was talked out. As one Gaelic activist reported at the time:

It took five hours of long-winded debate to establish that Gaelic is a charming language, spoken by charming people, whose needs would in no way be helped by such workaday things as parliamentary action... Ironically it was Welsh-speaker, Thomas Hooson, Conservative for Brecon and Radnorshire, who was on his feet speaking in criticism of the Gaelic bill when the allotted debating time expired and along with it the bill.

There was special anger afterwards at the actions of the then Conservative MP for Argyll and Bute, John Mackay. His contributions to the debate were described by various pro-Gaelic groups as 'venomous, outrageous and unsympathetic'. Mr Mackay afterwards claimed to have voted for the bill at an earlier stage and that he only wished to modify some of it in committee. Tory MPs such as Albert MacQuarrie and Alex Pollock both backed the bill as did Labour's Hamilton MP, George Robertson – now the defence minister. Later in 1981, the committee considering the Scottish education bill threw out a proposal for instruction in the language in Gaelic-speaking areas, by nine votes to six. But the failure of Donald Stewart's bill gave impetus to another young Finlay Macleod – better known as Fionnlagh Strì – who set up the Gaelic playgroups umbrella body Comhairle na Sgoiltean Àraich. More than anything else, that group has ensured that there is still some opportunity to save the language.

But the up-shot of all this was that activists saw the need for a new approach to language development and for lobbying the state. Since 1886 that work had been done by An Comunn Gàidhealach – the Highland Association. It was set up by urban Gaels in 1886, but with its then upper echelons dominated by landlords and gentry figures. The body, nevertheless, had organised the National Mòd and similar localised festivals, supported Highland light craft industries and published some Gaelic books. By the early 1980s the body was in the doldrums and seen as a spent force. Its leaders, then and now, would strenuously deny the charge. But it was a voluntary body and tied so closely to the Mòd that Gaeldom's young Turks did not see it as the vehicle to revive the language and carry it into the next century.

In the early 1980s the Gaelic-medium business college at the south end of Skye was finding its feet. Set up around 1973, the college has now developed to the stage where physical expansion is the norm almost every year. It was, and to a great extent still is, the first seat of higher education using the language since the days of the semi-autonomous Gaelic kingdom of the Lordship of the Isles five centuries earlier. (Incidentally, Sabhal Mòr Ostaig's founder, Sir Iain Noble, used his own network of business contacts to help the establishment of the college and the present college directors are legendary for their networking skills and ability to target key individuals in key funding organisations.) On the fringes of the emerging language-revival movement were the young members of the group Ceartas (Gaelic for justice) who carried out essential improvements to English-only road signs across the Highlands and were fined, probably for carrying out the modifications with red paint.

The government in 1965 had set up the Highlands and Islands Development Board and although its social remit was often held to include Gaelic, it gave little real support for the language until a slowly-growing trickle of applications by Gaelic initiatives for funding led to the establishment of a Gaelic working party. Significantly, its members were all Gaelic-speakers. They saw the need to work in the private, public and voluntary sectors and published a report written by broadcaster and journalist Martin MacDonald, entitled *Còr na Gàidhlig*. It recommended the setting up of a body tying together these sectors and working to promote the language in a number of fields. In 1985, Comunn na Gàidhlig, or CNAG as it is better known, was set up. Crucial to its effectiveness was that it included elected representatives from local councils – Strathclyde Region, Highland Region and Western Isles Island, councils. That meant that senior local politicians were members of CNAG. It also meant that CNAG had access at the higher political levels to these bodies. And that is a crucial distinction to make: instead of being marginalised and reactive, Gaels were now insiders and proactive in relation to these powerful institutions.

CNAG quickly agreed four priorities: Gaelic-medium education; the Gaelic arts; broadcasting; and business. Let us remember that in 1984 there were no real Gaelic-medium classes, a minuscule amount of Gaelic television programmes and a fragmented radio provision. It is easy to forget how few services there were. Had CNAG not been set up, things might have moved in a very different way. Anne Lorne Gillies, in her paper on education, fills out the details of how Gaelic-medium education began and developed but the following is a thumb-nail sketch of part of that story.

In 1983–84 parents in Lewis, Glasgow and Inverness were discussing how to emulate the Welsh model of bilingual education in Scotland. There was a growing feeling that the only short-term possibility was to create fee-paying Gaelic-medium schools. But the establishment of CNAG suddenly provided lobbying strength and confidence that the state sector could be persuaded to provide Gaelic-medium education. Real progress occurred in Glasgow and Inverness. But there was a real struggle. By spring 1985 parents in Glasgow were at loggerheads with Strathclyde Regional Council. There was similar resistance by education officials at Highland Regional Council, which lead one parent in Inverness to threaten to break the law by not sending his child to school if the education was not through the medium of Gaelic. Strathclyde education officials had been asked to write a feasibility study, after parents working at grass-roots level surveyed young families in the city and proved there was significant interest in Gaelic-medium education in Glasgow. A meeting was set up with the council education committee convenor Charles Gray. It was clear, ahead of the meeting, that the officials had written a negative report and were opposed to the establishment of such provision.

But CNAG privately lobbied Charles Gray. As a Labour-controlled local authority, they argued, Strathclyde surely had to be seen to carry out the party's policy of being in favour of the language's development. And as a body which liked to boast of being at the cutting edge of innovation in local democracy, and was strategically important to the survival of the language, how could the authority *not* support a Gaelic-medium education provision? That line of argument succeeded. At the meeting, Mr Gray stayed quiet as officials poured cold water on the idea. Parents and a young, long-haired activist, Brian Wilson, expressed disappointment. But at the end Charles Gray told them that a political decision had been made and he instructed the officials to go and make it happen. The meeting was in May 1985. In August a Gaelic-medium unit opened in Sir John Maxwell School on the city's south side. Highland Regional Council were also prevailed on that year and the Western Isles Council followed suit with their first Gaelic unit in 1986 at Breascleit, on Lewis.

Let's look at the dynamic behind the Glasgow victory. Anne Lorne Gillies has insider knowledge of much of it but I am told that the following is true of that momentum: there was grass-roots support and activity with parents lobbying and surveying their peers who had young families; 'high' politics where CNAG had previously lobbied all political parties including Labour to make pro-Gaelic noises; 'local' politics where Strathclyde were urged to maintain their cutting-edge image in local government circles as the innovators and risk-takers; and the CNAG structure with direct links to the local authorities allowing discreet and non-confrontational lobbying.

Moving quickly on, the arts priority was being dealt with and a major report by Dr Finlay Macleod led to the creation of the national Gaelic Arts Project in 1987. Although closely associated with CNAG, the Arts project is now to all intents and purposes autonomous from that body. Its main achievements to date have been the creation of a professional national Gaelic Theatre Company – Tosg – and the nurturing of the *feisean* movement. Unlike the national and local Mòds these are local non-competitive tuition festivals for school-children. Malcolm MacLean will explain that these and many other arts project initiatives focused on the critical need for community-based progress in language development.

As I mentioned, another key aim of CNAG's was to give Gaelic a professional dimension. This would be in both senses of the word 'professional' – that the interface between the linguistic community and the state should be at an institutional level with paid officials working on its behalf; and that there should be language-related employment created before the Gaelic-medium pupils came onto the jobs market. The need for employment located in and relevant to the linguistic heartland dovetailed with the desire to deal with the 20th century's greatest cultural bull-dozer – television. A few series of light entertainment programmes in Gaelic and one series of current affairs discussion had appeared sporadically in the 1970s. But in the mid 1980s CNAG were very aware that there was no regular prime-time presence of any kind for the language. They knew that Professor Ken MacKinnon, on socio-linguistic field-work in Barra, Uist and Harris in the 1970s was told again and again that the quality and quantity of Gaelic spoken by school-children declined from the arrival of television in the Western Isles in 1965.

Then CNAG and Thatcher's Britain found out in 1987 that a new broadcasting act was on the way. CNAG had formed a relationship with the two main ITV companies – Scottish Television and Grampian, as well as the BBC. This had produced marginal increases in the number of hours broadcast, but more importantly, partners in the future campaign for a Gaelic television service. But the wrong result from the bill could destroy all progress made for the language. And the task of achieving the right result would not be easy – a tiny, historically-oppressed, marginalised and only recently-politicised linguistic minority, had to think and argue in terms of seizing opportunities from the broadcasting revolution rather than defending the status quo.

The Annan and Crawford Committees, as well as a paper by Martin MacDonald and John Murray for the BBC's Gaelic Advisory Committee, had recently made well-argued arguments for an enhanced profile for Gaelic on television. But these were on the basis of linguistic and human rights – hardly the main philosophical icons of Mrs Thatcher's government. CNAG were wary of continuing that line of argument in the campaign that had to be fought. The campaign was waged across a wide number of fronts and had both overt and covert manifestations. The overt side of the struggle was that CNAG pushed the message home at public meeting after public meeting and in press release after press release, that this really was the wake-up call. The shake-up of television offered by Mrs Thatcher meant that for the first time in a generation there was the chance to influence the government's provision for the language before events rather than afterwards.

In one sense, the campaign for the television fund marked the culmination of the strategy of ending the old-style amateur, part-time approach where Gaeldom's spokesmen carped from the sidelines *after* any change took place, to the strategy of being in among the network of decision-makers and opinion-formers. CNAG's working group realised that the case being made wasn't chiming with government thinking. And it became clear that crucial as the Scottish office and Scots secretary Malcolm Rifkind were to be, the overall debate on the broadcasting revolution was being driven from London. Reluctantly it was decided to enter the big bad world of lobbyists, think-tanks and influence-wielders. Twelve lobbyists were given a specification and the firm chosen had a key figure on its board who had been an adviser to Mrs Thatcher in the run-up to the 1987 general election.

Within a few months there had been a flurry of meetings with civil servants and ministers in London and Edinburgh, a greatly-heightened media profile for the CNAG campaign, and even questions asked on its behalf in Parliament. The organisation prepared a discussion paper written by Martin MacDonald, The case for a Gaelic broadcasting service. In the paper, sixteen recommendations called for a more structured approach to ensure the language survived in the new broadcasting eco-system. Both main ITV companies in Scotland – Scottish Television and Grampian – had backed that broad statement. Mackay was able to go into talks knowing that on paper at least there was no opposition on the part of the two broadcasters.

The CNAG recommendations asked the government to recognise that the current type and level of provision for the language was totally inadequate. They asked for a structure to be put in place which would ensure the future funding, production and transmission of Gaelic programmes. In addition, they called specifically for the establishment of a Gaelic Broadcasting Council to manage the funding, commissioning and scheduling arrangements of the new service, a body which would work closely with the broadcasting authorities and broadcasting companies. Most importantly they recommended that the minimum requirements of such a service be 520 hours per annum (or ten per week) by the year 1995; that a minimum of £21 million be made available annually; and that programmes be show at peak viewing times.

Martin MacDonald's paper got positive noises and support at first but an ominous silence developed from the government end of CNAG's spectrum of contacts. A lobbyist can only present a case and however well he or she does so, they are limited by the effectiveness of the case being made and in late 1988 the government White Paper on Broadcasting had clearly not gone far enough. There was a warm welcome for the fact that the word 'Gaelic' was mentioned at all but wiser heads pointed out that the technological solutions proposed – microwave transmitters and satellite channel – were not really an answer at all. Either the PR had failed or the case being put was wrong. CNAG saw that raw economics had to be put at its centre for there to be any chance of success. As one activist reminisced to me during my research for this paper, 'After the White Paper we needed a lot of Touche Ross and just a little Saatchi and Saatchi'.

What they settled on was a director of the pro-Thatcherite think-tank, the Institute of Economic Affairs. Jento Velanowski was flown to the islands, not for a Prince Charles-style potato-planting session, but to see for himself that Gaelic was about a real community with an under-developed linguistic resource. He was given the challenge of making the economic case for a Gaelic television service. Although the rhetoric from the Gaelic lobby had been for a Gaelic opt-out on BBC2 or Channel 4 along the lines of the Welsh-language channel S4C, that was a non-starter according to Velanowski. In the time available he did not foresee that battle being won. CNAG already knew that the BBC and Channel 4 were fiercely resistant to the proposal; the latter had a greater audience reach in Scotland than in the rest of the UK and certainly did not want to undermine that advertising revenue source. In any case neither the BBC nor Channel 4 were totally germane to the national debate – Mrs Thatcher's broadcasting revolution was aimed at shaking the very core of the ITV network.

CNAG therefore needed a feasible political solution within strict time-limits. Velanowski was told to target the issue of why ITV revenue was going out of Scotland at that stage to fund the Welsh S4C while Scotland's own linguistic minority had not a television service to speak of. His case was built on two thrusts – the economic benefits to small communities, and a deal where the Scottish ITV broadcasters' existing Gaelic output was maintained in the new broadcasting set-up but topped up by several hundred hours of government-funded Gaelic television programmes.

The argument was won; in December 1989 Malcolm Rifkind announced there was to be a Gaelic Television Fund worth £8.5 million per annum administered by the Gaelic Television Committee. It slowly emerged that the ideologist par excellence of the Scottish Tory right, Michael Forsyth, had also lobbied for the language. Almost ten years later that body is now called the Gaelic Broadcasting Committee to reflect more recent legislation which allowed it to fund radio programmes both in the BBC and community sectors. Up to 500 people – many in the West Highlands and Islands heartland – are indirectly or directly employed through the committee's economic foot-print and everyone in Scotland is aware of a language called Gaelic. But the committee is ham-strung by not being able to schedule or even commission programmes – although it has influence in these matters they are still under the control of the broadcasters, and the committee's main role is as a *funder* of programmes. The 1989 act's stipulation that 'a suitable proportion' of its funded programmes be broadcast at peak viewing times was not implemented to the satisfaction of the Gaelic community and the lack of definition remains a real stumbling-block.

But what is behind the 1989 story? There was, of course, a rich mix of high politics, grass-roots support, the creation of a coalition of churches, universities, local authorities and other institutions who all wrote to the government asking for a Gaelic television service. And there were students who marched in the streets, gathered a 10,000-name petition, delivered it to 10 Downing Street and later threatened Welsh-style civil disobedience. I have asked some of those involved in that campaign and one clear answer as to the reasons for its success is that it was not so much the tactics as the dynamic between them – the way people and events interacted and could perhaps be influenced. One brief example, with real names left out. After a bruising public meeting in a Highland community about setting up a Gaelic-medium unit in the local school, the CNAG official made the discovery that one cabinet minister who was proving something of a stumbling-block in the broadcasting campaign happened to own a holiday home there. One of the leading lights among the parents who'd fought for the Gaelic-medium unit just happened to be the person from whom the government minister usually hired his car while in the community. Needless to say the CNAG officer suggested that she say a quiet word to the minister about small cultures fighting globalisation. Within forty-eight hours the cabinet minister – who actually arrived unannounced the following day – was being told by his wife – by this time also briefed – to 'jolly well sort this out'.

There will be moments of what appear like sheer good luck, but several people have suggested that working at a number of levels, keeping your eye on the ball, grabbing the chance if you happen to be in the right place at the right time are all important too. Perhaps the lesson for the Belfast revival movement may be that repeating every step taken in Scotland would be wrong but that keeping up the momentum of inter-locking campaigns is more important.

## Gaelic in law

A working group set up by CNAG has spent many months preparing the case for what they called 'Secure Status' for the language in law. The emphasis in the final proposals is on the feasible rather than the adventurous. In March 1997, CNAG announced that their focus would be on '*Inbhe Thèarainte*' – Secure Status – which they said would 'move the language issue from questions of basic survival and maintenance to purposeful and progressive development in the normal domains of a modern living language'. The general aim would be to provide the right to use Gaelic wherever possible in dealing with the state. The objective was to 'give Gaelic an official measure of status through achieving equal validity with Welsh, thus enabling the language to achieve its full potential.' CNAG stated that the overall thrust would be one of facilitation rather than coercion.

The external rhetoric of CNAG's argument has been laid out on a human rights matrix. Much of the internal rhetoric directed at the Gaels themselves has been based on the fear that fiscal pressures in the brave new world of the Scottish Parliament could see recent advances for the language reverse or disappear. 1996 and 1997 saw real threats to Gaelic-medium units in South Lanarkshire, Edinburgh and Highland Regional Council. One Gaelic-speaking Highland councillor argued that Gaels had to accept cuts like everyone else. When parents persisted in lobbying to prevent the cuts, he issued an astonishing press release complaining of 'whinging Gaels'. That attitude and the real fear that a Scottish parliament might replicate some of the anti-Gaelic prejudice occasionally visible in the letters and opinion sections of papers such as *The Scotsman* – despite welcome recent advances such as the fortnightly Gaelic page – show there is some basis to that fear. There have been some indications by Brian Wilson that Gaels seeking secure legal status might not have to wait for the establishment of a Scots parliament, as the pre-election messages suggested.

It is a little-known fact that there are at least nine acts of parliament which in one way or another mention the language and provision for it. The Small Landholders (Scotland) Act of 1911 stipulated that one member of the Scottish Land Court be a Gaelic speaker. A vaguely-worded couple of lines in the 1918 Education (Scotland) Act allowed teaching in the language but seems not to have been implemented. More recent acts dating from the 1980s allow the secretary of state to approve bilingual road signs, allow the government to fund arts, community and education projects and a 1986 regulation amending the Education (Scotland) Act 1980 allows the secretary of state to make specific grants for Gaelic.

In the run-up to the May 1997 general election, all the main political parties in Scotland made what since the late 1970s have been traditional pro-Gaelic noises. Indeed the all-party Gaelic group in parliament had tabled a commons early day motion on the day of CNAG's March 1997 announcement on Secure Status. The group backed the CNAG report and stated the belief that the proposals would 'contribute to consolidating the enormous progress made with cross-party support in recent years'.

The all-party group was chaired by Western Isles MP Calum MacDonald, and among others was signed by the SNP's Margaret Ewing and Roseanna Cunningham; the Conservative party's Allan Stewart and Charles Kennedy and Ray Michie from the Liberal Democrats. The commitment by politicians has moved from the lip-service of 1981 to the personal backing and tangible political will, seen today, to do something. But despite the obvious Gaelic credentials of people like the SNP's Anne Lorne Gillies and Labour's Brian Wilson, there was intense pre-election lobbying of key figures in the Scottish parties over Secure Status. Some individuals pushed Labour to include legal status for the language in the legislation setting up the Scottish parliament. Fearful of only a small majority in the house of commons, the party hierarchy made clear in such discussions that they would not risk the devolution bill by also including in it the hostage to fortune which matters other than the parliament and its relationship to Westminster, would represent.

However it may be achieved, legal status is only useful if the rights enshrined are used. Gaelic-speaking lawyers, such as Roddy-John Macleod, Wilson Macleod, and Rob Dunbar who lectures in Glasgow University's law faculty, helped draft much of the discussion paper and proposals drawn up by CNAG. But Mr Dunbar has warned that rights on paper mean nothing if they are not exercised.

That point draws me on to summarise some of the recent developments in the form of a strengths, weaknesses, opportunities, and threats (SWOT) analysis. I would like to suggest that the same phenomena may simultaneously *be* strengths, weaknesses, opportunities and threats.

## Strengths

Almost 2000 children are now in Gaelic-medium education. Well over that number are in Gaelic playgroups or nurseries. In terms of ensuring that another generation of bilingual children is growing up, then, the language is much more secure than other linguistic minorities. Pro-Gaelic policies are pushed at the highest level in Scottish political life. Literacy is improving and there are new initiatives to place the language at the heart of the radical new high-tech University of the Highlands and Islands. There are still villages where just about everyone can speak Gaelic and where even small-scale public meetings for locals are in the language and other public institutions such as church meetings, grazing committees and community councils use it.

The 'Gaelic mafia' – that network of old university friends and colleagues dating to the late 1970s – has matured. No longer does internal criticism or media probing automatically meet with cries of betrayal. There is an increased self-confidence among the senior figures. Yes, there are still squeals of protest if someone suggests there is too much bureaucracy and too many organisations in Gaeldom. But that very suggestion by writer Iain Morrison last year met with little of the old-style comments such as, 'Don't say that – what will the Scottish Office think?'

## Weaknesses

The Gaels are good at tactics but not so good at strategy. The amount of public relations effort on the part of the language is small; there is an over-emphasis on publicity at the expense of networking and 'outreach' work; Gaeldom fails to utilise sufficiently public expressions of support by the friends in high places which CNAG and others have no doubt won: political lobbying tends to concentrate on those in power; and without naming names there is a lack of attention to quality and track record in some of the services provided.

Professor Ken MacKinnon's research and analysis of 1991 census data shows the real collapse of the language among young people in the Western Isles. As one living there, I would say that without universal Gaelic-medium education being the norm within the next five years, then there will only be a few pockets or individual villages within the islands where it will be anything like the community language in ten years' time. For me to talk up the growth and excitement that does really exist among Gaelic activists at the moment, would be pointless without looking these facts straight in the eye. Most people under thirty-five in the Western Isles – if they are bilingual – are English-dominant bilinguals. Only a quarter of primary-school children are in Gaelic-medium education. Linguistically-mixed marriages are the norm.

## Opportunities

Out-migration from the heartlands of the language may be halted by the 'Air an Oir' initiative – On the Edge. This was announced earlier this month and aims to give young people in the so-called 'remote' areas of the Highlands and Islands a better chance of getting a job, house and land in their own communities. Oil development west of the Hebrides may have some limited spin-off for island industries and help underpin rural communities.

A new broadcasting bill is about two years away. Overall control of that issue will remain in London. But there is thorough research going on into the potential for digital channels. Indeed the argument for a designated level of peak-viewing time presence for Gaelic on one of the digital multiplexes has already been accepted. The establishment of a Scottish parliament offers the opportunity for a new politics and a new self-image for Scotland. Many hope that the autonomy soon to be enjoyed will lead to a flowering of the arts, community and political life of Scotland. Catalonia's flowering after autonomy is seen as one parallel. At the basic level of social justice, the ability to focus on tackling poverty and housing were key arguments made in the referendum on devolution. Gaelic *may* benefit from having a legislature nearer to its base and more accessible to lobbying.

The economic arguments for Gaelic development and investment in the Gaelic arts have clear public support in the heartlands, as shown by the in-depth opinion survey carried out for the National Gaelic Arts project by Caledonian University's Dr Allan Sproull and published earlier this month.

## Threats

Both Brian Wilson and Western Isles MP Calum MacDonald have indicated they will not stand for the Scottish parliament. It may be that too much emphasis is being placed on today's key players, who in reality have very limited time to make a difference. It only takes one decision by the prime minister and these two pivotal figures could be working in Westminster long before the Scottish parliament is set up. Another threat, as I mentioned earlier, is that the language could be regarded with hostility in the new Scotland; or seen by most in the new parliament as unworthy of time, investment or even the 'Secure Status' being sought. It should not be over-stated, but there is real ignorance and in some cases antipathy towards Gaelic by some Lowlanders. Ancient prejudices have not completely gone, no matter what some of Gaelic plc's spin-doctors would have us believe.

It seems likely that the 1991 census total of around 65,000 Gaelic speakers will, at very best, fall slightly at the 2001 census. The demography is still top-heavy towards older age-groups. Unless Gaeldom is ready for these figures with sound, reasoned arguments, then the party may be over. And that leads me on to the main threat that I see, as someone living in the Western Isles and mixing with the residual native Gaelic communities on a daily basis. Five years ago, a common phrase in describing Gaelic development was the Gaelic mafia. Today the rhetoric is often about the Gaelic *economy*. In some ways that reflects a welcome mushrooming of job prospects. But there is a real danger that the language is seen as a passport to a job with no further commitment required by the learner or native speaker. What was a family culture may one day soon become only a career option or marketing tool. There is a danger in taking the view that with all these wonderful job opportunities, then the language must be thriving. But as one young man from Barra commented recently: 'In the 1980s we spoke *in* Gaelic, in the 1990s we speak *about* Gaelic'.

Although John Angus Mackay and others in the early days of CNAG did follow some of his ideas, the writings and ideas of that great American soci-olinguist Joshua Fishman remain a closed book to most of official Gaeldom. Fishman stressed the need for language revival to concentrate on the hardest part of society to change: the interaction of parents with children. As the Gaelic poet and television lecturer Angus Peter Campbell said recently: 'One Gaelic-speaking mother is worth more than 1000 development officers'.

## Postscript

Since this paper was written, there have been some significant developments. Following the 1999 election to the new Scottish Parliament, the ruling Labour-Liberal democrat coalition in Edinburgh appointed Western Isles MSP and native speaker, Alasdair Morrison, as minister for Gaelic, Highlands/Islands and tourism. The inter-party concensus on Gaelic partial-ly collapsed on 7 June 2000 when the language's place in the Standards in Scotland's School Bill went to a vote. SNP Gaelic spokesman Michael Russell and Lib-Dem John Farquhar Munro failed by sixty-two votes to thirty-six in their bid to make local authorities provide Gaelic-medium education where there was reasonable demand. The government amendment, placing a statu-tory duty on councils to explain their plans for the introduction or expansion of Gaelic-medium education, was carried. The subsequent post-mortems on the row focused on the failure to lobby widely prior to the vote and the absence of a Gaelic lobbyist based at the Scottish Parliament. The political consequences of the expected drop in the number of Gaelic-speakers at the 2001 census became a matter of concern. The language's role was accepted within legislation covering the creation of national parks. The act requires the authority running each park to take account of the literary and linguistic aspects of local culture in the interpretation of each area. The summer saw demands for the Scottish Executive to bring forward legislation for Secure Status. A task force set up to look at the structures and effectiveness of the publicly-funded language development agencies added tension to the debate: its recommendations were expected to be implemented before April 2001.

# Legal and Institutional Aspects of Gaelic Development

Robert Dunbar

Tormod Caimbeul has provided much essential information on developments in Scottish Gaeldom over the last twenty-odd years. I have tried to keep any duplication to a minimum, and have sought to explore some of the ideas Tormod raised and, perhaps, expand on a few of the themes he touched on. Tormod began his paper by saying that the views expressed were his alone, and in no way reflected those of his employer, the BBC. I would like to express the same caveat with respect to my remarks.[1]

## Scottish Gaeldom as a 'land of plenty': a realistic appraisal?

From the point of view of a Canadian Gael such as myself, or, I dare say, an Irish Gael living in Northern Ireland (though not, probably, from that of an Irish Gael living in the Republic of Ireland), Scottish Gaeldom appears to be in a much favoured position. Without question, support for Gaelic has come a long way over the past fifteen years.[2] In 1984, for example, there were no Gaelic-medium primary school units and only a handful of Gaelic-medium pre-schools: CNSA, the Gaelic Pre-School Association, was then just in its infancy. In 1998–99, there are about 2200 pupils being taught in Gaelic in over seventy schools, at both the primary and secondary school level (CNAG 1999). In 1984, there was very little Gaelic-medium radio programming, and only about seventy-five hours of Gaelic-medium television programming per year. In 1998–99, there is a Gaelic-medium radio service, Radio nan Gàidheal, part of BBC Scotland, which broadcasts about forty-four hours per week of Gaelic-medium programming, and there is about 250 hours of original

1. I am a director of three Gaelic organisations, Comhairle nan Sgoiltean Araich (CNSA), the Gaelic Pre-School Association, Comunn an Luchd-Ionnsachaidh (CLI), the Gaelic Learners' Organisation, and Comunn na Gàidhlig (CNAG), the chief Gaelic development agency in Scotland, and am also Chairman of the CNAG working group that has put together a set of proposals for *Inbhe Thèarainte*, or Secure Status, for Gaelic. The views expressed here, however, are solely my own.
2. See Tormod Caimbeul's contribution to this volume for a good chronological summary of events.

Gaelic-medium television programming offered over the two BBC services, and the private sector Grampian Television, Scottish Television and Channel 4 (Fraser Production and Consultancy 1998: 3–9, appendix 1). Much of this programming is funded by a Comataidh Craolaidh Gàidhlig (CCG), or the Gaelic Broadcasting Committee, set up under the Broadcasting Act (1990: 42), which currently has an annual budget of £8.5 million. In 1984, the Gaelic college in Skye, Sabhal Mòr Ostaig (SMO), had just become the first full-time establishment offering higher education through Gaelic, and had seven full-time students on course. In 1998–99, The SMO is part of the new University of the Highlands and Islands, will be a full degree-granting institution, has a new Arainn Chaluim Chille campus, and has over seventy full-time students.

In the cultural sphere in 1984, aside from the Mòd, a week-long festival of musical competitions which takes place in a different location each October, there was some local activity, but very little taking place on a co-ordinated and properly funded national basis. In 1998–99, there is Proiseact nan Ealan (PNE), the Gaelic National Arts Agency (founded in 1987), which receives a grant of almost £40,000 from the Scottish Office to promote and co-ordinate Gaelic arts developments, Fèisean nan Gàidheal (set up in 1991), which co-ordinates and develops over thirty Gaelic community festivals (*fèisean*) catering to over 3500 children throughout Scotland, and there is a Gaelic theatre company, Tosg, which tours the country.

Finally, in 1984, a national Gaelic development body, Comunn na Gàidhlig (CNAG), had just been founded. In 1998–99, CNAG received over £250,000 from the Scottish Office, and has, over the years, spearheaded many of the other developments just discussed, including the creation of the CCG and other Gaelic organisations. It is currently behind the drive to attain legislative protection for the language, a topic to which I shall return below. CNAG's annual *Comhdhàil*, or Congress, held every June, continues to be the one place where all those active in Gaelic development meet and discuss their various initiatives. As CNAG's chief executive, Allan Campbell, has often said, the annual Congress is as close as we come to a 'Parliament of the Gaels'.

The increased recognition of the Gaelic fact in Scottish life can even be seen in the new Scottish Parliament, created by the Scotland Act (1998: 48) although it is not yet clear whether this recognition is real or symbolic. Nonetheless, the Scottish Executive – essentially, the cabinet – includes a minister for Gaelic, the native Gaelic-speaking Labour member for the Western Isles, Alasdair Morrison.[3] The standing orders for the Scottish Parliament –

---

3. This follows the practice first instituted in 1997 by the Labour Government of designating a Scottish Office minister with special responsibility for Gaelic. The first such minister was Brian Wilson, who was replaced in June 1998 by Calum MacDonald, the Labour member from the Western Isles at Westminster.

essentially, its rules of procedure – provide that members of the parliament may speak in Scots Gaelic[4] and that members and others appearing before committees and subcommittees may also do so.[5] Members must take their oath of allegiance in English, but may repeat it in Gaelic, a choice which several of the 129 members did, indeed, exercise, including the two native Gaelic-speakers.[6] The signage for the parliament is fully bilingual.

And yet, when one looks at the situation in which Scottish Gaeldom finds itself in 1998–99, we cannot say that the picture is a pretty one. The reality is that government support for this linguistic community is very limited, and that such support as does exist is insecure. More fundamentally, the Gaelic community itself has very little, if any control over any of the levers of power in the crucial areas of its day-to-day existence. And against all this must be set the steady decline in numbers of Gaelic speakers. Based on census figures, there were 69,510 Gaelic speakers in Scotland in 1991, a drop of about 13,000 from 1981. CNAG itself is expecting that the next census, in 2001, will show at least as sharp a loss in numbers of speakers, and estimates that in 1999 there are only about 54,000.[7] Thus, we are looking at a net loss of Gaelic speakers at a rate of well over 1000 per year. Most troubling, perhaps, is that CNAG estimates that even with the recent rapid expansion in Gaelic-medium education, there would have to be an almost four-fold increase in the present 2200 children enrolled in such education simply 'to sustain a reproductive Gaelic-speaking population'. CNAG notes that this higher figure implies a minimum intake of over 500 children per annum, which, given the numbers being lost each year, may still be too small an intake.[8] So, the situation is, simply, critical.

At present, Gaelic has no 'official' status, and only very limited legal protection under a handful of acts of parliament. The approximately £12 million that the Scottish Office will spend on Gaelic-medium services in fiscal 1998–99 looks very impressive, until one recognises that this represents less

---

4. Edition 2 of the standing orders, made by resolution of the Parliament of 9 December 1999, in accordance with section 22 and schedule 3 of the Scotland Act 1998; see rule 7.1.1 and 7.1.2.
5. Ibid, rule 7.8.1. The likelihood that much Gaelic will be used is, however, small. Gaelic is not permitted in many important types of parliamentary business: the standing orders provide that motions (rules 8.2.2(a) and 8.5.2(a)), petitions (rule 15.4.3) and, most importantly, questions to the Scottish Executive (ie, the cabinet; see rule 13.3.3(c)) must be made in English. There is no provision about the language of draft legislation, but it is certain that only English will be used. Even the use of Gaelic in debate is subject to the discretion of the Presiding Officer (ie, the Speaker), and it is expected that those wishing to use Gaelic will have to provide some prior notice so that a translator may be found. A long notice period will almost certainly ensure that Gaelic will be rarely used. The standing orders are not, however, final, so the question of a symbolic versus real presence for Gaelic is still an open one.
6. Ibid, rule 1.2.2; in addition to Mr Morrison, the Labour member for the Western Isles, John Farquhar Munro, the Liberal Democrat member for Ross, Skye and Inverness West.
7. CNAG, p 43.
8. Ibid, p. 10.

than one-tenth of 1 per cent of the total Scottish Office budget of over £14 billion for that same fiscal year. As total British government spending in Scotland is almost certainly in excess of £25 billion, spending on Gaelic-medium services represents perhaps only one-twentieth of 1 per cent of total government spending in Scotland. And this, for a community which repre-sents approximately 1.4 per cent of the total Scottish population. There are slightly over 3 million taxpayers in Scotland, which means that only about £4 of every Scottish taxpayer's taxes goes directly towards Gaelic-medium serv-ices.[9] And the amount of spending on Gaelic-related services for each Gaelic speaker is roughly £200 per year. These figures render laughable the sugges-tion often made by those opposed to Gaelic that Gaels are subsidy junkies. There is, quite simply, no subsidy for Gaelic. Indeed, if there is a subsidised language in Scotland, it is English. Unfortunately, mention is almost never made of the 'English subsidy' which Scottish Gaels have had to bear for many long decades – of having to fund through their taxes things like English-medium education in Gaelic-speaking areas. And, of course, we must not for-get that this £12 million is not statutorily-protected; it can disappear as easily as it has appeared.

To understand the real constraints under which Gaels operate, I should like to take a closer look at two areas which, most will agree, are of crucial importance to the survival and revival of Gaelic: education and broadcasting. In both areas, we suffer not only from a serious shortage of funding, but also from having almost no control over the major levers of policy and planning. I suggest that until such time as Gaels are able not only to receive services in their own language, but exercise real control over the shape and content of those services, we will be a long way from turning the corner to establishing a truly secure and healthy language community.

Take the case of broadcasting. Nothing upsets the critics of Gaelic more than the mention of Gaelic-medium broadcasting. They guffaw at the mil-lions spent on the soap opera *Machair*. And there is no question that some Gaelic programming is weak, based on almost any measure of quality one wishes to apply. Some is also excellent, again by any measure. The same is, of course, true of much English-language programming. But the reality is that the production of television or radio programming of whatever quality is a very expensive business, and the £8.5 million received by the body charged

9. The word 'directly' is used because the £12 million of Scottish Office direct funding does not repre-sent total Scottish Office and central government funding. For example, the salaries of those working at BBC's Radio nan Gàidheal and at the BBC's Gaelic television service are funded through the BBC, and the salaries of teachers in Gaelic-medium units, as well as many of the other costs of Gaelic-medium education, are not paid out of the Gaelic-specific grant but by the local education authorities themselves. Still, one suspects that the £12 million does represent the largest share of government funding of Gaelic-medium services, and so the point remains valid.

with funding the production of such programming, the CCG, is really quite a paltry sum. Gaelic broadcasting has become an easy target; last year, *The Scotsman*, Scotland's self-styled 'national newspaper', suggested that money should be diverted away from the CCG and towards Gaelic-medium education. Indeed, the government had already used this ploy – in December 1997, the first minister with responsibility for Gaelic, Brian Wilson, announced that the funding of the CCG would be *cut* to £8.5 million from its previous level of £9.05 million. For young Gaels considering a career in broadcasting, or entrepreneurial Gaels who may have been considering the creation of a production company to make Gaelic-medium programming, what sort of signal does such an arbitrary cut send?

The problems facing Gaelic-medium broadcasting are much more fundamental than this. The CCG can only fund the production of Gaelic-medium programming; it has very little control over how, when and even if such output is aired. That power lies with the broadcasters, and neither the Gaelic community nor the CCG has much power over them. Although regulations under the Broadcasting Act 1990 and 1996 create certain obligations with respect to the number of hours of Gaelic programming the BBC and the independent broadcasters must air on a weekly and annual basis, these are very limited – about 300 hours per year – and are largely at the broadcasters' discretion. The Gaelic comedy show *Ran Dan* was not too far off the mark when it showed a Gaelic household waking in the small hours of the morning, putting on the tea and racing downstairs in their night-clothes to see the half hour of Gaelic programming. The crucial point is this: it is the broadcasters, not the CCG or the Gaelic community, who have ultimate control over when and what is broadcast. This being the case, it should not surprise us that Gaelic-medium television programming will be directed in subtle and not-so-subtle ways by the needs and interests of those outwith the Gaelic community. You might think that this is something which the Scottish Parliament may be able to deal with, but this is not the case: under the Scotland Act 1998, sole responsibility for broadcasting will remain with Westminster.

When we look at Gaelic-medium education, we are once again tempted to think that all is well. After all, a scheme of specific grants was established in 1986 under the Education (Scotland) Act 1980 to fund the development by local education authorities of Gaelic-medium education. That fund stands at what looks like an impressive £2.434 million for 1999–2000. Additionally, some £300,000 has been set aside for Gaelic pre-school education, £200,000 for a course to increase the supply of Gaelic-speaking secondary school teachers, £80,000 for the staffing costs of a national resource centre for

Gaelic teaching materials, and £25,000 for the development of Gaelic secondary courses. In 1999–2000, there are some fifty-nine Gaelic-medium primary school units attended by some 1831 students, and some thirteen schools at which at least some Gaelic-medium classes are offered at the secondary level, which courses are attended by some 232 students. In August 1999, Scotland's first Gaelic-medium primary school opened in Glasgow.[10]

Yet, this has all taken place in the absence of any firm statutory basis, and is based mainly on the hard work of interested parents, of people in Gaelic organisations such as CNSA, Comunn nam Parant (Naiseanta) (CnamP(N)), the organisation for parents of children in Gaelic-medium education, and CNAG, and on the goodwill of certain key local councillors, and, occasionally, national politicians who have been willing to support the language. In the world of education, the Gaelic community is, I am afraid to say, little protected and totally at sea. Until the advent of the Scottish Parliament,[11] power with respect to education lay primarily with a Scottish Office minister, a small number of bureaucrats in the Scottish Office Industry and Education Department (SOIED), and local education authorities, which are essentially a branch of the various local councils which control the provision of primary and secondary education in Scotland. The Scottish Office (now the Scottish Executive), through the Gaelic-specific grant, could (and still can) help local education authorities to provide Gaelic-medium education, but it cannot force them to do so. And what duties are these local education authorities under with respect to Gaelic? The answer is: not many.

The Education (Scotland) Act 1980 does place an obligation on these education authorities to provide Gaelic instruction, but the extent of this obligation is extremely unclear. Specifically, subsections 1(1) and 1(5) make it an obligation of education authorities to provide for 'the teaching of Gaelic in Gaelic-speaking areas'. Unfortunately, the act does not explain what is meant by 'the teaching of Gaelic', nor does it describe how one determines what is a 'Gaelic-speaking area'. With no decided case law which interprets these terms, this provision provides parents seeking Gaelic-medium education for their children with a rather blunt weapon. Certainly, one can expect local education authorities which do not want to extend Gaelic-medium education to take a restrictive view of the potential application of this provision to them.

---

10. Comhairle nan Eilean Siar, the Western Isles Council, also recently announced that it was designating two schools under its control as Gaelic-medium schools.

11. Education is a devolved matter under the Scotland Act 1998 and therefore this is a state of affairs which the new parliament may be able to change, if it is willing. At present, however, the replacement of a Scottish Office minister with an education minister in a Scottish Executive responsible to a Scottish Parliament has made little difference. Indeed, one of the first pieces of draft legislation put before the parliament in the summer of 1999 was a draft education bill, which contained not a single reference to Gaelic or Gaelic-medium education; see the postscript (p 84) for a description of the progress of this bill.

And certainly, as parents of children in Gaelic-medium education in areas as widely separated as East Kilbride, Skye and Lochalsh and Edinburgh have recently found, this provision has not given them a sufficiently powerful tool with which to challenge decisions and threatened decisions of school authorities to which they are opposed.

A crucial problem is that the decisions with respect to both the retention of existing Gaelic-medium units and the extension of Gaelic-medium education are solely within the hands of 'education authorities'. Subsection 35(1) of the Education (Scotland) Act 1980 tells us that the 'education authority' is essentially the regional or isles council. In practice, the education authority appoints an education committee to deal with its statutory responsibilities. At least half the committee must be composed of regional or island councillors belonging to the council. The committee must also include at least two teachers employed by the education authority and three people interested in the promotion of religious education. Yet, even in education authorities which offer Gaelic-medium education, there are not necessarily any representatives of the Gaelic stream on an education authority, the body which takes many of the key decisions regarding Gaelic-medium provision.

In fact, for most education authorities and education committees, Gaelic-medium education is at best a minor issue. I learned this personally in Glasgow. I have attended meetings on behalf of parents of children in Gaelic-medium education. I have found little ill-will directed at Gaelic among the committee members I have met, although I am sure that there are members of education committees in many parts of Scotland, even (perhaps especially!) the Highlands and Islands who harbour some ill-will towards Gaelic. But I have found little ill-will in Glasgow. What I have found, however, is a remarkable ignorance, both of the fact of Gaelic-medium education and the needs and issues facing such education. This is not surprising. In an education authority such as Glasgow, which has responsibility for over 60,000 students and many hundreds of schools, the handful of students in Gaelic-medium education must represent a rather marginal concern, particularly given the huge financial pressures that are currently bearing down on even English-medium schools in Glasgow.

There is no question that the Gaelic-specific grant scheme has helped to bring about a substantial expansion in Gaelic-medium primary school provision. However, the funding of the scheme has not kept pace with increasing demand for Gaelic-medium education. For the current year, applications by local education authorities have outstripped available funding. In these circumstances, who decides which education projects go ahead and which do not, and on what basis are these decisions made? The answer is that, since the

SOIED administers the project, it is bureaucrats at the Scottish Executive who are making the decisions. Perhaps they are guided in these decisions by the new Gaelic minister in the new Scottish Executive. Although this minister, Alasdair Morrison, is a native Gaelic-speaker, comes from an Island community, and is the member of the Scottish Parliament for the Western Isles constituency, it cannot be said that he either represents or speaks on behalf of *the entire* Scottish Gaelic community. He was appointed Gaelic minister by the Scottish First Minister, Donald Dewar, leader of Mr Morrison's party, and not by the Gaelic community. Certainly, unelected Scottish Executive bureaucrats cannot claim to represent the interests of the Gaelic community. Thus, once again we have decisions of fundamental importance to the future of the Gaelic community made by people who cannot in any meaningful sense be representative of or be held directly accountable to that community. The minister and the SOIED may listen to the Gaelic community; but there is nothing that compels them to obey or respond to that community. We are reliant on their goodwill, their largesse. This, I suggest, is a fundamentally unhealthy situation. Once again, the Gaelic community has almost no power over Gaelic-medium education, which all recognise is crucial to the very survival of that community.

## The need for a legal framework: Inbhe Thèarainte

In 1996, CNAG set up a working group to investigate the possibility of developing legislation which would provide support for Gaelic. A set of proposals, entitled '*Inbhe Thèarainte dhan Ghàidhlig/ Secure status for Gaelic*', was presented to the government in December 1997, and a draft Gaelic language bill, based on those earlier recommendations, was developed by the CNAG working group and presented to the new Scottish Executive in the summer of 1999.[12] The following is a summary only; the proposals are too detailed to be covered in the space available.[13] The principle upon which the proposals are built, however, is that the provision of Gaelic-medium services of various sorts is a basic right which should be statutorily protected through an act of the Scottish Parliament. Because Gaelic is one of the national languages of Scotland, the proposals envision a certain level of services throughout Scotland, but also seek to impose heavier obligations with respect to the pro-

---

12. The author is chairperson of this CNAG working group, and helped draft both documents. The draft Gaelic language bill expanded on the earlier proposals in only a few areas, particularly that of enforcement of the provisions of any future legislation. It also took into account certain changes which were necessary to reflect the changed legislative structures in place after the passage of the Scotland Act 1998.
13. Copies of both the December 1997 recommendations and the draft Gaelic language bill are available from CNAG.

vision of Gaelic-medium services where users of Gaelic-language services are either a significant proportion of the local population, or are present in sufficient numbers (though they are small in proportion to the wider population) to justify a broader range of such services. In those local government areas where Gaels constitute at least 30 per cent of the population, Gaelic and English are to be treated on the basis of full equality in all areas of local authority business.[14]

Specifically, both sets of proposals recommend that the legislation should establish a basic principle of equal validity for Gaelic and English in Scotland. There are several recommendations relating to the use of Gaelic in the Scottish Parliament, some of which, as noted above, have been acted upon. It is also recommended that all local governments and public bodies draw up Gaelic policies which are to be scrutinised and approved by the Scottish Executive. There is provision for use of Gaelic in legal contexts; in particular, before the courts of law. With respect to education, it is recommended that the obligation of local education authorities to provide Gaelic-medium education be made absolutely clear by the imposition of a duty on them to provide such education when certain set levels of demand had been reached. Finally, with respect to broadcasting, it is recommended that the legislation create a cohesive Gaelic broadcasting service with the capacity to grow to meet audience needs.[15]

CNAG's approach has been guided by two processes. The first is an increasing recognition of the need for a rights-based approach to minority protection. Such recognition is a feature of both the domestic law of many multi-ethnic, multi-lingual states[16] and, increasingly, international law.[17] The second is a growing recognition among Gaels of the precariousness of the Gaelic-medium services which they are presently receiving. In 1996 and 1997,

---

14. At present, the only local authority which would come within this requirement is Comhairle nan Eilean Siar, the Western Isles Council; although this council has a bilingual policy, it falls well short of full bilingualism in practice. Significant levels of Gaelic-medium services would also be required of public bodies active in local authority areas where Gaelic speakers make up at least 10 per cent of the population or number 2500 in total.

15. Because broadcasting is not a topic within the legislative competence of the Scottish Parliament, legislation in this area would be required at Westminster. The government has already commissioned a task force, headed by the former director-general of the BBC, Alistair Milne, to consider the case for the creation of a dedicated Gaelic digital channel.

16. Canada, where minority-language rights, particularly rights to minority-language education, are constitutionally-protected: See, for example, Hogg (1992), or Schneiderman (1989). For a good overview of constitutional protection of minority languages in the domestic law of various states, see de Varennes (1986).

17. See, for example, article 27 of the United Nation's *International Covenant on Civil and Political Rights*, as well as interesting developments in the Council of Europe, in particular, such as the *Framework Convention for the Protection of National Minorities* and the *European Charter for Regional or Minority Languages*. There have also been developments at the UN and within the Organization for Security and Co-operation in Europe. See, Robert Dunbar, *Minority Language Rights in International Law* (forthcoming).

uncertainty surrounded the future of Gaelic-medium primary school units at East Kilbride in South Lanarkshire and in Edinburgh, and Gaelic-medium educational services at schools in the Highland Region.[18] In 1998, one Gaelic-speaking Highland councillor went so far as to argue that Gaels had to accept cuts like everyone else. When parents of children in Gaelic-medium education persisted in lobbying to prevent the cuts, the councillor issued an astonishing press release in which the parents were labelled 'whinging Gaels'. And, as noted above, the budget of the CCG has, in fact, been subject to a significant cut, this at the hands of a minister, Brian Wilson, who has been a prominent supporter of the language community.

As is noted in Tormod Caimbeul's paper, in the run-up to the May 1997 British general election, all parties supported a preliminary statement of general principles on secure status that had been released by CNAG in March 1997. And as he also noted, in January 1998, there were some indications by Brian Wilson in the debate on the Scotland Bill[19] that Gaels seeking secure status might not have to wait for the establishment of a Scottish Parliament, as the earlier pre-election messages suggested. In October 1998, the next Scottish Officer Minister with responsibility for Gaelic, Calum MacDonald, announced at the Royal National Mòd in Portree that he was instructing Scottish Office officials to meet with CNAG with a view to advancing the proposals for secure status. In the election campaign for the Scottish Parliament in the spring of 1999, three of the four major Scottish parties – Labour, the Scottish Nationalists and the Liberal Democrats – all gave support in their electoral manifestos to CNAG's campaign for secure status, and subsequent to the election, the coalition agreement between Labour and the Liberal Democrats pursuant to which the present new Scottish Executive was formed described secure status for Gaelic as one of the new government's legislative priorities. In the heady days following the formation of the new Scottish Executive, there was even some speculation that a Gaelic language bill would be one of the first eight pieces of legislation the government hoped to introduce in the first session of the new Parliament. This was not to be, although the minster with responsibility for Gaelic in the new government, Alasdair Morrison, reaffirmed the government's commitment to secure status at the CNAG *Còmhdhail* in June 1999. In September 1999, however, the Scottish Executive released the government's legislative priorities for the next several years. Entitled 'Making It Work Together', secure status for Gaelic was not listed as one of those priorities; indeed, secure status was mentioned only in passing, and the government pledged merely to 'work towards' it, with no

---

18. See Tormod Caimbeul's contribution to this collection.
19. The legislation under which the Scottish Parliament was created.

target date specified. Thus, the possibility of early legislative action is looking increasingly unlikely.

Professor Donald Meek of the Celtic Department at Aberdeen University has said that secure status, if and when it comes, could be the single most important development for the Gaelic community since the passage of the Crofters Holdings (Scotland) Act 1886. This is, in my view, a fair assessment. Yet there are still many in Gaeldom who lack the imagination to see what a difference strong legislative protection for Gaelic could make. In Tormod Caimbeul's contribution to this conference, he gives an entertaining account of some of the successful campaigns that have been waged over the last fifteen years for certain Gaelic services, most notably, the creation of a Gaelic television fund. Like Tormod Caimbeul, I salute the skill, even the *seòltachd* – the ingenuity or cunning – of the Gaels who were involved in these successful campaigns. The Gaelic community needs this sort of political craftiness. But we must also recognise that there is something horribly wrong when the provision of what I regard as simply a basic right – the provision of basic public services in one's own language, and a language native to the country, at that – depends on knowing the right people, and, indeed, sheer good luck. So, I suggest that the time is right to put these political skills to work to obtain real statutory protection for the Gaelic language community, so that in future Gaels can direct their intellect and energies to the building of the community, not playing the roulette wheel of political lobbying.

Gaels should also remember, though, that even the acquisition of fundamental legal rights will not be the end of the story. The existence of such rights will not guarantee greater goodwill towards the language among politicians, bureaucrats, or voters who are not part of the Gaelic community; indeed, it is precisely because such goodwill can quickly evaporate that secure status is of such importance, for it provides a measure of protection to the Gaelic community in spite of ill-will, cutbacks, changing fashion and so forth. And, if legal protection is to be of any value, there will come the day when such linguistic rights will have to be put to the test. This will require Gaels to develop a new set of skills, a new activism, and a new sense of self-reliance and self-confidence. Secure status can, in my view, be a very important tool for advancing the interests of the Gaelic community. But it is only a tool. It needs a human hand to put it to use. If the Gaelic community feels that legal protection somehow absolves it from the need to organise and press to fully realise its legal rights, the battle may have been won and the war lost.

## Gaelic, politics and party politics

The foregoing demonstrates that the core issues with respect to Gaelic in Scotland are essentially political ones. This is, I am sure, also true of Irish in Northern Ireland, or of virtually any other minority language one may wish to name. In my experience, however, there has not yet emerged a widespread recognition in the Scottish Gaelic community of this reality that language revival and development is a struggle which lies in a fundamental way in the always tough and often dirty world of politics.

I shall conclude by addressing a few aspects of this political dimension in Scotland: first, the issue of the relationship between the Gaelic and non-Gaelic speaking communities in Scotland; second, the issue of the relationship between Gaelic activists and the major political parties; and third, and the political possibilities presented by the new Scottish Parliament.

In his paper, Tormod Caimbeul notes that one of the threats to Gaelic is that the language could be regarded with hostility in the new Scotland, or seen by most in the new Parliament as unworthy of the time, investment or even 'secure status' being sought. As he notes, there is real ignorance and, in some cases antipathy towards Gaelic among non-Gaels. Old prejudices die hard. As I noted when speaking at the 1997 CNAG *Comhdhàil*, even in the two and a half years that I had then been in Scotland, I had seen pieces written about Gaelic in the press – both tabloids and the so-called quality press – which were offensive and which simply would not have been written about other minorities in this day and age. In one memorable tirade, for example, Alan Brown wrote in the autumn of 1997 in the pages of the *Sunday Times'* Scottish supplement that everything about Gaelic and those who promote it is 'loathesome'. There are many, many other examples. One still often hears Gaelic speakers called 'teuchters', a term described in one of the standard dictionaries of the Scots language as 'mildly disparaging'. These views have a long pedigree, and space does not permit a fuller discussion of how Gaels have been perceived in the wider Scottish context. And while we are commonly told that attitudes of non-Gaelic speakers towards Gaelic are more positive than ever, there is still some way to go before we reach a point where there is full understanding and acceptance of Scotland's Gaelic fact. For too many in Scotland, Gaelic is still essentially considered to be 'foreign'; something not perceived as truly part of a national heritage, but only part of a regional one. The crucial point for our purposes is simply that such attitudes do have political implications for Gaelic. For one thing, they make it easier for people like the Gaelic-speaking Highland councillor, referred to above, to marginalise the concerns of 'whinging Gaels'. So, while it would be inappropriate to suggest that there is the same level of polarisation of attitudes with regards to Gaelic that there may exist with respect to Irish in Northern Ireland, Scotland does have its own internal contradictions.

Perhaps the most peculiar thing to a Belfast audience about the interface between Gaelic and Scottish politics is the degree to which Gaelic has, in fact, remained non-politicised. There are individuals in all four of the major Scottish political parties who are strong supporters of Gaelic (although it must also be admitted that each of these parties is also home to people who are seriously opposed to Gaelic and the aspirations of Gaels). In spite of this, however, no party has given Gaelic issues very much prominence in its manifesto, and none of the parties has, at least in recent elections, pledged anything in respect of Gaelic that is remarkably distinctive. Usually, Gaelic is simply not considered at all in mainstream political discourse. In some respects, of course, this is not surprising. The Gaelic community is a small one, concentrated in sufficient numbers to actually matter in only one or two constituencies, such as the Western Isles, or Ross, Skye and Inverness West (interestingly, the only two Gaelic-speaking members of the Scottish Parliament, Alasdair Morrison and John Farquhar Munro, represent these two constituencies), and those constituencies are rural ones, far from the centres of power. It could be argued, though, that the Gaelic community has done itself few favours. It has not, for example, shown the inclination to organise itself at the ballot box as a united and powerful political voice since the 1880s, and on that occasion, the issue was principally one of crofters' land rights, not language rights per se, and led to the election of four MPs who formed the 'Crofters' Party' at Westminster.[20] In the 1999 elections to the Scottish Parliament, for example, a new political party emerged, called *Cairdeas*, or The Highland Alliance. Though Gaelic was only one of many issues of particular relevance to the Highlands that *Cairdeas* sought to advance, the party garnered little support and elected no members.[21] Gaelic, then, is simply not much of a political issue, and is certainly not one which has thusfar divided sharply on party-political lines.

20. See, for example, the seminal work on the issue: James Hunter, *The Making of the Crofting Community*, (Edinburgh, John Donald, 1995), p 160.

21. Parliament is, as noted earlier, composed of 129 members, seventy-three of whom are elected in the traditional 'first-past-the-post' manner from Scotland's existing seventy-two Westminster constituencies. (Orkney and Shetland were split into two constituencies under the Scotland Act 1998, and, presumably because of their distinctiveness, they cannot, unlike any other existing constituency, be redefined out of existence by any future changes to constituencies by the Electoral Commission.) One would have thought that the Western Isles constituency – the one constituency in which Gaels are a majority – would have been similarly protected from changes in electoral boundaries which would compromise its distinctiveness, but such was not the case. Given its relatively small electoral roll, and that the number of Scottish constituencies is due to be significantly reduced, it is entirely possible that the Western Isles could be grouped with a part or the whole of another constituency or constituencies, thereby reducing the Gaelic character of the constituency and, significantly for our purposes, weakening the potential of a Gaelic voting block, were such a thing to ever emerge.

One aspect of the foregoing which may be noteworthy for a Belfast audience is the notable lack of exclusive association between Gaelic and nationalist politics. This is not as surprising as it may seem, however, for the Scottish identity is a complex and multi-layered one. This is partly a result of history, partly a result of historiography and ideology, and partly the result of political realities. Indeed, the relationship between Gaelic and party politics could itself be the subject of a paper, and so I need not delve too deeply into the matter. But I would suggest that in the absence of a coherent national identity, or at least in the absence of strongly integrative national myths, the linkage between one strand of that national identity – Gaeldom – and a particular brand of national – or nationalist – politics is a difficult one to make. Even if there was any great groundswell of support among Gaels for nationalist politics, for example, this would pose some problems for a nationalist party which must appeal to a much wider and more numerous cross-section of the population, and one which has, as described above, no real affinity for Gaeldom nor any strong sense of having a Gaelic heritage.

This is not necessarily a bad state of affairs. It allows, for example, for the sort of tactical flexibility that Tormod Caimbeul describes very effectively in his paper. But in order to advance Gaelic as a political issue, Gaels will, in my view, have to do at least three things. First, they must identify supporters in all parties and help such supporters to build cross-party coalitions of support. There is an informal all-party parliamentary working group on Gaelic at Westminster which has provided some support to organisations such as CNAG. Such a grouping, comprised as it is of members of all the four major parties, is a good start at coalition building, and in the absence of a formal Gaelic committee or sub-committee at the Scottish Parliament (one of the CNAG secure status proposals), the development of such an informal grouping of MSPs in Edinburgh would be welcome. Such a cross-party group has now been established at the Scottish Parliament.

Second, Gaels must help supporters in all parties to convince their colleagues of the importance of Gaelic; as noted, opposition can come from colleagues as well as members of other parties. This sort of coalition-building will, however, require both tactical skill and strategic planning. Tormod Caimbeul argues in his paper to this conference that Gaels have been good at tactics but not strategy. This may be a fair analysis, but is not surprising. Tactics, after all, are often the only device available to the weak. Indeed, all of the Gaelic organisations face two considerable obstacles which impinge even on their tactical flexibility, to say nothing of their ability to engage in serious strategic planning, and both relate to funding.

One major obstacle relates to levels of funding; Gaelic organisations have relatively few resources available to them.[22] It is, for example, often assumed that the various Gaelic bodies have armies of people working for them. This is simply not the case. CLI, CNSA, CNAG and the CCG all employ only a handful of people between them. They simply do not have the financial resources to employ more. Those that are employed must generally deal with day-to-day operational issues, or with administration. To effectively lobby the various parties on an ongoing basis, or wage an effective ongoing public relations effort, or to engage in significant 'outreach' work is difficult without sufficient staff and other resources. CNAG and the various other Gaelic bodies have, for example, recognised the desirability of having a parliamentary affairs officer in Edinburgh to monitor the Scottish Parliament and engage with politicians, bureaucrats and other public- and private-sector bodies which have a presence in the capital. Due to present expenditure commitments and limited overall budgets, Gaelic organisations simply do not have the resources at present to engage such an officer. Even a major campaign, such as CNAG's campaign for *Inbhe Thèarainte*, has had to rely in significant measure on the efforts of volunteers.

The other obstacle that Gaelic organisations face is the source of funding; a quick glance at the financial statements of any of the Gaelic organisations would show that virtually all of their funding comes from the public purse, and significant amounts from the Scottish Executive and local governments. Yet these are the very people whose policies the organisations are trying to shape. It is difficult to put very much real pressure on the people who pay your bills, and therefore the scope for tactical manoeuvring is extremely limited. Greater freedom to operate would come if the Gaelic community financed the various Gaelic organisations themselves, such that they were relatively independent of government, but the community has thus far shown neither the ability nor the inclination to do so.

The third thing that Gaels must be aware of is the opportunity to use whatever voting power they have to advance Gaelic issues. Most politicians do not enter politics with a particularly well-defined political agenda, but they do respond to issues which represent a significant opportunity to pick up votes or a significant risk of losing them (or both). Where Gaels do exist in sufficient numbers, then, they should be thinking carefully of how to exercise their voting power to extract concessions from local candidates. As Gaels constitute a majority of voters in the Western Isles and a significant minority in con-

22. See, for example, the information with respect to funding set out in part 1 of this paper. The figures there reflect Scottish Executive funding only, and most Gaelic organisations are also partially funded by local councils, public agencies such as Highlands and Islands Enterprise (an economic development agency) and other public and quasi-public bodies. Nonetheless, Scottish Executive funding is a significant part of total funding.

stituencies such as Ross, Skye and Inverness West, and Argyll and Bute, these are three constituencies in which Gaels could, if they wished, push Gaelic issues and demand strongly pro-Gaelic candidates. The question is, will they? As noted above, Gaels have not shown a strong inclination for this sort of strategic voting for quite some time.[23] At the same time, there is almost certainly a small but significant number of voters in these and other constituencies who harbour irrational fears about so-called 'Gaelic fanatics' bent on 'forcing us all to speak Gaelic' (there are, no doubt, a number of Gaelic-speakers who also fall within this camp!), and who are willing to loudly proclaim such views. This combination of weak political consciousness and solidarity among Gaels and strong, vocal opposition is almost certainly a recipe for political inaction on Gaelic; a politician who voices strong support for Gaelic may not necessarily win much additional support from Gaels who would otherwise be inclined to vote for other parties, and could alienate supporters who are suspicious of Gaelic. A far safer strategy for the sensible politician is one of mild appeasement: speak in warm but general terms about Gaelic, and if action must be taken, support measures which tend to be symbolic rather than fundamental. Politicians who pursue such a path cannot be blamed too much for this; after all, why should we expect them to be more adventurous and bold than the Gaelic community itself?

To fundamentally alter this state of affairs will require a sea-change in the political behaviour of the Gaelic community. Quite simply, Gaels must begin to make strong support for Gaelic a *sine qua non* of their political support; a significant number of Gaels must begin to vote as Gaels first, and Labourites, Scottish Nationalists, Liberal Democrats, or Tories second, and they must elevate Gaelic issues to the top of the list of political priorities. Also, non-Gaelic speakers must still be won over. As noted, significant progress on Gaelic issues will be more easily advanced in an atmosphere in which the political costs and dangers associated with the support of strongly pro-Gaelic measures are small. Changing broader public opinion will require, however, that Gaels begin to engage in the dreaded world of public relations. In particular, the benefits of Gaelic language revival for the wider Scottish public must be

---

23. It must be admitted that any definitive statements about voting patterns and political attitudes of Gaels have to be made with considerable caution; as is true of so much else relating to the Gaelic community, a detailed and rigorous study of voting patterns and preferences among Gaelic speakers, broader political attitudes, and so forth, has yet to be made. The views of the author are therefore based on the next best thing: in-depth discussions with a range of people active in the Gaelic community, first-hand observations, and so forth. It is worth noting, though, that in leading academic texts on modern Scottish politics, issues relating to the Gaelic language, and Gaelic-speaking voters, get barely a mention: see, for example, Alice Brown et al, (1998) in which Gaelic and Gaels are notable by their absence. This reflects both the general irrelevance with which Gaelic is treated by non-Gaels, and the relative lack of political importance attaching to Gaelic.

made more obvious. These include cultural, social and economic benefits, and, in fairness, it must be said that Gaelic organisations have already made some progress in convincing the public about the advantages of Gaelic in each of these areas. But the Gaelic community and its representatives must also convince the public that there are real costs to all Scots involved in language decline, and Gaelic organisations have not, perhaps, emphasised these enough. This is, however, largely because we simply do not know these costs ourselves. Such costs include all of the social costs involved with the decline of a community, including social problems like alcohol and drug abuse, poorer than expected economic performance, higher than expected levels of out-migration, and so forth.

I would like to conclude by noting that the next year or two is a crucial time for Gaelic, a time of real opportunities but also of real threats. With the new Scottish Parliament, everything is, in a real sense, up for grabs. While the first few months of the new Parliament have not given Gaels a clear signal that the new arrangements will produce immediate improvements for the language, all involved in this new venture in democratic politics, from politicians and bureaucrats to journalists and lobbyists, are still finding their way. As noted, though, much will turn on the ability of the Gaelic community as a whole to become more politically dynamic and on the ability of Gaelic organisations, in particular, to interact effectively with, on the one hand, the community they represent in order to build this dynamism, and on the other hand, the politicians and bureaucrats in Edinburgh with whom the political power now lies. The latter will be difficult to for Gaelic organisations to do without some sort of ongoing presence in Edinburgh, in the form of, say, at least one parliamentary affairs officer to represent them. Such an officer would be far more than a 'lobbyist'; he or she would be responsible for providing 'political intelligence': for example, the early identification of issues which may have an impact on Gaelic, the identification of those with real, as opposed to de jure power, an awareness of the written and unwritten rules and procedures under which such players play, the identification of potential political allies and enemies and the manner in which effective alliances can be built, and so forth. As noted above, Gaelic organisations are hampered in the appointment of such an officer by resource and other issues, but a way around these issues must be found.

The interaction between Gaelic organisations and the broader Gaelic community will be just as important, perhaps more so: a weak linkage between the two robs the community of an important source of leadership on Gaelic issues, and robs the organisations of a sense of legitimacy which, in turn, makes their representations easier for politicians to ignore. One of the great dangers I see in Gaeldom is a certain apathy, even cynicism. While the professionalism of the various Gaelic organisations to which Tormod Caimbeul refers in his paper has been essential to much of the positive measures of the last fifteen years, it has also allowed certain members of the Gaelic community to sit back and say: 'Let CNAG do it', or 'let CNSA do it', or 'let CLI do it', or 'let the CCG do it'; 'after all, they are the ones who are getting paid to promote the language.' In my view, this is a dangerous view which compromises the political dynamism of the community as a whole and weakens the hand of the organisations themselves. Ultimately, this can only be addressed by ensuring that our various organisations are as open and democratically accountable to the Gaelic community as possible. This, however, is a topic for another day, and another paper.

## Postscript: June 2000

As noted in my article, endorsement of secure status by three of the four major parties in their 1999 campaign manifestos and a reference to it in the ruling coalition's plan for government heightened the expectations of Gaelic campaigners that legislative measures to implement the CNAG proposals were imminent. These hopes were, perhaps, somewhat overly optimistic. In autumn 1999 for example, an education reform bill, the Standards in Scotland's Schools (etc.) Bill (the 'Schools Bill') was tabled by the Executive; in spite of the fact that a significant portion of the secure status proposals dealt with educational issues, including the creation of a statutory right to Gaelic-medium education where reasonable demand existed therefor, there was initially no reference at all to Gaelic in the Schools Bill.

In December 1999, Alasdair Morrison's first major move on the Gaelic front was not a legislative initiative but, to the surprise of some, the establishment of a five-person task force, to be chaired by John Alick Macpherson, deputy director of the CCG, with the remit of examining the arrangements and structures for the public support of the Gaelic organisations in Scotland (such as CNAG, CNSA, Comann an Luchd-Ionnsachaidh (CLI), the Gaelic Learners' Association and CnamP(N)), with a view to advising Scottish ministers on future arrangements. The task force was to have reported by 30 April 2000, but the report is not expected until summer. While the various Gaelic organisations welcomed the review, it must be said that, given the present circumstances of the language, minute scrutiny of comparatively small organisations (all except the CCG receive less than £1 million in public funding per year), the work of many of which is carried out in significant measure by volunteers, is hardly a serious priority.

In winter 2000, an ongoing campaign by parents in Edinburgh to win the establishment of a Gaelic-medium school in the capital was encountering significant opposition from the local council, and was turning increasingly bitter. There was still no discussion whatsoever by the Executive of its intentions with respect to secure status for Gaelic, or any comparable legislative or other language maintenance strategy for the language. Given reports that the 2001 census could show a precipitous drop in the number of Gaelic speakers, perhaps as large as 20,000 from the 1991 figure, there was an increasing sense of urgency among many Gaelic activists.

It was within this context that CnamP(N) decided to press the Scottish Executive for the inclusion of a statutory right to Gaelic-medium education, based on the secure status proposals, in the Schools Bill. Through its use of the public petition mechanisms of the standing orders, CnamP(N) was able to get the issue before the committee scrutinising the Schools Bill, and representatives of CnamP(N), CNSA and CNAG were asked to give testimony before this committee on 2 May 2000.

What followed was a remarkable five weeks of activity which can be only briefly summarised here; however, these events serve to highlight a number of the themes I raised in my article. It is clear that the Gaelic community and, indeed, the various political parties have crossed a Rubicon of sorts.

On 3 May, after the testimony of the Gaelic bodies, John Farquhar Munro of the Liberal Democrats tabled an amendment to the Schools Bill which was based on the CnamP(N) petition. Following intensive discussions between the Scottish Executive Deputy Minister for Education, Peter Peacock, and CNAG, this amendment was withdrawn by Mr Munro, on the understanding that the Executive would itself table an amendment which would not create a statutory right of the sort the Gaelic organisations had been campaigning for, but which would include Gaelic within the School Bill's framework for improving standards in education. The following week, considerable dissent emerged within CNAG; many activists were concerned that acceptance by CNAG and the opposition parties of the Executive's amendment would scupper any future chances of a more substantial scheme for Gaelic-medium education, including a statutory right thereto, and without any Executive commitment on a Gaelic language bill to implement the secure status provisions, it was feared that the Gaelic community would come away with too little, at a time when resolute action needed to be taken before it was too late for the language.

After an extraordinary poll of its board of directors, CNAG announced on 2 June that it welcomed the Executive's proposed amendment, which had been slightly enhanced to also place a statutory duty on local councils to report on their provision of Gaelic-medium education and on their plans for the development thereof. However, CNAG also noted that, given the parlous state of the language, stronger measures were now needed. Michael Russell of the SNP and John Farquhar Munro then tabled a further amendment which, among other things, would have created an obligation on local councils to provide Gaelic-medium education where there was 'reasonable demand' therefor. The amendment was rejected by sixty-two votes to thirty-six, with seventeen abstentions. The amendment was universally opposed by the Executive, including Alasdair Morrison, and the Scottish parliamentary Labour party; it was universally supported by the SNP, and by the single Green party and Scottish Socialist MSPs and the one independent. Mr Munro, the two other Liberal Democrat MSPs representing Highland constituencies, and one other Liberal Democrat supported the amendment; the other Liberal Democrat MSPs supported their coalition partners. It had initially been suspected that the Tories would vote with the Executive against the Russell/Munro amendment; ultimately, they abstained. Indeed, it emerged that they might have been convinced to support the amendment, but ultimately did not in part because they felt they had not been adequately consulted by Russell and Munro and, in particular, by the Gaelic organisations.

The Schools Bill amendment produced considerable recrimination within the Gaelic community; the deputy convenor of the Western Isles Council, Roddy Murray of the Labour Party, was highly critical of the role played by CNAG, as was Alasdair Morrison himself. Ominously, Murray called upon Mr Macpherson's task force to scrutinise CNAG' s future role very closely, apparently oblivious to the fact that it was CnamP(N) which had been instrumental in forcing the issue. However, the episode has forced Gaelic organisations, the Gaelic media and, perhaps, the wider Gaelic community to confront the dire situation which faces the language, and has forced Gaels to consider what steps are now necessary to reverse the decline.

The episode has also put the question of Gaelic firmly within the political arena. For many, the present author included, this is entirely appropriate, for questions such as linguistic rights and the linguistic development of a community are matters of public policy and are, of necessity, political in nature. The Schools Bill also showed that clear differences are beginning to emerge between the political parties, particularly between Labour and the SNP, on how to approach Gaelic. This has been highlighted in the passage of another bill, on national parks, which is currently wending its way through the parliament; Michael Russell of the SNP has tabled a number of amendments with respect to the inclusion of reference to and provision for Gaelic in this bill, and although the Executive has indicated that it is willing to table some form of amendment in response, it is not yet clear whether it is willing to go as far as the SNP. In the wake of the Schools Bill, the SNP, the Tories and some Liberal Democrats have all raised the possibility of introducing a Gaelic language bill in the near future as a private members' bill; if they are able to come to a set of joint proposals which garner the support of many of the Gaelic organisations, this could put considerable pressure on the Executive to reconsider its approach and its timing on this issue. Indeed, Michael Russell announced on 7 July that he had lodged a proposal within the Parliament to introduce a Gaelic language bill.

Finally, the episode has once again highlighted the need for Gaelic organisations, and CNAG in particular, to appoint some sort of parliamentary affairs officer, stationed at the Parliament full-time. Had the Tories been involved in the process at an earlier stage, their support for the Russell/Munro amendment might have been secured; this would have made the vote a very close one. More thorough lobbying at an earlier stage in the process may have allowed the Gaelic organisations to at very least obtain more significant commitments from the Executive, and may perhaps have won greater support from the Liberals and even dissident Labour MSPs which would have added to their clout. It may also have helped to avoid some of the mistakes which had been made by all the parties involved. Such sustained lobbying by CNAG or any of the other Gaelic organisations was almost impossible, given their present limited resources, and shall remain so until such time as they have a full-time professional present at the Parliament.

My conclusion remains the same: the next year or two is still a crucial time for Gaelic, a time of real opportunities but also of real threats. The Scottish Parliament has created an entirely new dynamic, has ensured that the issue of Gaelic will remain in the political arena and will require Gaels to develop new attitudes, skills and ideas, whether they like it or not. Much will depend on how Gaels themselves, rather than politicians, respond to these challenges.

# Taig Talk

Aodán Mac Póilin

You have been given a vivid overview of the current situation of Gaelic in Scotland. In this brief response it would be foolish to try to give an equally comprehensive account of how Irish is faring on this side of the Sheugh. So I have narrowed the field; first to the Northern Ireland context, and then narrowed the account further by concentrating mainly on the issue of how the Irish language is perceived in this society.

Minority languages can be contentious enough anywhere in the world, and Gaelic in Scotland and its first cousin in the Republic of Ireland clearly face a number of daunting challenges. In an overwhelmingly Anglophone world, as we all know, the chief reaction to Irish and Gaelic ranges from various levels of negativity through indifference towards a vague and unfocused instinct to be moderately supportive leavened by pockets of fervent enthusiasm. In Northern Ireland, however, the language question is also implicated in the deep religious and political polarisation of our society. This presentation attempts to show how the language issue in Northern Ireland is arguably both more intensely felt and more divisive than in Scotland or the Irish Republic, to hint at why this may be so, and to point out some of the dilemmas facing the language movement.

The following extracts, chosen to illustrate one pole of the debate, are from an unpublished survey on Protestant attitudes to the Irish language carried out on behalf of an Irish language group in Derry. Non-natives may need some background information to interpret the material, but I will be as brief as possible, and try to summarise an extremely complex situation in three short paragraphs.

The first point is that the issue which dominates all others here is whether Northern Ireland remains in the United Kingdom or becomes integrated into a united Ireland. As a result, every question becomes the constitutional question; every issue is ultimately interpreted in the light of how it may affect the constitutional issue.

Second, the term 'Taig' may be unfamiliar to some of you. This is of course the once common Christian name 'Tadhg' which survives in Scotland in the surname MacCaig, and in Ireland as McTague and its variants. In Northern Ireland 'Taig' belongs to an impressive litany of terms, among them 'Fenian', 'Mick', 'Popehead', 'Papist', used to describe an 'Arsie' (= RC; = Roman Catholic).

Point three relates to the high correlation between religious identity and political affiliation in Northern Ireland. In practical terms, this translates into an almost immutable perception that Protestant equals unionist equals loyalist, and Catholic equals nationalist equals republican. In this context, the link made by the interviewees between religion, politics and linguistic loyalty is not entirely without foundation, if rather extreme in its expression. Most Irish speakers in Northern Ireland are Catholics; the 1991 census returns showed that fewer than one in twenty of those who identified their religious persuasion and claimed a knowledge of Irish were Protestants (Census 1993: 28). If Irish speakers are predominantly Catholic they are also presumed to be nationalists. Irish is therefore seen by many unionists as a Catholic, nationalist language, and therefore subversive of the polity.

The first interview was with 'Mark', a 19-year-old unemployed Belfast man:

*Question*: 'Have you, or any member of your family learned the Irish language?
*Mark*: No.
*Question*: Would you ever consider learning it?
*Mark*: No.
*Question*: Why not?
*Mark*:    Because it's Taig talk, that's why.
*Question*: Why did you say that?
*Mark*: Because only Taigs talk it, that's why.
*Question*: Given the current peace situation, could you ever see a time when it could be used in the unionist community?
*Mark*: No way, it's for the Taigs and not us.'

The interviewer presented Mark with a list of thirty-six words, ranging from the benevolent to the hostile, asking him to pick the five he thought were most appropriate to describe the Irish language. Mark picked out 'anger', 'Catholic', 'republican', 'dead', 'sectarian'. The next question:

*Question*: 'Why did you give those responses to that question?
*Mark*: Because that's what I feel about it, and that's what you asked me to tell you.

*Question*: You also said that you hated anyone using it. Why?

*Mark*: Because they're all in the IRA and I'm a loyalist, and that's the story.

*Question*: Would you be suspicious of anyone using it?

*Mark*: Yes.

*Question*: What images do you have of those using it?

*Mark*: They're all Taigs.'

There is a short note at the bottom of the page: 'Interview duration – eleven minutes. It was abandoned after the interviewer received a lot of vitriolic abuse from the respondent' (Kerr 1994, No 12).

This was the most dramatic of the interviews in the survey, but it was by no means unique. Working-class interviewees in particular, but also one 39-year-old civil servant, gave a similar pattern of responses. One 17-year-old girl, who thought the Irish language was 'basically more for Taigs than [for] us', when asked if she had seen any Irish language programmes on the television, responded:

> I have never noticed any, but I am sure if they were on the television my da would have them off right away. He wouldn't stand it. He is not what you would call a supporter of anything Irish. He wouldn't even watch the Irish playing football, and he loves football. (Kerr 1994, No 4)

Some unionist politicians are equally hostile. Jim Shannon of the Democratic Unionist Party, and a prominent supporter of the Ulster Scots movement, which he appears to identify solely with Presbyterianism, said, 'We are Ulster Scots, descended from a proud and fiercely independent people with a longer tradition than that promoted by nationalists – their language is a dead language for a dead people' (*Irish News*, 25 September 1996). It is ironic that Jim Shannon's surname is derived from the Irish Gaelic Ó Seanáin (Black 1993: xxxix, 720).

This type of response is not universal. While it is worth knowing that the Irish language can produce a reaction at this level of hostility, it is not the complete picture. In a 1991 survey, 23 per cent of Protestants agreed that all secondary school pupils should have to study Irish language and culture (Stringer and Robinson 1991: 18); study of the Irish language at secondary level is restricted almost exclusively to the Catholic education sector. The Opsahl Report of 1993 noted:

> The commission was made aware of a real desire by many Northern Protestants to regain their sense of Irishness, and to reacquaint themselves with Irish history, culture and the language,… we believe that Irish culture has a great potential for uniting people in Northern Ireland, and urge all its proponents to ensure that it is made unthreatening and attractive to Northern Protestants (Pollak 1993:122).

A major survey carried out in April 2000 found that only 21 per cent of Protestants regarded the Irish language and culture as fairly offensive or very offensive – the alternatives were 'neither offensive or inoffensive/fairly inoffensive/very inoffensive' (*Belfast Telegraph*, 5 April 2000). While these examples may illustrate an increasing level of tolerance to the language, reflecting a new spirit of acceptance of cultural diversity, it is important that we do not underestimate the level of suspicion or hostility which still exists.

To put unionist hostility to Irish in a historical context, it is worth noting that the perception that the language is exclusively associated with Catholicism and nationalism is of recent origin. The chain of office of the Lord Mayor of Belfast bears the inscription '*Éirinn go Brách*' – 'Ireland for Ever' (the chain of office of the Lord Mayor of Dublin has King William of Orange). When Queen Victoria came to Belfast in 1849, she noted in her diary: 'I have all along forgotten to say that the favourite motto written up on most of the arches, etc. was 'Céad Míle Fáilte' which means 'a hundred thousand welcomes' in Irish… They often called out Céad Míle Fáilte and it appears in every sort of shape' (Ó Bléine, *Irish News*, 21 November 1991). One of the shapes was an enormous floral display of dahlias on which the greeting was spectacularly mis-spelt. While the loyal burgers of the city were not necessarily Irish speakers, their use of the language for symbolic purposes reflects a very different attitude to the Irish language among unionists than that of the majority of unionist politicians through most of the 20th century.

Irish language activists emphasise that the Irish language is the common heritage of anybody who wants to learn it or speak it, no matter what their political or religious affiliation. This principle is deeply ingrained in the ideology of the language movement, and goes back to the founding of the Gaelic League in 1893. It should be said, however, that this inclusivity of principle is not always followed by an inclusivity of action. The reasons for this may be worth examining.

Most Irish language activity takes place in Catholic nationalist areas. This is not accidental, but is equally not necessarily due to a deliberate attempt to exclude Protestants and unionists. Because support for the language movement is an integral part of Irish nationalist ideology, the language is inevitably stronger in nationalist areas. Unionist ideology does not have that imperative, and, in fact, was actively hostile to the language for generations. As the language tended to be taught only in Catholic schools, the pool of speakers, semi-speakers and learners is overwhelmingly Catholic. Reinforcing these elements is the social structure of the Catholic community. Catholics, in the years in which they had been largely marginalised in Northern Ireland, responded not only by evolving a strong sense of social cohesion and an ethos of self-sufficiency, but had created institutions which passively resisted the institutions of the state. The Irish language movement was one of these institutions.

In addition, in a society in conflict, there is the question of personal safety. It remains the case, even today, that it is less dangerous to be involved in Irish language activities within Catholic areas. I live in a small Irish-speaking community in Belfast, which also developed the first Irish-medium school in Northern Ireland. The community is situated in Catholic West Belfast, in what is possibly the largest ghetto in western Europe. Regrettably, it is unlikely that this community or its school could have survived the worst of the Troubles anywhere but within a ghetto. It is almost certain that the school would not have survived for thirteen years as an independent non-funded school without the unstinting financial support of the large community of English-speaking Catholic nationalists around it.

The dynamic which all these factors created is of a language movement which aspires to be inclusive, but which is composed overwhelmingly of Catholic nationalists, with a tiny minority of Protestants, some of whom are also nationalists. One other element may be worth mentioning. Many Irish-speaking nationalists assume that Protestants who become involved in the Irish language movement, even if they begin as unionists, will ultimately become nationalists. This usually unspoken assumption is one of which unionists are profoundly aware, and itself is a barrier to greater unionist involvement. It is also a barrier which is passionately denied by most language activists. For those who wish to study this issue at a deeper level, a more complete account of the practical and psychological barriers to Protestant involvement in the language will be found in Gordon McCoy's article, 'Protestant learners of Irish in Northern Ireland' (McCoy 1997).

Those of us who are involved in the Irish language but who strive for a more inclusive language movement face an uncomfortable dilemma. We are aware that the language movement, while remarkably dynamic in the circumstances, is much weaker than we are prepared to admit in public. We are faced with two main choices.

One option relates to living out the implications of an ideology which claims that the Irish language belongs to everyone in Northern Ireland. Personally I always find it difficult to embrace that rhetoric and then fail to create access to the language for people who, for historical reasons, have been denied access, or who have been brought up to regard the language with suspicion. For me, to talk of inclusiveness while maintaining the conditions where inclusiveness is impossible, is hypocrisy.

The alternative is to accept the reality of the linguistic situation, to recognise how fragile the language movement is, and that the language's survival depends on strengthening the language community where it is already comparatively strong, within Catholic and nationalist areas. These areas provide social cohesion, an ideologically-supportive community, physical protection, a tradition of activity, and a relatively high proportion of Irish-speakers to build on. In a situation where resources are limited, there is a very strong argument for putting most of those limited resources into those communities where people are most interested in the language, and where there is a realistic chance of success.

These options are not, of course, mutually exclusive. The organisation I work for, ULTACH Trust, strives to find a balance between the two priorities. In practical terms, this involves about 80 per cent of our funding going to projects which operate more or less exclusively within the Catholic community, while about a third of the staff's time is spent in addressing the issue of inclusivity. To our surprise, this emphasis has led to a high level of hostility from a section of the Irish language movement. I have personally been described as 'Stormont's Irish language spy', 'the man from the NIO' (Northern Ireland Office), and as someone who, on behalf of the Ulster Unionist Party, is trying to block the development of the language. In fact, I have been described in print as a unionist. This is not a particularly comfortable situation for anyone who lives in Catholic West Belfast, although it would be much easier to live with if I was, in fact, a unionist. What is even more galling is that the debate on this extremely important question is conducted at such a reductive level that the central issue is never really addressed.

Before I finish, I would like to touch briefly on the dynamics of language movements in general, and the relationship of minority language communities with the majority culture and with the centres of power.

Minority language communities often live through two languages and two cultures within a broader monoglot society. Monoglots have only one window on the world, but our dominant, unilingual, unifocal, one-window majorities tend not to know that other windows exist. Nor do they have any idea what it is like to belong to a threatened culture, to a tradition that has been attenuated and half-broken. The reaction of many of the majority to a minority culture can range from simple incomprehension to downright loathing, but as often as not takes the form of a sadly blinkered, but instinctive and often unconscious arrogance. We cannot ignore the majority, we do not have the option of pulling up the drawbridge and pretending they do not exist, for they control our society.

But how do we engage with them? Confrontation may have its uses, and in some cases is the only option; we can demand recognition, demand our

rights as a minority and cite every international convention and every international precedent we can lay our hands on. But it seems to me that persuasion can be just as effective and in some cases more effective, and that the
more allies we can find the better. It seems to me that we must work strenuously to find intelligent and sophisticated ways to persuade as many of the
majority as possible of the value of our language and our culture.

We must also engage with the structures which directly control society, the
decision-makers and those who control the purse strings. There are two ways
of approaching the latter; you can work with them or you can work against
them, you can either head-butt or you can infiltrate. Most language organisations tend to do one or the other.

Welsh language activists have a wonderful two-handed system that has
lasted for three generations. The pattern goes something like this. Between
their mid-teens and their late 20s they are involved in the radical language politics of the Welsh Language Society. This involves grass-roots activism and
organised passive resistance, usually focused on a specific issue. Past campaigns have involved painting out English language signs in Welsh-speaking
areas to raise public awareness that these communities were in danger of
being destroyed. One particularly successful campaign involved the destruction of television studios to encourage the establishment of a Welsh-language
television station.

When they get to about 30 and have a couple of children, most activists
join the establishment. Joining the establishment has three effects on those
who join. They lose their grass-roots credibility, everybody who is not in the
establishment hates them, and they develop an enormous guilt complex.
However, they also believe in the Welsh language and they work the system
from the inside as best they can. They also have the advantage of having the
next generation outside roaring at the gates, who they can use to influence the
people who have the real power and could not care less about the language.

The Irish language movement in Northern Ireland was, until very recently, composed entirely of outsiders. Until recently, in fact, we were not allowed
inside the gate. This began to change in the late 1980s, and the government
began to look for safe ways of funding the language movement. In 1990 I
began to work for ULTACH Trust, the first Irish language organisation to
adopt a consensual approach to government rather than an oppositional one.
We were the first, and for a long time the only, Irish language insiders in
Northern Ireland. There is now a shift in emphasis, and things are beginning
to change slowly. A commitment to support the language has now been
enshrined in legislation, supported by statutory funding. There is a potential
in the future for an unspoken partnership between the activists, the outsiders

if you like, and guilt-ridden insiders who have sold their souls working quietly in the background. The survival of the language may depend on such a dynamic.

To conclude, just one word of warning to language activists – don't believe your own propaganda, unless it's true.

# Creating Culture

ANNE LORNE GILLIES

My Gaelic-speaking grandfather William Gillies (Liam Mac Gilliosa) died in 1932. According to his obituary he had 'among his old and intimate friends… as many Irish as Scots' (Ua Briain 1932, lxv). Ua Briain continues:

> Many a scheme… Liam and I elaborated for the purpose of bringing the Scots and Irish together again. Amongst others, a project for a joint gathering in Iona on St Colm Cille's Day. That came in days which were too troubled to permit us to more than propound the project to a few friends on either side of the Sea of Moyle. But I see in front of me a book, *Iona – a History of the Island*… presented to me by Liam Mac Giolla Iosa as a souvenir of our still-born project, and hoping that some day other Gaels might bring it to fruition. (ibid.)

So I would like to dedicate my remarks today to Liam Mac Gilliosa and Art Ua Briain and to the dream that they hatched away back the other side of that troubled sea. And perhaps the 'fruition' those two old friends anticipated may be seen in this conference and all the other new links that we have been forging in these celebrations for Colm Cille – all these healthy new shoots which have been reaching out across the Sea of Moyle, like the branches that linked Deirdre and Naois across eternity.

As you will already have guessed, I am going to give you a very personal, experiential version of this 'creating culture' theme. Because like all of you I work very hard, very full-time, at trying to maintain, define – or even create! – Gaelic culture. Theorising about our aims – taking stock of where we're going and why – is a luxury we do not get very often.

As in Ireland, Gaelic speakers in Scotland are spread very thinly: we turn our hands to whatever is needed at the time. I have often wished I had more time to look backwards to my grandfather's generation, to revisit their ideals and aspirations, their knowledge and richness of cultural idiom: to find substance and direction for my work. But then I have turned to look at my children's needs and interests and the rich diversity of their knowledge and skills, and the roads in both directions are littered with the shades of work as yet undone. Today's young Gaels have huge advantages, yet we of my generation have one overwhelming advantage over them: we have had to fight every inch of the way.

I learned Gaelic by a not uncommon route: the secondary school taught me grammar and introduced me to annual singing competitions; the university Celtic department taught me 18th-century literature and introduced me to 17th-century vowel shifts. It's all a very far cry from our children's linguistic experience, thirty years later, years in which the language base has shrunk to parlous levels but official support, especially in education and the media, has grown beyond the wildest dreams of those of us who have helped to make it happen. They are encouraged to communicate: we were belted for talking in class. We were surrounded with real live Gaelic speakers and story tellers and singers; they have Gaelic television and books and computer programs, and talk to each other by e-mail.

Gillies (*Gille Iosa*: 'the servant of Jesus') is an archetypal Gaelic surname, found throughout the north-west of Scotland, especially in the islands of Skye, Raasay and Harris. But mine is not a conventional island Gaelic background. As far back as we can trace them, to the mid 18th century at least, my Gillies ancestors came from Galloway, in the south-west, where Gaelic had lost its hold as a commonly-spoken language by the end of the 17th century (Withers 1984: 40). I myself was born in Stirling, but was taken at an early age to live in Argyll – *Earra-Ghàidheal* – 'Territory of the Gaels' and well-spring of Scottish Gaelic culture from the time of Colm Cille onwards. Here, I confidently assumed, I was going to learn Gaelic. But though there was plenty of Gaelic in and around Oban in 1950 there was none to be heard in the primary school classroom. I could sing in the Gaelic choir, or learn a few words by listening to the neighbours, but learning the language properly had to wait till I reached the high school.

On the face of it Oban High School in the 1950s was a bastion of Gaelic. The Rector (or head teacher) was the brother of Somhairle MacLean, the internationally celebrated Gaelic poet. Himself an erudite man with a talent for translating ancient Greek poetry into Gaelic metre, he was also a piper and the source of many of the traditional Gaelic songs I have treasured to this day. The head of the Gaelic department was also the president of An Comunn Gàidhealach and a well-known champion of linguistic rights. English lessons were enlivened by the hilarious asides of Iain Crichton Smith, acclaimed poet and novelist from Lewis. Even the maths teacher's brother, poor soul, had been customs officer in Uist when the SS *Politician* went down full of 'whisky galore'!

Oban High School had a long-standing tradition of success in Gaelic competitions – academic, musical, literary and sporting. The four school 'houses'
were known as 'clans', and owed their names to Celtic heroes (Ossian, Fingal,
Diarmid and Somerled). The school catchment in those days included the
Gaelic-speaking islands of Lismore, Mull, Iona, Colonsay, Tiree, Coll, Islay
and Jura. In short, the ethos of Oban High School was palpably 'Gaelic'. And
yet the number of pupils studying Gaelic – either native speakers or second
language learners – was in fact comparatively low: the high perceived cultural
or sentimental value of Gaelic did not outweigh its low societal status and
poor perceived instrumental value (Hunter 1990: 32–3).

Gaelic was taught as a discrete subject, timetabled against French. Though
the first language of many pupils, it was not classified as a 'modern' or
'European' language. Gaelic-English bilingualism was not considered to be an
advantage in learning other 'proper' languages: indeed choosing to study
Gaelic automatically disqualified pupils from taking up German at a later date.
Small wonder then that most of the 'bright, academic' pupils opted to study
French, while Highland history – the history of our own people – was seen
as 'definitely unimportant and probably untrue' because it was taught in the
Gaelic class while all the 'proper history' of the Romans and the Tudors and
the Roundheads took place somewhere else, in another country, another
classroom (Fraser 1989: 4–5).

The majority of the 12-year-olds in my S1 Gaelic class were native Gaelic-
speakers: home-sick hostel-dwellers transported from distant rural communities in Ardnamurchan or Morvern, or hollow-eyed travellers from Luing,
Appin, Ballachulish or Dalavich. Typically they were fully competent as
regards Gaelic comprehension and oral production, though more or less illit-
erate in the language. Yet they found themselves in a class alongside complete
beginners with no previous experience of the language at all. You, in
Northern Ireland have also come up against this problem I know, with the
transfer to secondary of the first few batches of your *bunscoil* pupils. The
Gaelic teacher responded to this impossible situation by teaching Gaelic as a
classical language: rich, poetic, unutterably precious – but effectively dead. We
all struggled through declensions and conjugations, and then graduated to the
poetry of Donnchadh Bàn, 18th-century Argyll game-keeper, peering myopi-
cally into every nook and cranny of his misty mountains. But the everyday linguistic experience of the boy from Ardnamurchan or the girl from Morvern
– the authentic living Gaelic culture of that time – was less useful in the
Gaelic class than a knowledge of Latin grammar.

Nowadays you will travel many a weary mile before you will find a single
native Gaelic-speaking child in Ardnamurchan or Lismore. Yet Gaelic-medi-

um education is now taking root in primary schools in Argyll and elsewhere in Scotland, not as cultural or linguistic maintenance, as would have been appropriate thirty years ago, but as cultural and linguistic regeneration. Like snowdrops sprouting through ground too hard to till, 'Gaelic is creating its own unlikely springtime not only in Argyll but also in parts of Scotland where the winter has been even longer, the ground even more forbidding' (Gillies 1990: 24). Places like Glasgow and Edinburgh, Aberdeen and Cumbernauld, where real deserts surround the educational experience of the children, and where attitudes, though we hope changing for the better, can still be less than supportive. My son, born and raised in the city of Glasgow, is now 25. At the age of 3 he was a fluent, irrepressible and, we thought, monolingual, Gaelic speaker. One day a Glasgow taxi-driver was berating me for speaking Gaelic to him: 'You'll ruin that wee boy's life speaking that language. You'll hold his education back if you don't teach him to speak English.' With that, my son struck both me and the taxi driver dumb by intoning, very distinctly, the undying words, 'Sit well back in your seat for safety and comfort'. (It occurs to me that that might have been a good title for this conference!)

At four, my son was given a place in an English-medium nursery school – unexpectedly, for local authority nursery places were scarce. It was some time before I discovered that his place had been offered because he was perceived to have 'a linguistic disadvantage'. This seemed very funny at the time: after all we perceived him to have a very great linguistic advantage! Believing early education to be very important, and blissfully unaware of the likely linguistic outcome, I brought my son every day to the nursery, past the 'Multicultural' notice in the foyer:

> Strathclyde Regional Council acknowledges the importance of mother tongue maintenance. Therefore books and audio-visual materials are available on request, in the following languages: Urdu, Punjabi, Cantonese...

No Gaelic, of course. My son quickly learned English – the language of football and television and books and games and friends. Of course I had expected this. What I had not anticipated was that within a very short time he became unwilling to speak Gaelic at all, associating it with parents and grandparents and '*sèid do shròn is ith do churrain*' ('blow your nose and eat your carrots'). He is now one of the many who 'understand some but don't speak it at all', his early advantages revealing themselves only in an above average penchant for languages in general.

It was as a result of negative experiences like ours that, in 1982, Comhairle nan Sgoiltean Àraich (the Gaelic Playgroup Association) was formed. CNSA was to become an enormous source of support and advice for isolated parents

struggling to maintain the language within the family. It was especially important in involving Gaelic-speaking women in responding to completely new
challenges. I am unwilling to suggest that Gaelic-speaking women in any way
form a single homogenous group. However I believe few would argue if I
suggested that, in the past, many of us were comparatively diffident both personally and politically, and relatively inexperienced in committee work, business management, finance, and in dealing with officialdom. CNSA provided
us with that experience – and we learned it through the medium of Gaelic. We
became empowered. Many of us, through Gaelic, found self-confidence and
jobs in Gaelic, and have not looked back since then. But I suspect that some
people might suggest that that is exactly what we should do: that we should
*look back* and weigh the importance of that empowerment, and the impact of
those Gaelic playgroups on our children, against the cultural implications of
successive generations of women adopting patterns of work (or should I say
workaholism) which are just as anti-social as men's. After all, women have
always been instrumental in transmitting culture, language, tradition to their
young children: who will take over this role in future? And who will decide the
syllabus?

The Gaelic playgroup movement also provided us with the support and
self-confidence to lobby the officials for the continuation of the Gaelic-medium process into the primary school and beyond. Suddenly we had parent
power: no more hanging back and being deferential – we were tax-payers,
constituents, ready and able to play the political parties off against one another, more powerful than all the language agencies put together. We also had a
solid piece of research (Grannd 1983) to back up our arguments: Seumas
Grannd, then of Glasgow University, had surveyed Gaelic-speaking parents
to see if they would consider sending their children to a Gaelic-medium mainland school if such existed, and his findings appeared to indicate a very high
level of parental interest. But in Strathclyde we found it an uphill struggle to
convince the regional council that these figures were authentic. We had to
work hard to convince them that we ourselves were not a Machiavellian, or
even, (perish the thought) middle-class pressure group sent to try them in
times of economic stricture but rather a bona fide group of parents with real
children and real cultural and educational needs. But when, in 1985, the council finally agreed to countenance us – albeit on an experimental basis – things
began to happen at a speed which left us all breathless and unprepared.

Of course we had blithely filled in Seumas Grannd's questionnaire: of
course we would send our children to a Gaelic school – after all it will never
happen, will it? Of course I had lobbied Strathclyde with all my might and
main: I am a parent, I want a Gaelic school, I am entitled to a Gaelic school,

the Gaels have been discriminated against for long enough, the Welsh have their Welsh-medium schools, the Irish have Irish-medium schools... Well, they won't give us one anyway, will they? But when the moment of truth comes and suddenly you are looking at unfamiliar, uninviting premises; worrying about the lack of resources, teacher training, methodology; when it's your children who are about to be used as guinea-pigs – then it is a different matter. We lacked a body of knowledge or expertise upon which to base our first faltering steps. The Western Isles, heartland of Gaelic, had been operating a bilingual policy since the late 1970s, but would reading material and environmental studies developed for rural communities be relevant to the city-based child's experience, let alone their level of linguistic competence? How would children fare in a community where Gaelic is seldom if ever heard outwith the school? How could we foster a sense of identity and common purpose among families scattered across a big city? How would the Gaelic language fare if exposed to hurried adaptation to and sustained usage in non-traditional contexts? In a city where a system of segregated schools exists, would religious differences make for difficulties undreamed of in rural contexts? Suddenly we realised that we were creating culture as we went along, and we did not know what criteria to apply. In the blur of those stressful days we made what I have long thought to have been a considerable strategic mistake.

At first we were offered a school in the centre of town – an urban wasteland behind the bus station, not near to any recognisable community at all, let alone a Gaelic one, nowhere near the homes of any of the families concerned. A huge, ugly, prison-like building with outside toilets, where we were assured that the roll was falling sharply and that we would soon have the run of the place. But we resisted – risking accusations of shaky commitment or, even worse, middle-class snobbery – and our Gaelic Unit ended up within another declining school, but this one a warm, friendly place in the heart of Pollokshaws, a long-established working-class area. Perversely, numbers in the host-school revived almost as soon as the unit opened within its walls. As parents we were reassured by the atmosphere in the host-school, by the well-stocked English resources and bright, shared facilities. Clearly such a scenario is also attractive to the authorities on grounds of cost. But with hindsight I think most of us have regretted that initial decision: regretted losing the opportunity of establishing an all-Gaelic school, where we could have promoted a clear cultural identity, where children could play together in Gaelic in the yard, where teachers could speak Gaelic together in the staff-room without incurring the wrath or misunderstanding of non-Gaelic speaking colleagues. A school where they could delay the introduction of reading without having to suffer invidious comparisons with English-medium peers; where they could use the television or the gym whenever they wanted to, because Gaelic-medium education depends so much on a wide range of stimuli; where the children were not the minority in the school, would not feel 'different'; where the janitor and the lollipop lady and the visiting music teacher and the minister and the priest and Santa Claus and the Easter Bunny could all speak Gaelic all the time; where all the important things – the parties and the sports days and the assemblies and the sales of work and the plays and the carol services and the fire drills – could all be in Gaelic and not just the lessons: in other words, avoiding the '*sèid do shròn is ith do churrain*' syndrome ('blow your nose and eat your carrots').[1]

In 1989, while working as National Education Development Officer for Comunn na Gàidhlig, I was invited to the island of Tiree to address parents on the benefits of Gaelic-medium primary school education. Irony sat beside me all the way to the island. (Gillies 1990). As a teenager I had spent holidays in Tiree, the guest of a school friend and her family. The granny of the house refused to speak English to me, which provided much-needed reinforcement of my nervous communicative skills. Thirty years later the meeting in the school had to be held in English, as few of the Tiree parents now spoke Gaelic: city-born parents; island-born parents who had lost their Gaelic along the way and incomers who wanted their children to be part of a Gaelic community. All queueing up for the Gaelic playgroup, all wanting to be told that they could, through their children, regain something whose value they had never realised until they had lost it. What was it they were reaching for? Surely not just majority culture, majority values, majority experience translated into Gaelic? But then again, surely not a mere recreation of times long gone, before young people surfed the waves and the internet all around Tiree? Anyway, the one dissenting voice that night, accusing me of 'coming with political intent to introduce divisions into our peaceful little island', had a strong Northern Irish accent.

In Scotland we are so fortunate when compared to your community, where language has religious and political connotations and sectarianism has so long and so obdurately obscured such valuable work and, if I may use the word, *love* among ordinary men and women and children. A community, however, does not lightly abandon the language and culture which defines it. Historically we have little to be complacent about. The odds stacked against Gaelic in the past were so steep that many – often the most conscientious – parents and teachers felt justified in protecting the children in their care from

1. Since this speech was delivered, funding has been provided for the establishment of an all-Gaelic-medium primary school in Glasgow: a chance to create within its walls a culture with past, present *and* future perspectives.

what they saw as its *negative*, or even *malign* influence. Even now Gaelic struggles to reach the ordinary people of Scotland across a no man's land of genuine ignorance – withheld or mis-reported history, neglected or discredited scholarship, anglo-centric media and centrist educational policies – punctuated by the occasional land-mine of 'linguicism' (Phillipson 1990: 43–50) or other form of prejudice (Gillies 1989: 34–5).

Twenty years ago Gaelic had no locus in any public domain except perhaps the church and the BBC. It was still the predominant language of communities in the Gàidhealtachd, used naturally by young and old across most areas of everyday life. But its status in education was low, and research suggested that it was declining sharply as a spoken language, especially among young people, though the community was (understandably) inclined to dismiss these findings as negative scare-mongering. On television, Gaelic songs were introduced in English, and the only other Gaelic output was a weekly current affairs programme and a few hours of Gaelic radio. Gaelic church services were available in most Gaelic-speaking areas, though they might, anomalously, be replaced by English services in the summer months out of respect for the tourist. Twenty years ago the prime objective of Gaelic language activists was to protect and support Gaelic in the Gàidhealtachd – the Gaelic-speaking heartland.

Today Gaelic bilingualism is acknowledged as a definite career asset in areas like education, the media, journalism, community development and, in some places, local government, clerical employment and the caring services. Some degree of Gaelic-medium primary education is now available throughout the Gàidhealtachd, and it is now possible – if you are willing to undertake a certain amount of strategic island-hopping! – to learn through the medium of Gaelic at every stage from pre-school to tertiary education. We are now having to redefine the term 'Gael', with so many young Gaelic-speakers emerging from non-Gaelic speaking households throughout Scotland.

The introduction of Gaelic-medium education into English-dominated areas was of enormous significance to the status of Gaelic. It not only constituted a major departure from the official mindset of at least 500 years – an acknowledgement that Gaelic language and culture is of interest and relevance to the nation as a whole, including its centres of administration and commerce: it also caught the imagination of ordinary people who would otherwise have had no access to Gaelic. Though the first moves were made by Gaelic-speakers like myself, determined to maintain our children's identity as members of a discernible though scattered linguistic community, the children of non-Gaelic speaking parents are now in the majority in our urban-based Gaelic units. Such parents appear to be motivated not only by interest in languages, bilingualism, etc, but also in many cases by the desire to reaffirm a sense of national identity. Though, of course, feelings like these are notoriously difficult to pin down and measure, it seems that many Scottish parents experience a sense of dislocation (varying in the degree and manner of its conscious articulation) from their own cultural heritage, which they believe can be bridged through their children's involvement in Gaelic education (Fraser 1989).

As educators, as television producers, as politicians, as writers and artists and fund-holders – in short as the creators of culture – we have an awesome responsibility. For a language both reflects and shapes a culture. And in promoting our language we must try to reconcile the needs and strengths of women and men with the needs and interests of children; the tensions of past and future with spiritual and economic necessities.

And somehow, in our pell-mell rush hither and thither, with our mobile phones and our electronic organisers, we must not lose the essence of the very thing we are trying to preserve: what Yeats called the 'simplicity and musical occurrences' of a people,

> ...for whom every incident in the old rut of birth, life and death has cropped up unchanged for centuries; who have steeped everything in the heart; to whom everything is a symbol... With us, nothing has time to father meaning, and too many things are occurring for even a big heart to hold. (WB Yeats, quoted Kiely 1994: 13)

# Parallel Universes:
# Gaelic Arts Development in Scotland, 1985–2000

Malcolm MacLean

## Abstract

This paper describes the origins of the Gaelic Arts Agency, Pròiseact nan Ealan (PNE), and reviews its role as Scotland's national development agency for the Gaelic arts. It summarises the historical context and goes on to outline the range of activity and some of the guiding principles that have underpinned the organisation's development strategy.

PNE was established by the Scottish Arts Council (SAC) in 1987 with a national remit to identify new approaches to Gaelic arts development. The organisation has evolved and expanded significantly over the years and continues to design, develop and deliver new initiatives in the Gaelic arts. It has adopted a multi-disciplinary approach to a variety of artforms and worked in various sectors such as education, the media and tourism. A variety of delivery styles have been employed, ranging from professional flagship productions to community collaborations and the creation of independent companies to sustain delivery of Gaelic arts services.

Some of these initiatives are described in the context of overall Gaelic language development. Some parallels and divergences between the Scottish and the Irish Gaelic arts experience are highlighted and the paper concludes by indicating areas of potential Scottish/Irish collaboration.

## Introduction

There is a 'parallel universe' quality to the Gàidhealtachd regions of Scotland and Ireland. An Irish colleague used the term to describe the duality of his first encounter with the Scottish Gàidhealtachd – the sense that the culture he found there was both the same and different, both familiar and exotic. This is equally true for Scottish Gaels visiting Ireland. There is an immediate sense of affinity with so much that is instantly recognisable alongside so much that seems completely new. Our geographical, historical, cultural and linguistic affinities and discordances are rich, resonant, intriguing and, above all, complex.

This paper sets out to give an overview of recent developments in the Gaelic arts in Scotland. It will also touch on the opportunities created by the re-convergence of the Gaelic communities of Scotland and Ireland and especially the potential for creative interaction through the Gaelic arts. The ideas thrown out here are informed by a strongly held personal belief that the mutual rediscovery of the other half of the Gaelic world will create exactly those conditions in which creative interchange can flourish.

It may be useful at this point to identify for Irish readers three particularly important ways in which Gaelic Scotland differs from Gaelic Ireland. Unlike the Republic of Ireland, the Gaelic language in Scotland has never enjoyed the support of the modern state; until the late 20th century its only legitimate role in public life was in the church. Another striking contrast is that the majority of Gaelic speakers in Scotland, about 80 per cent, belong to the Protestant faith. The most immediately obvious difference is that, in contrast to Ireland, Scottish Gaelic has no special associations with nationalist politics and is seen as a cross-party political issue. There are clearly many more points of difference and some will emerge in the course of this paper while others await further exploration.

For those unfamiliar with Gaelic Scotland I will begin with a very compressed, 'cartoon history' of Gaelic on our side of the Sea of Moyle. I will go on to focus on the role that the Gaelic arts have played in support of Gaelic language planning since the 1980s and outline some of the principles that have guided arts development strategy. I will conclude by touching on some of the implications of the renewed cultural connection between Gaelic Scotland and Ireland.

I will offer a description as opposed to an evaluation or a structural analysis. These are issues that will be tackled elsewhere.

## Historical context

Scotland's Gaels came originally from Ireland and settled in the west Highlands and Islands from the 5th century. By the 10th century they had united the other Scottish tribes to create the independent kingdom of Scotland in which Gaelic was the language of the Royal Court. By the 15th century the Gaels had lost control of the Scottish Court and been pressed back into the Highlands and Islands where, however, they enjoyed a high level of autonomy under the Lordship of the Isles. The union of the two crowns, followed a century later by the Act of Union of 1707, brought Scotland increasingly under London's control. By the mid 1700s the great Jacobite misadventure had foundered at Culloden, the last battle fought on British soil, and the British state was determined that these Gaelic barbarians would never again pose a threat to the stability of the state. By the mid 19th century the combination of military, legal and cultural repression had been compounded by famine and the forced evictions of the Highland clearances. The clan system, the social fabric of the Highlands and Islands, was destroyed and a pattern of emigration was established that continues to this day.

Until the middle of the 20th century the contraction of the Gaelic community into the west Highlands and Islands, coupled with the decline in the number of Gaelic speakers, was a consistent but gradual process. Despite language-shift from Gaelic to English, usually over three or four generations, there had always remained a strong, if shrinking, Gaelic heartland. Although the language enjoyed no legitimacy in public life in terms of the law, the schools, commerce or politics, it seemed relatively secure as the first language of Gàidhealtachd homes, workplaces and church.

Between 1891 and 1971 the Gaelic population fell gradually from 254,415 (5.2 per cent of the Scottish population) to 88,415 (1.8 per cent). The census of 1981, however, confirmed a changing dynamic. Between 1971 and 1981 the total number of Gaelic speakers fell dramatically by 5795, a fall of 6 per cent, to 82,620 (1.7 per cent). The cultural pressures were intensifying and the decline in the number of Gaelic speakers was accelerating, even in the remaining heartlands. The option of slowly 'singing ourselves to sleep' over the next few generations was suddenly replaced by the sobering prospect of imminent terminal decline. As awareness of this crisis sank in it prompted independent reactions from both the Gaelic community and government agencies.

## Grassroots

In the course of the 1980s a number of new initiatives emerged spontaneously and independently from within the Gaelic-speaking community. As these have been the foundations of further developments they are worth mentioning.

The first Gaelic playgroups were set up in 1981 and rapidly became networked into a playgroups movement with its own organisation, Comhairle nan Sgoiltean Àraich (CNSA), which now represents more than 120 playgroups. This was followed by a drive to establish Gaelic-medium education in Scottish schools led by parents who went on to form their own organisation, Comann nam Pàrant (CnaP). The first Gaelic-medium unit opened in

Glasgow in 1987 and Gaelic-medium education is now available in more than 50 primary schools and 15 secondary schools across Scotland.

The Gaelic college at Sabhal Mòr Ostaig on Skye emerged from disused farm steadings in the early 1980s and is now a cornerstone of the University of the Highlands and Islands.

Other parents on the Isle of Barra came together in 1982 to create Fèis Bharraigh, a new form of Gaelic arts tuition festival for children. This has grown into a network of thirty community festivals with their own umbrella organisation, Fèisean nan Gàidheal. The first Gaelic arts centre and art gallery, An Lanntair, ('The Lamp') opened in Stornoway in 1985. This award-winning community enterprise has gone on to create international touring exhibitions and has acted as a model for similar arts centres on Skye, North Uist and Mull. The international success of Gaelic artists such as Sorley Maclean, Iain Crichton Smith, Capercaillie and rock group, Runrig, confirmed that Gaelic was far from dead despite the falling numbers.

## Inhabiting the system

This 'grassroots' activity was complemented by new attitudes emerging from national government and public agencies.

The local authority for the Western Isles, Comhairle nan Eilean Siar, only came into existence in 1975 with the re-organisation of local government but it had rapidly moved to establish a bilingual policy. Highland Regional Council also developed a Gaelic policy and by the 1980s other agencies were beginning to take a more positive and sympathetic approach to Gaelic issues. These included the Scottish Office Education Department, the Scottish Arts Council and the regional economic development agency the Highlands and Islands Development Board (HIDB) – Scotland's closest equivalent to Údarás na Gaeltachta although without a specific Gaelic brief.

All of these agencies already had a nominal responsibility for Gaelic, although it could be argued that few of them had taken their linguistic responsibilities seriously. Their potential to deal effectively with Gaelic issues was undermined by a lack of experience of Gaelic culture and a lack of clarity regarding their responsibilities to the Gaelic community. The Census figures, however, had confirmed that unless some radical action was taken they were about to preside over the extinction of an indigenous language and culture. There was now an urgent need for the authorities to find new ways of doing something for Gaelic, or, at the very least, to appear to be doing something for Gaelic.

The key initiative was taken by the HIDB who appointed a Gaelic Report Group whose report, *Còr na Gàidhlig* (*Language, Community and Development: the*

*Gaelic Situation*), was published in 1982. This recommended that '… a new agency, of a radically different kind from those already in existence, is needed if realistic progress is to be made in further Gaelic development' (Macdonald 1982: 6). By 1984, respected representatives of the Gaelic community had come together with the HIDB Scottish Office, and local authorities to launch a new Gaelic development body, Comunn Na Gàidhlig (CNAG), with a remit to take a fresh and more developmental approach to Gaelic.

CNAG's initial strategy was to support parents and Gaelic activists in achieving their aspirations by acting as advocates and advisers to local and national government and other public agencies. Decades of clamouring for Gaelic recognition 'from the outside' had failed to achieve any meaningful progress. CNAG's aim was to 'inhabit the system' and build Gaelic into the fabric of public policy. In key areas this approach was to prove highly effective. In the late 1980s, for example, CNAG mounted a highly successful, cross-party campaign for a Gaelic television service, which led to the creation of a £9 million Gaelic Broadcasting Fund. CNAG, although not a statutory body, is Scotland's closest equivalent to Ireland's Bord na Gaeilge, and is currently leading the campaign for Secure Status for Gaelic within the Scottish Parliament.

## 'A Way Ahead'

CNAG's original brief embraced all aspects of Gaelic development with the critical exception, however, of the Gaelic arts. The Scottish Arts Council, were disappointed that the Gaelic arts were excluded from this new approach to Gaelic development and, in 1985, they commissioned their own report from Dr Finlay MacLeod. This report, *The Gaelic Arts: A Way Ahead*, was published the following year and remains an important and highly readable document. It presents a snapshot of the realities of Gaelic arts and culture in the mid 1980s and goes on to propose the creation of a Gaelic arts development project.

Implicit in the report were two complementary principles. One was that the promotion of the Gaelic arts could not and should not be divorced from the wider context of the promotion of the language. At the same time it was emphasised that the development of the Gaelic arts, while an integral part of the broader issue of language development, required a distinctive and innovative approach.

The MacLeod report highlighted serious structural weaknesses in Gaelic cultural support provision and noted that what structures did exist tended to depend excessively on competitions. Although a number of highly successful, non-competitive initiatives had been undertaken they had mostly worked in a vacuum and some of them had made no long-term impact. These 'nodes of excellence' indicated a high level of dormant artistic skills. However, there was little continuity even within individual groups, no cycle of events to facilitate forward planning, and minimal networking among groups. As a result, the lessons learned in one community or within initiatives were rarely passed on.

Although the report recognised that there were '... an increasing number of organisations with an interest in promoting some form of Gaelic arts' (MacLeod 1986: 7) it also recognised that the fragmentation of Gaelic arts activity made it difficult for funding agencies to develop any consistent funding pattern. Most agencies had adopted a purely reactive approach that could be problematic where plural-funding partnerships were involved. In other words, no matter how high the level of Gaelic arts goodwill that emerged among funding agencies, they had no developmental overview, no developmental policy, and no developmental programme.

The MacLeod report recommended the creation of a three-year project that would identify new ways of providing continuity and coherence for Gaelic arts development. The SAC created the National Gaelic Arts Project, now the Gaelic Arts Agency, Pròiseact nan Ealan. This new body initially worked to a Steering Group comprising SAC, CNAG and the Gaelic membership organisation An Comunn Gàidhealach. I took up the post of Gaelic arts development officer in August 1987.

Our original brief could hardly have been wider: 'To co-ordinate, develop and promote the traditional and contemporary Gaelic arts, including film and television, throughout Scotland'. Our total budget was £25,000 a year, inclusive of wages and all project expenses. Although we jokingly re-christened ourselves 'the Cosmic Gaelic Arts Project' we recognised that this was a major advance for the Gaelic arts and set out to seize the opportunities it presented.

## Research

Our first year was spent exclusively on research to identify needs, wants, potential resources and new ideas. We contacted artists, arts organisations and language activists, and consulted extensively with the Gaelic-speaking community, conducting well over 100 interviews. We also identified existing and potential funders and support structures, and began to analyse funding levels and patterns of provision for the Gaelic arts.

This last exercise threw up some interesting results. Gaelic publishing, for example, was comparatively well supported through the Gaelic Books Council but there was no mechanism for dealing with book distribution.

Gaelic music was partially supported through mainstream commercial recording companies, but these were often ignorant of the tradition and bastardised the music and songs to make them 'more accessible' and increase sales. Gaelic drama had no support structures at all. There was no professional Gaelic theatre activity and no mechanism for identifying, encouraging or training new performing arts talent.

By our second year we had drafted a three-year development plan. The research and consultation process had identified more than 100 ideas which the development plan narrowed down to fifteen specific projects that were targeted for development over a three-year period. We proceeded to design, develop and deliver these fifteen projects.

## Funding strategy

The funding strategy involved identifying a wide range of potential funders and clarifying their remit, budgets, funding cycles, grant criteria and current priorities. The development plan was presented as an integrated programme but individual projects were budgeted independently so that each specific project sought a tailored funding package from a variety of funding sources. This enabled us to target funding from the arts, education, media, community and economic development sectors depending on the nature of the project. Funders were invited to invest in plural funding partnerships that enabled them to achieve their aims in a sector where they had previously been somewhat adrift. We tried to present funders with solutions as opposed to problems.

Generally speaking, the funders responded positively. We offered a cost-effective approach, which enabled them to make specific investments in individual projects that collectively formed a strategic development plan. Investment was modest and the risks were shared with other funders. Equally important was the arms-length relationship with Pròiseact nan Ealan – we took the blame for failure and they shared the credit for success. We offered a toe-in-the-water approach to funding the Gaelic arts and what the CIA calls 'deniablity'.

This strategy rapidly broadened our funding base and drew a number of agencies and funding committees into direct engagement with the Gaelic arts for the first time. By levering in additional funding we increased our budget and our credibility. Our low level of initial funding had reflected a degree of official scepticism that progressively diminished as we established professional relationships with key officers in other agencies.

## Project strategy

The fifteen targeted projects were selected on the basis of clearly identified needs or opportunities – such as the Gaelic Youth Theatre and the *fèis* support network Fèisean nan Gàidheal. As a package they were designed to be mutually reinforcing – our Gaelic Writer-in-Residence would work with the Theatre-in-Education company which would promote the Youth Theatre and so on. There was a particular emphasis on provision for young people such as the Gaelic comic *'Smathsin*! and the Dealbhan Beò ('Moving Pictures') film-animation-in-schools project.

Project design and planning were given a high priority. Time was invested in detailed planning to ensure the highest quality standards would be achievable within the human and financial resources available.

Our initial constraints compelled us to engage in rigorous forward planning and forced us to be inventive and flexible in our developmental approaches. We became better at turning negatives into positives. We have never, for example, been funded to dispense grant-aid and have thus avoided becoming a funding agency. Instead we have developed considerable expertise in the design, development and delivery of projects and in forming sustainable project funding partnerships.

Projects were progressed in collaboration with other organisations wherever possible. We have acted as a catalyst and focus for individual and community creativity; co-ordinated and integrated a wide variety of approaches; and represented the sector by presenting coherent arguments to funding bodies.

Although it is not always achievable our projects aim to become free-standing and ultimately independent of Pròiseact nan Ealan. Funding partnerships are designed to be sustainable once the pilot development period is over and the project's viability is, hopefully, confirmed. The prospect of independence encourages a greater sense of ownership, responsibility and motivation within a project and ultimately frees up our resources to move on to develop new initiatives.

## Outcomes

Evaluating arts development is a tricky process. One simple indicator of progress, although not necessarily the most significant measure, is the level of funding invested in the Gaelic arts and this has increased significantly.

Scottish Arts Council funding of Gaelic arts activity has grown from less than £100,000 per annum in the late 1980s to approximately £650,000 in the late 1990s. Pròiseact nan Ealan's annual turnover has grown from £25,000 in 1988 to £400,000 in 1998 with SAC funding accounting for approximately 35 per cent. The balance of our income comes from the regional development agency Highlands & Islands Enterprise (formerly HIDB) and the Local Enterprise Company network, the Scottish Parliament, the Gaelic Broadcasting Committee, the National Lottery, local authorities and an annually increasing proportion of earned income from sales and services. Independent companies that Pròiseact nan Ealan has either initiated or developed in collaboration with others now have a combined turnover of more than £1 million per year.

Another simple indicator is the unique range of national and international awards achieved by Pròiseact nan Ealan projects and associated initiatives. These include a BAFTA for the best Scottish arts and music television programme, the Scottish Tourist Board's Thistle Award for Excellence in Cultural Tourism, a Civic Trust Award and the Scottish Natural Heritage Supreme Award for Environmental Regeneration.

Flawed and imperfect as our original development plan was, it initiated a process that has driven Gaelic arts development for the past ten years. The projects have changed, the priorities have shifted, our circumstances are significantly different, but we still work to a three-year development plan that is reviewed and renewed annually. This process continues to provide a stable and productive framework for Gaelic arts development. We still have problems but our problems are now better problems.

## Synergy

The process I have described for the Gaelic arts, involving comparatively modest beginnings and significant increase in momentum, has been replicated in Gaelic education, broadcasting and economic development. We do not see the Gaelic arts in isolation from these other aspects of Gaelic development and we have consistently sought synergy by attempting to integrate our work with that of other sectors. Gaelic arts development has educational, broadcasting and economic dimensions as well as the vital community development dimension. These interconnections are important extensions of our central function of fostering creative talent and promoting high-quality artistic activity.

It may perhaps be helpful to give some indication of how we work with some of these other sectors. This is not always simply a one-to-one relationship between arts and education, arts and broadcasting, arts and tourism, arts and community development, and so on. It is in the nature of the arts that they can sometimes involve several of these areas simultaneously. I will try to illustrate some specific interconnections with education, broadcasting, tourism, community and economic development but with the health warning that this breakdown by category will itself begin to break down almost immediately.

## Arts and education

I will begin with education. For those of you familiar with the Irish situation it may come as a surprise to find how far behind Scotland was in developing Gaelic-medium education. There has been extensive Irish-medium education in the South since the 1920s, and first Irish-medium school in Northern Ireland opened in 1971, even if it was not funded until 1984. Although Scotland has an extensive Gàidhealtachd there was, incredibly, no Gaelic-medium education in Scotland until 1987. The growth to our current situation of almost 200 Gaelic-medium centres at pre-school, primary and secondary level is a remarkable feat.

To support the work of Gaelic-medium education Pròiseact nan Ealan piloted the first issues of the Gaelic children's comic *'Smathsin!* The English language term 'smashing', popularised by DC Thomson in the *Beano*, the *Dandy* and the *Sunday Post*, originally comes from the Gaelic *is math sin* ('that's good'). The pilot editions and the funding package for the comic were passed on to Acair Publishers and *'Smathsin!* is now in its tenth year of circulation to Scottish Gaelic-medium schools.

We also developed a children's theatre company, which toured to all of the Gaelic schools to great effect. The great thing about drama is that it involves all of the arts and offers a wonderful medium for engaging children's attention. Most of the plays were based on Gaelic reading material with which the children were already familiar, including characters and storylines from the *'Smathsin!* comic. The theatre company made the books come alive in a completely different way and the drama workshops that followed each performance, combined with the supplementary tuition materials developed for teachers, enabled the children to create their own drama productions long after the theatre company had moved on.

Another educational initiative was the film-animation-in-schools project, Dealbhan Beò. Two film animators from Edinburgh Film Workshop Trust spent two weeks in each of ten Gaelic-medium schools. They would use the first few days to work with the kids, showing them how to make pictures that appeared to move and demonstrating different forms of film animation technique. The children would then write the scripts, provide the voice-over, invent the sound effects, perform the music, create the artwork and come to grips with the science and arithmetic of producing their own three-minute film with support from the experts. BBC TV broadcast more than forty of the films and BBC funding sustained this schools' project over several years.

The Dealbhan Beò film archive is possibly the largest body of children's films in the world, and several have picked up international prizes.

## Arts and broadcasting

Our interaction with Gaelic broadcasting has taken a variety of forms. Until 1991 Scotland had no real Gaelic television service to speak of. The BBC's Gaelic television department did good work but only broadcast a couple of hours of programming per week. The commercial broadcasting companies occasionally broadcast good Gaelic programmes at reasonable times and even attracted respectable audience figures. Their general approach, however, could at best be described as minimalist and became offensive to many Gaels. Legally they had an obligation to broadcast twenty-six hours per year of Gaelic programming, up to thirteen hours of which could be repeats. Latterly the general practice was to produce thirteen hours of the cheapest programming, broadcast it in the middle of the night, and then repeat it six months later – again in the middle of the night. Things changed significantly with the 1991 Broadcasting Act, which led to the Scottish commercial broadcasters having a legal obligation to broadcast 200 hours per year of Gaelic programming and the creation of an annual fund of £8 million to support the making of Gaelic programmes.

Pròiseact nan Ealan worked closely with CNAG throughout the campaign for a Gaelic television service. We marshalled cultural arguments and sought support for the campaign from the Scottish Arts Council and other cultural agencies. We helped promote the economic argument that Gaelic television development would draw new resources into Scottish broadcasting and represent a significant investment in Scottish arts and culture. Television is by far the biggest sponsor of the arts in the world today. Before a television programme goes on screen, before anyone says a word, a composer has been paid for composing the title music, musicians have been paid for playing the music, a writer has been paid for the script and a designer has been paid for running up the graphics. This is before taking into account the employment of performers, directors and editors, never mind sound, light and camera technicians.

Media 'sponsorship' of the arts, however, is usually attributable to commercial exploitation as opposed to arts development. Television tends to view the arts as a form of cost-free research and development process. An arts sector that is often chronically underfunded, continues to generate new ideas and new talents that are creamed-off by broadcasting companies and converted into programming. The substantial profits generated by commercial broadcasting are rarely re-invested in arts development despite the growing interdependence of the arts and media sectors. Such short-termism has numerous negative implications.

Since the creation of the Gaelic Broadcasting Fund we have worked closely with the Gaelic Broadcasting Committee, Comataidh Craolaidh Gàidhlig (CCG), to challenge the predatory nature of television's relationship with the arts. We have argued that Gaelic television will not survive without the Gaelic arts. If television does not invest in creativity it becomes progressively more mediocre and ends up haemorrhaging audiences. Broadcasting in any language is dependent upon creative thinking and creative skills across a wide range of art forms. Television has a voracious appetite for ideas and it is those companies with the best ideas and strongest creative talent that will thrive in the international media marketplace. Cultural vitality converts directly into economic benefit in terms of media markets.

The Gaelic Arts and Media Training Programme grew out of our Gaelic Youth Theatre summer school established in 1989. Getting funding for this first summer school was like trying to squeeze blood from a stone. Funders had no real enthusiasm for the project, and some councillors were so sceptical that their comments got front page coverage in the local press. Once the Gaelic Broadcasting Fund was announced, however, the penny began to drop that a youth theatre fostering performing arts talent could be a key factor in creating and sustaining Gaelic drama on television. We built on our experience with the youth theatre to develop other short courses over a period of several years.

Following our early TV Comedy Writing courses, BBC Television commissioned two series of comedy shows from the young writers involved. Broadcasters began to realise that, what for them was a relatively modest training investment, could pay significant programming dividends. The Arts and Media Training Programme is funded by the National Lottery, CCG, BBC and the HIE/LEC network and currently has a budget of £250,000. It offers a series of integrated master-classes for Gaelic writers, actors and musicians. It emphasises hands-on practical experience and links training to production and broadcast. This is a good example of how a modest strategic investment, in this case in youth theatre, can snowball into a considerable investment from other sources. It has also enabled us to develop a major database of Gaelic speaking actors, writers and musicians and led to a contract to provide actors and extras for the soap-opera *Machair* and other media services.

We also helped initiate and develop the television programme *Tacsi* which won the BAFTA Award for the best Scottish Arts and Music programme produced in 1997. *Tacsi* was chosen for the BAFTA award, not by Gaelic activists, but by a jury of mainstream, English-speaking, professional broadcasters. It represents a significant shift in the image of Gaelic culture. In the past the image of a Gaelic arts and music programme would have been the White Heather Club. (For those of you too young to remember black and white television, the White Heather Club was a BBC programme where everyone wore kilts and no-one spoke Gaelic but Andy Stewart sang 'Donald Where's Your Troosers?') The best of Gaelic television programmes are now presenting an image Gaelic culture which is less stereotyped, more complex, more contemporary in outlook and much more attractive to young people.

## Arts and tourism

PNE is the only organisation to have won the Scottish Tourist Board's annual Thistle Award for excellence in cultural tourism on two separate occasions. The first award was for a major visual arts exhibition based around the theme of the Calanais standing stones that was jointly developed with the Stornoway art gallery An Lanntair and which toured throughout Scotland and into mainland Europe. The second, in 1999, was for the annual, week-long, Ceòlas summer school in South Uist which offers a holistic approach to masterclasses on Gaelic music, song and dance and forges links with Gaelic Canada. We are currently developing new exhibition ideas and new summer school proposals.

## Arts and community development

In 1989 we brought together the four community *fèisean* which existed at that point. The *fèisean* are community-run, non-competitive Gaelic arts tuition festivals for children. They run for a week or two weeks in the school holidays providing children with tuition in music, dance, drama and Gaelic song. We worked with the *fèis* activists to create an umbrella association, Fèisean nan Gàidheal, and managed the organisation for the first four years of its existence. Fèisean nan Gàidheal is now an independent community enterprise that has worked hard to support and develop the *fèis* movement into a network of thirty *fèisean* across the Highlands and Islands. Fèisean nan Gàidheal now has its own staff providing a variety of services such as a tutors' directory and tuition materials, tutor training provision, an extensive instrument bank and block insurance cover.

It is worth mentioning in the context of Irish/Scottish interaction that one of the key reference points for Fèisean nan Gàidheal was the development of traditional music tuition in Ireland, and especially the work of Comhaltas Ceoltóirí Éireann. Although the *fèisean* focus on a wider range of tuition than music alone, their initial stimulus came from the Irish experience and offer a good example of positive cross-fertilisation of ideas and experiences between Scotland and Ireland.

Another initiative involving tuition and community development as well as tourism was also modelled on an Irish precedent. The previously mentioned, Ceòlas summer school in South Uist brings together leading experts to explore and restore the relationship between piping and *seann nòs* ('old-style') singing, and *puirt-a-beul* ('mouth music'; vocal dance music) and traditional dance. Ceòlas, which began in 1996, is largely modelled on the example of the Willie Clancy Summer School in County Clare and benefited enormously from the generous advice given to us by its organisers, Muiris Ó Rocháin and Harry Hughes. The success of Ceòlas has generated a new community confidence in South Uist and a recognition of the Gaelic arts as a vital resource in the social and economic development of the area. New proposals have emerged for a full-time, certificated, Gaelic music and language course and the creation of a Gaelic music centre. In 1999 Ceòlas was selected as a case study for an as yet unpublished Scottish Office study of the arts and community regeneration.

We have been supportive of, but less active in, the area of amateur community drama. That the number of drama groups competing at the National Mòd has drastically diminished is sometimes seen as a crisis for Gaelic community drama. There have, however, been some large-scale and remarkably successful community drama projects in recent years that have had nothing to do with the traditional amateur drama competitions. One of the new non-competitive community dramas involved more than 100 participants preparing a spectacular Gaelic music and drama performance based on the warrior queen *Sgathach,* and was a huge success both locally and in Inverness where it filled the Eden Court Theatre. This suggests that it may not necessarily be community drama that is in crisis but the competitive festivals. Pròiseact nan Ealan's drama development has prioritised professional theatre skills and, following a series of pilot touring productions, we launched the independent touring theatre company Tosg (from *tosgaine* 'emissary') in 1996.

## Arts and economic development

We have attempted to clarify and highlight the economic dimension to Gaelic arts and cultural development. At a time when many of the traditional sectors of the Highlands and Islands economy seem to be in slump, the cultural industries remain one of the few growth sectors. The idea that the arts create jobs is now being taken more seriously.

For years the Highlands and Islands have lost their most talented young people because they could not find employment in their home areas. This trend has not yet been reversed, but there are now considerably more opportunities for creative people to find employment in the Gàidhealtachd and thereby contribute to the cultural vibrancy of their own communities. This can bring important social benefits to economically depressed areas; communities with a vibrant cultural life can cope more confidently with economic hardship. Our Gàidhealtachd areas have never been wealthy, but the richness of Gaelic arts and culture has enormously enhanced the quality of life and sustained Gaelic communities through good times and bad. Communities with an active cultural life are more likely to retain their young people even if those young people are not themselves directly engaged in creative artistic activity.

The extent to which attitudes are shifting on issues of art and culture was highlighted in the recent economic survey by Glasgow Caledonian University, *The Demand for Gaelic Artistic and Cultural Products and Services* (Sproull 1998). This study surveyed a massive sample of more than 2000 homes, or 6 per cent of the population, in the Western Isles and Skye and Lochalsh. The report records that 80 per cent of the business community in the area believed that the Gaelic arts and cultural industries stimulate new jobs and two-thirds believed that the Gaelic arts have a positive impact on tourism. A similar proportion believed that the Gaelic arts boost levels of confidence in local communities, encourage local people to stay in the area and/or attract those who have left to return:

Sixty per cent of respondents agree or strongly agree (34 per cent plus 26 per cent) that the regeneration of Gaelic art and culture is *essential* for the future economic development of their own area or island group. The figures for a similar question on whether Gaelic is *essential* for social development were 69 per cent (34 per cent agree, 35 per cent strongly agree) (Sproull 1998: v).

The study concluded that: 'Gaelic arts activity is making a substantial contribution to many of the main objectives set by public agencies dedicated to economic, social and linguistic development...' (Sproull 1998).

## Guiding principles

It will be clear from what has been said so far that Pròiseact nan Ealan considers the arts to be much more central to language development and community cohesion than is generally supposed. The extent to which the Gaelic arts can act in support of other sectors should not obscure the fact that they also have a powerful intrinsic value. Gaelic survived for centuries largely because the Gaelic community was sustained and inspired by a rich and distinctive arts and music heritage that was fully and unselfconsciously integrated into the way of life. There is an undisputed consensus that Gaelic-medium education and Gaelic economic development strategy are essential for linguistic and cultural survival in the modern world. There is no evidence, however, to suggest that these factors alone are adequate. The arts and media are the arena in which cultures will live or die in the 21st century. A clearer understanding of the energising value and inspirational role of the arts will be a critical factor in the success of future Gaelic cultural and economic development strategy.

Pròiseact nan Ealan has concentrated on development rather than conservation, on living creativity rather than museum culture. Traditions survive because they get reinvented and we are continually looking for new ways of delivering new cultural expressions to new audiences. We develop contemporary arts initiatives as well as support for the traditional arts and, over and above our advocacy and advisory roles, we are cultural entrepreneurs. We have tried to nourish an ethos in which practitioners and communities reclaim a sense of ownership of the Gaelic arts and Gaelic arts organisations.

We have tried to take a holistic approach that links the local and the international. If I were to try to summarise the principles which have underpinned our approach to Gaelic arts development the keywords would include collaboration, synergy, multiplier effect, infrastructure, networking, evaluation, timing, prioritisation and quality. Some of these, such as collaboration and synergy, have been illustrated in the earlier part of this paper, and need not delay us. Nor is there a need to argue the importance of multiplier effects or spin-off benefits that will enhance and extend the impact and value of a project. Some other headings may need further elaboration.

*Cultural infrastructure* has been a key development focus *for* Pròiseact nan Ealan. We have wonderfully talented Gaelic writers but without publishers to print, distribute and promote their work the talent never reaches its audience. We have wonderful artists but without galleries or a system that promotes their artwork in the wider world it is not seen or fully appreciated. We have wonderful musicians but their talent alone will not be sufficient to achieve success without an educational, archival, recording, promotional and distribution infrastructure.

*Networking* is especially important in the Scottish Highland and Islands where communities are widely scattered and communications can be highly problematic. Our networking activities, however, range much more widely. At its simplest, this involves linking communities, organisations and individuals with each other and with funders and politicians, and is sometimes merely a matter of keeping funders informed of what is happening. A more complex dynamic involves trying to understand the systems in which the funders function, and attempting to link the aspirations of the community to the priorities of the funders and the politicians who ultimately control the purse strings.

*Evaluation* involves a number of levels of activity including independent professional assessment, participant questionnaires, internal reporting. etc. The skills we learned in the early years for assessing project potential have served us well. We embark on new projects only after we have looked very carefully at their sustainability and are convinced that they have a fighting chance of success. A related, but somewhat different, evaluation is undertaken while projects are in operation. Our three-year plan is reviewed and renewed every year. This review is exhaustive and involves considering new approaches to issues and sometimes changing priorities, identifying new opportunities, and being, if necessary, ruthless in cutting out projects where we are not delivering. We work on the principle that self-assessment and self-criticism is essential and that without a hard and honest look at the weaknesses as well as the strengths of a project, it will be incapable of achieving its full potential or adapting to changing circumstances. Although some of the organisations with whom we collaborate can be impatient with the process of looking at all the possible pitfalls and weaknesses, we have found that this discipline not only diminishes the chance of failure, but also prepares us for external evaluation by funding bodies.

Evaluation also takes place in the context of the broader picture. First, this involves an awareness of how the Gaelic arts are meshing, or failing to mesh, with the broader issues of Gaelic development. This generally involves formal and informal interaction with other Gaelic organisations. Another approach is to actively commission or support rigorous research in key areas such as the 1998 Glasgow Caledonian University study from which I have quoted above. An important spin-off from independent studies and in-house self-evaluation, such as participant questionnaires, is that they provide raw data that can greatly facilitate further research. The Ceòlas summer school, for example, has been selected for two major independent case studies; one by the Scottish Tourist Board (1999) on cultural tourism, and the other by the Scottish Office (2000) on community regeneration through the arts. Both studies have been extremely positive, but the availability of primary evaluative data was a key criterion for selecting Ceòlas for further study.

*Timing:* the Gaelic demographic clock is ticking and time is against us. This generates an inevitable sense of urgency and highlights issues of timing, pacing and prioritisation. People, quite rightly, have ambitious aspirations for their language and their culture. They are impatient for things to happen immediately. The idea of working to a three-year plan before you can demonstrate concrete results does not come easily or comfortably to many of us. Funding agencies must also be willing to take this kind of long-term view, and will be critical to the self-image and cultural self-confidence of a younger generation of Gaels growing up in a multilingual, multicultural world.

## Alba agus Éire

There are exciting new opportunities opening up for co-operation between Ireland and Scotland. Our cultural infrastructure has developed significantly and the next challenge is to make that infrastructure work to best advantage. In this context our links with Ireland are becoming increasingly important. The peace process in the North has opened up the possibility of renewing Gaelic connections that are so many and so varied that there is enormous creative potential for all sorts of development. I will highlight a only few key areas of linkage.

Gaelic broadcasters in both Scotland and Ireland are already co-operating successfully and new media and the internet are opening up new forms of communication, new forms of archiving and new forms of cultural commerce. The geographical barriers and distance factors that used to handicap areas like the Highlands and Islands and the Irish Gaeltacht are beginning to disappear. Geography is becoming history. This will create new challenges and new opportunities for us both.

Our shared Gaelic arts and music tradition is a key area of potential collaboration. I have already highlighted the extent to which Scotland has learned from the Irish experience in terms of music tuition, but we have, as yet, no equivalent to the Irish Music Archive in Dublin. We remain deeply envious of the extent to which Ireland has developed 'Celtic music' into a multi-million pound export industry while simultaneously maintaining the authenticity and integrity of the tradition and according respect and prestige to the tradition bearers. Celtic music is clearly rooted in the Gaelic tradition but it has not been calcified by some rigid orthodoxy and can grow, experiment and develop without losing its authenticity. We believe there is great potential for tapping into this energy and linking the international language of music more effectively to Gaelic language development.

The current *Leabhar Mòr na Gàidhlig* ('The Great Book of Gaelic') project involves 100 Gaelic poems, 100 visual artists and a team of calligraphers from Scotland and Ireland who are currently working on a 21st century equivalent of the Book of Kells. The *Leabhar Mòr* will tour widely and have a radio, TV and tourism dimension. It offers a major opportunity to educate a new generation and a wider public about the significance of the pan-Gaelic connection.

We also have Iomairt Chalum Chille/The Columba Initiative, and for the first time in centuries we have the formal commitment of both governments they can be even more difficult to convince. This was a particular problem in our early years, in that funders were reluctant to work to a long-term development timescale. We have, however, worked extremely hard to achieve a level of credibility that will convince funders to invest in projects that will bear fruit in the longer run. It is also the case that even the very best of ideas need to find the right moment in time.

*Prioritisation* is essential given the scale and diversity of the arts sector. No matter how much funding for the Gaelic arts may have increased in recent years, resources are still limited. Against a background in which everything is desirable but not everything is possible, in which the process of community development and the creation of high-quality product are both essential, in which external support depends on goodwill and goodwill depends on measurable success, we must be as careful now in developing our strategy as we were when we first began. To put it another way, our task is to prioritise simultaneously on a number of levels. We have to maximise impact in the shortest possible time and maximise sustainable high-quality arts provision in the longer term. We have to maximise the impact of whatever funding is available now and convince funders of the value of future, longer-term commitment. We must also be adaptable, seizing opportunities wherever they present themselves, while integrating new possibilities into a coherent development plan.

*Quality* is possibly the single most important consideration. Although we are mindful of the significance of funding, marketing, distribution, promotion and PR, etc, it is ultimately quality that counts in the arts. The pursuit of excellence is common to all artforms across all cultures and it is the international currency of cultural exchange. The sheer quality of Sorley MacLean's poetry has lent enormous status to Gaelic culture throughout the latter half of the 20th century. It is also extremely important that high-quality art is given the recognition that it deserves and we have worked hard to maximise the exposure of Gaelic arts to an audience beyond the Gaelic community. Our series of *seann nòs* concerts at the 1997 Edinburgh International Festival were presented alongside the very best of the world's opera and classical music. The shows sold out well in advance and received rave reviews from the non-Gaelic critics. The Gaelic/Scots/American English theatre production *Craobh nan Ubhal* ('The Aipple Tree'), filled Glasgow's Tramway Theatre for three nights, and the visual arts exhibition, *As an Fhearann* ('From the Land'), toured coast to coast across Canada for two years.

These successful projects have had a subtle but important effect in undermining sterile and stereotyped anti-Gaelic attitudes within Scotland and reinforcing an image of Gaelic that is associated with quality. This is not simply an issue of external validation. Gaelic associations with quality and excellence to renew and reinforce the linkage between Gaelic Scotland and Ireland. Iomairt Chalum Chille is already active in promoting projects in the arts, education, academia, cultural tourism and sports. It sponsors an exciting programme of community exchanges involving substantial numbers of people and linking areas such as Ness with Connemara, and the Uists with County Clare and Donegal. These exchanges are developing new relationships, opening new perspectives, creating new cultural opportunities and prompting new interest in our parallel universes. One of my hopes for Iomairt Chalum Chille is that it will provide a forum for sharing our experiences, negative as well as positive, and exploring the dynamics behind both our successes and our failures.

Looking to the future it is obvious that the scale of the challenge is enormous, although there may also be grounds for optimism. The dispersed nature of the Scottish and Irish Gaelic communities, for example, has created major historical disadvantage and communication problems. New ways of working, new support networks, new technology and new media may yet offer new solutions. Given the wealth of creative Gaelic talent it may yet be possible for us to achieve our full cultural potential. If we are to do so, however, it will be essential for a new generation to develop new skills in arts management, marketing, promotion, community development and cultural co-operation.

## Conclusion

I would like to conclude by highlighting the fact that the three Arts Councils in Scotland and Ireland invest many millions of pounds of public money in the arts and cultural development each year. A key challenge for the Gaelic community in the new millennium will be to secure the resources necessary for the Gaelic arts to achieve their full potential. This is not simply a question of funding levels. Other important questions include how the Gaelic arts are to be supported; what will be the role of the Arts Councils; what policies do they propose to develop; what philosophy underlies the policies; and how will they monitor the effectiveness of those policies.

The EC sponsored *Linguarts* report produced by the Barcelona-based Interarts Observatory summarises this key issue:

> One of Europe's great riches is that of the great diversity of both languages and cultures. On the other hand, this very diversity has led to some of the most bitter and violent wars, both civil and national, in history. How may we contribute to that diversity without provoking additional separations between peoples, often divided as they already are? One way is to use both language and cultural policy as a single tool instead of the separate policy tools that they

are at present. All too often it may be seen that language policy limits itself to the sphere of education and that cultural policies rarely, if ever, address language issues. Both policy areas need to be made aware of the strengths and opportunities to be gained by working hand in hand (Interarts 1999: 15).

It is not yet certain that our arts councils actually have a real and lasting commitment to developing Gaelic arts and culture. One of the many tasks of those of us who are active in arts development is to alert the powerful to their cultural responsibilities. We will continue to argue that the arts councils should have a clearer commitment to Gaelic and that they should demonstrate that they take that commitment seriously by providing adequate funding, developing sensitive support structures and creating appropriate monitoring mechanisms. We would hope to do this in conjunction with Irish language arts bodies in Ireland.

Our own language community has a shared responsibility in this process. There is an onus on Gaelic language policy-makers to take the arts more seriously. We need to identify how the arts can best contribute to Gaelic language development and how the Gaelic community can best support the development of the Gaelic arts. The Gaels of Ireland and Scotland can, and I believe should, work together on these issues.

# The Gael is Dead; Long Live the Gaelic: The Changing Relationship Between Native and Learner Gaelic Users

Peadar Morgan

Adult learners; adult learners as a language movement – I sometimes think learners are a Celtic phenomenon, though the Basques and others may disagree. There are even two languages that are for now totally in the hands, and in the mouths, of learners.

But maybe it is easier for the Manx and Cornish, because the term 'learner' is (in Scotland at least I would argue) both ambiguous and loaded: how fluent does a new user need to be before he or she ceases to be a learner? Is it the height of their linguistic ambition to earn the yes-but label of 'fluent learner'? It can be fairly insulting to the person who has been able to make Gaelic the first language of his or her daily routine, with the ability and desire to use it in each and every possible circumstance encountered, to be lumped in with those stuttering through their first few sentences.

And what of the native speaker who lost the language at school age and seeks to recover it later in life – a familiar situation these days as a result of recent educational prejudice, of Anglo-American youth culture and of increasing English use in the family home. Is he or she not a learner? Perhaps the term 'learner' can even apply to fluent speakers pushing their language into improved literacy or new domains – or for that matter, apply to every user of a language, as he or she expands knowledge during the course of life and tries to keep up with the dynamism of the language itself.

'Native speaker' is also an ambiguous and, to some, a loaded term. Interestingly, there is no real Gaelic equivalent unless it is the problematic 'Gael'. Problematic in that it is a term sometimes applied to, and claimed by, non-speakers who were brought up in a Gaelic community or exhibit some perceived qualifying characteristics.

With universal English fluency, increasing community pride understandably encouraged by Gaelic organisations – and the end of rural isolation, it is perhaps inevitable that the Gaelic identity becomes confused with regional culture. Locals without Gaelic do not want to be alienated; local Gaelic speakers identify as one of themselves someone with the same sense of humour, musical tastes, geographical and occupational experiences, regardless of which of their two languages is used. Encounters with such restricted and restrictive views, downplaying the central role of the language, can lead some learners equally to downplay the role of native speakers in their Brave New Gaelic World.

'*Fileantach*/fluent speaker' has been proposed as a PC term for the upper end of the fluency scale, from whatever background and whatever the route taken to reach that level. It certainly has its attractions in certain circumstances, but the term and its implications have yet to catch on and cannot hide the differences I will shortly address. Nor does it allow, in its English form, for the learner phenomenon of those who are fluent in literacy but not in conversation. However, it is possible that this term may yet win out.

Last week I was in Wales and heard another term which might well be worth considering, even if a wee bit cumbersome – 'first language speaker'. However, those I heard using this phrase retained 'native speaker' to distinguish those fluent speakers who came from Welsh-speaking households, whether their parents were native or not.

The membership organisation of which I am director is burdened with the plural of 'learner' in its title, Comann (ie, association) an Luchd Ionnsachaidh, though we tend to use the acronym CLI (pronounced klee), and to hedge our bets by saying that we are 'for Gaelic learners and supporters'. We aim to give them a co-ordinated voice, both by lobbying and, when necessary, activating support; we aim to give them and those working with them access to relevant information, in particular with databases for clubs, classes, courses and tutors, all but the latter now available on-line; we aim to encourage improved facilities and participation in the Gaelic world, through collaboration mostly but also now with our own Gaelic days and weekends. Our main plank is direct promotion of language, heritage and networking through the bilingual, parallel text, quarterly publications *Cothrom* (in Scots Gaelic meaning 'opportunity' and 'access').

But CLI is the poor relation of the Gaelic scene, with tight budget and tiny staff. Despite a quickly growing international membership now well past the thousand mark and picking up momentum, we remain dependant on the Scottish Office and the Gaelic powers that be for most of our funding. The Government is supportive, but I'm not sure if they really know what to make of Gaelic learners – we didn't feature in the recent boost in public funding for

Gaelic education, for instance. And the rest of the Gaelic world is generally sympathetic, but they are not always at ease when learners lay joint claim to the language and its future. I suspect that our very name has hindered our chances of being chosen to deliver wider services, building on our established information role and publishing success. It psychologically sidelines us more than comparative membership alone would justify.

To be fair, it could be asked whether learners themselves are clear as to what to make of the learner scene, if indeed they recognise it as a separate entity at all. If and when fluency starts to loom as a realisable target for an individual, learner institutions become merely a means of accessing the wider Gaelic world and cease to be an end in themselves. Some learners will even deliberately shun such institutions, in an attempt to go native in outlook, as much as in language, and seeing contact with other learners as diversionary, or culturally unsatisfactory, or linguistically polluting. And their choice has to be respected.

But go-it-alone or not, there is in all but a tiny number of cases a clear divide between the 'learner', in the sense of someone who has elected to come to Gaelic, and the 'native' speaker of traditional background. No matter how fluent we learners may become, I am sure that there is always something in the turn of phrase and in the production of sounds that will, in protracted communication, give the game away to the native speaker.

Then there is the choice of words, with the learner heavily reliant on 'book Gaelic', reading literature which until recently has tended to be archaic or peripheral, and relying inordinately on dictionaries that are archaic, peripheral and neologistical, but short on modern, vernacular vocabulary and idiom. Indeed the learner may make a point of using forms belonging to dead or dying dialects with which they personally identify; in the face of criticism of language usage and pronunciation from mainstream speakers, history or dialect can be quoted in a defence which allows the learner the possibility of being the alternative Gael. No-one can challenge your linguistic authenticity if you are the only user of an otherwise defunct dialect!

The learner will also look for the neologism rather than a descriptive phrase or (more often these days) interject English words or phases. This is perhaps a function of that other distinguishing feature, the linguistic energy evident in the learner – he or she has of course chosen Gaelic; the native speaker was all but born with it. The learner sometimes forgets this, and may not appreciate that the native speaker might have mixed or no feelings about the language and in all probability no grammatical expertise or interest. And, indeed, different grammar – the learner has to learn grammar twice; first to learn the conservative grammar of the books, then with more difficulty learn what grammar is left out in the modern tongue.

Not that book Gaelic, idiosyncratic Gaelic, neo-Gaelic and grammatical Gaelic are not Gaelic for all that, and the interplay between these and what could be called 'native Gaelic' can, in the right mix, be invigorating and provide the necessary drive for a dynamic, supple and poetic language, assuming the required conditions of tolerance and the confidence to experiment. But even if the differences between learner and native speaker were fundamental, the value to the language of learners of whatever level of fluency would still be great. They inflate the market for Gaelic products and services, add to lobbying contacts and weight, and of course boost the numerical justification for official support. Even those outwith Scotland have an important impact on these benefits, especially on the market for literature, tapes and now CD ROMs and websites.

But we should beware of exaggerating the distinction between native and learner. Some learners, though not many, have made their homes in Gaelic areas and have succeeded in being accepted into the community. A great many native speakers live outwith these areas and in their new communities have invested a tremendous amount of effort and goodwill in helping and encouraging learners. The linguistic difference is less important and more penetrable here, away from the dialect area, and indeed these exiled native speakers may be more open to being influenced by the language of the nouveau Gael.

And if Gaelic users of whatever description are all in some sense language learners, consumers and practitioners, and the language itself living and dynamic, then consideration of forms of fluency is reduced to individual tolerance. The learner–native speaker divide is not, as Scots Gaelic enters another millennium, the principal division. Neither is it a Highland–Lowland divide, nor a rural–urban one. The language has in fact no geographical limitation in appeal, though its detractors and some supporters often assume this to be otherwise – with an archaic view of a language ghetto or bulwark.

Reasons for learning the language are numerous and often collective, including place-names, poetry, politics, party songs, piss-ups, the past, pop-music, personal links. It doesn't start with a 'p', and it sends shivers up the collective Celtic spine, but yes, probably the romance of it all too.... Personal link by family member or residence in either the Islands or Highlands is not a factor for most, as a survey based on CLI members has indicated (Alasdair MacCaluim, unpublished 1995). In fact a fair number of learners don't even have a personal link with Scotland.

In my case I am indeed Scottish; half Highland, half Lowland. The census shows that one of my great, great grandfathers had Gaelic; while my surname seemingly came with the Dàl Riata Gaels from Ireland – but I was unaware of such things when I first became hooked on Gaelic and cannot invoke them as a reason for learning. If it really was a question of blood, then most Scots would be packing out classes in every hall across the land and there would be some interesting ramifications in this part of Ireland! But it is neither genetic nor geographic. My wife speaks Gaelic; yet she hails from rural North England, with no Scottish roots other than those she has put down herself.

Gaelic is the language of our home, the language of my office, the language which I listen to more often than not on the radio, the language which I frequently read in books and sometimes hear on the television. The next generation will have Gaelic as their first language and will receive at least all of their early education in Gaelic. But we are as yet rare as a nouveau-Gael couple, especially in the Highlands. And we could live in the Highlands all our days with very little, if any, contact with the language beyond the strange names on the map – we have had to mould our own mini-Gaidhealtachd around us.

But there are more and more nouveau Gaels – a term coined by those who would divide and rule the Gaelic movement – emerging around Scotland and indeed abroad, with concentrations in the cities only because of the truism that that is where the general population is concentrated. If older learner material had an almost exclusively rural feel, there is a danger that we are going too much the other way and presenting the language as a totally urban concern. Some of us actually live in the countryside, and the rural aspect to the language may be one of its romantic appeals to city dwellers.

It is also a mistake to imagine greater diversity and division among the surviving Gaelic communities than actually exists. Even in 1932, well before the levelling influence of BBC Radio nan Gaidheal and before Gaelic as a community language had effectively retreated to an all-island, all-crofting experience, Henry Dieckhoff could say in his dialect study of that part of the West Central mainland Highlands, that 'the people of Glengarry easily understand any Gaelic dialect except some of those spoken in the extreme north and in parts of Perthshire' in the Southern Highlands (Dieckhoff 1992). There is no major dialect issue in Scots Gaelic as there is in Irish; any problem is one of laziness on the part of the speakers or of local prejudice – usually directed against the numerically dominant folk of Lewis.

There is a common unity to the existing communities on which religious and dialect differences have little impact. A unity in which pressures of relative isolation, harsh elements and poor land quality are shared, as is dependence on supplementary small-holding agriculture and dominance by large estates. Most even vote in the same constituency and are served by the same local authority, the Western Isles Council – now officially known as Comhairle nan Eilean Siar. What threatens to dilute the strength of this modern-day Gaelic ethnic identity is the increase in language users with a different background and experience. Neo-Gaels who don't cut peat (ie, turf), don't have a love-hate relationship with CalMac ferries, don't think that the world revolves on a Glasgow-Stornoway axis, don't think that west is best. Few can aspire to be island crofters and most would probably not want to.

They have their own local cultures and traditions, their own economic and social patterns and, though each language carries an intrinsic heritage, their own perceptions of Gaelic's past and future. There is no need for them to give up these to speak Gaelic or to feel a strong sense of commitment to it. Nor is there a need to give up the Scots English which many of them will naturally speak or perhaps consciously acquire in parallel with their Gaelic. This then, I would argue, is the principal division in the world of Scots Gaelic today: between those living in the Gaelic communities and those living out a national renaissance of the language. Between the struggle for revitalisation and the struggle for revival.

Revitalisation is sadly relevant in precious few communities now – such a '*fìor Ghaidhealtachd*' should be defined quite strictly as where community-wide, inter-generational hope of language maintenance exists, rather than allow a political or sentimental fudge of the patch-work of realities within most islands. Of course the few locally resident learners, using and passing on the language, can be part and parcel of revitalisation.

But in the revival, where the needs are essentially the same, whether or not there is residual Gaelic in some localities, learners are a major if not majority element. The revival movement is national in character, even if some of its participants need to be constantly reminded of this. It is anything but uniform, with many work and home cultures represented and seeking new terminology and expression. As much as setting up the infrastructure by which individuals and families can tap into a 'virtual Gaidhealtachd' that exists nowhere but everywhere, the revival has to concern itself with selling itself, with promoting Gaelic as something that all Scots and friends of Scotland might want for themselves or their children, or at the very least accept in their local environment on signs and tannoy.

I believe it would be of value to recognise the difference in policy requirements between revitalisation and revival, and to target resources accordingly. But at the same time I am aware of the dangers of this division in the Gaelic world, and perceive a need to ensure that the two aspects are not allowed to develop along divergent paths. Indeed, moves should be made towards greater convergence in language usage and terminology. This is particularly acute in the Scottish circumstance, given the relative geographical isolation of the Gaelic communities from the centres of population and the lack of convenient and cheap travel and accommodation. The nearest many learners get to them is a short course in the south end of Skye, where Gaelic is no longer community-wide. And for the average resident of the more distant *fior Ghaidhealtachd*, encounter with a Gaelic learner is a rarity and a novelty.

The linguistic vitality and dynamism of what is left of such communities has to be shared: their slang and new turns of phrase broadcast to all Gaelic users. The exploration of new domains by the revival has to be broadcast to the communities. Gaelic-medium education and media already play an important role in this; books should be allowed to play a much bigger one, and the internet is showing great potential.

I would take the pure, revivalist line against use of English amid Gaelic – but would propose the absorption of many technical words from English or Scots or international vocabulary if they can easily take a Gaelic gloss. Easier for learners whether they like it or not, and easier to promote as a common term across all of Scottish Gaeldom. Such a stance, I'm afraid, has an impact on our relationship with Irish and Manx Gaelic. Irish can be but one source of ideas: convergence between the two languages could not be a priority, even if it were feasible.

However, even with more specific and concentrated effort on the *fior Ghaidhealtachd*, it is probable that the Scottish Gael is on his last legs. Should we pull it off, and any of the traditional Gaelic communities are revitalised, they will no doubt emerge much changed and certainly more reliant on, and aware of, the national revival.

And we will all by then be more aware of a growing influence from the ex-pupils of that product of the revival, the Gaelic-medium school unit. Many if not most of these will in effect be native speakers while not being members even by association of the Gaelic communities. Maybe we are witnessing the growth of a third world in the traditional Gaelic universe. A world that is at home in the diversity of the revival, but has the relaxed assuredness of the Gael. It is a world which I suspect is already beginning to generate its own terminology and language change. It is a world that, if allowed too much freedom will bring linguistic dangers, but if not over fettered promises great excitement too. Time will tell if it is to act as a wedge or a bridge between revitalisation and revival.

Whatever it is to be, it will still be an uphill struggle. The Gael may well die, but with luck and commitment his or her language will continue to feature as part of Scotland's national heritage and continue to adapt to being truly national again.

# Irish Language Enthusiasts and Native Speakers: An Uneasy Relationship

LARS KABEL

In his paper, Peadar Morgan differentiates between native speakers and learners of Scottish Gaelic and then describes how the term learner is 'loaded' in Scotland. This is not the case in Ireland, where there is greater awareness of language activists who have reached a high competence in Irish. Indeed, many teachers of Irish, if not most of them, have learned the language. Nevertheless, the interaction of native speakers and second language speakers is very similar in Ireland and Scotland. In this article, I classify speakers of the language in a slightly different manner from that of Peadar Morgan. I distinguish between *native speakers* on the one hand and *language enthusiasts*, also referred to as revivalists, Irish language activists, or *Gaeilgeoirí* on the other. There is a degree of overlap between both groups, as some native speakers consider themselves to be Irish language enthusiasts. However, most *Gaeilgeoirí* have learned Irish as a second language.

The impulse for the language revival, which began in the second half of the 19th century, did not come from the Irish language communities of the western seaboard, but rather from the Catholic urban middle class. The expression 'Gaeltacht', which originated among the bourgeoisie, became a generic term for unconnected rural communities in which Irish was spoken as a first language. The enthusiasm of revivalists for the Gaeltacht was not based upon linguistic considerations alone, for they also believed that the original and more authentic Irish culture survived in these communities.

Despite the fact that the Gaeltacht was endowed with a special status in the new Irish nation state, Irish is still in decline in its traditional heartland. Irish language districts are no longer as isolated as they once were. Many tourists visit the Gaeltacht, a process which encourages the use of English with strangers. Rural Irish speakers have become more mobile, fostering contacts with neighbouring English-language areas. Moreover, modern English-language mass media, such as newspapers, television, video and radio, have penetrated the Gaeltacht, and are often more popular than their Irish language counterparts.

Outside the Gaeltacht, the main burden of the revival fell on the schools which, as it transpired in the course of time, could not implement the desired language shift. In the north, Irish has been taught in many Catholic schools and has remained an important element of Catholic culture. Yet, despite the fact that almost everyone in the Republic and many northern Irish Catholics have a basic knowledge of the language, usually referred to as the *cúpla focal* ('a couple of words'), only a tiny minority actually achieves a high competence in Irish. This is because there is no out-of-school relevance of the language for most people. As there are no Irish speakers who do not understand English, an important incentive for learning another language is missing.

Enthusiasts who want to become fluent or practice their fluency, have to seek out like-minded people in order to do so. For them, Irish becomes the raison-d'être for communication conducted in the language. Very often, Irish language enthusiasts get in touch with other Irish speakers by joining a class or a local branch of Conradh na Gaeilge ('the Gaelic League'), although many of its members cannot conduct a complex conversation in Irish. Learners have fewer problems in the cities, where there are a larger number of language activists, than in the smaller towns or in the countryside. In Belfast, for example, Irish speakers can go to the Cultúrlann, an Irish language centre on the Falls Road, which includes a book shop and a café, where one can chat in Irish any time during the day. In the evening, Irish speakers can go to Cumann Chluain Ard, an Irish language club which has a bar and strongly discourages the use of English.

Sometimes Irish language enthusiasts marry each other and raise families through Irish, as happened in West Belfast in the late 1960s and early 1970s. Here, a group of young Irish-speaking couples built their own houses, which are nowadays known as the Shaw's Road Gaeltacht or locally as the 'Irish houses'. Other enthusiasts could be described as professional Irish speakers; their careers are related to the language, which may also be the medium of communication in their work environment. Professional Irish speakers can be found in the Irish language departments of universities and other third-level education institutions, Irish-medium schools, Irish-language media and organisations such as Bord na Gaeilge in Dublin or those based in the Cultúrlann in Belfast. Language enthusiasts who succeed in making Irish the language either of their work or their family (or indeed both) come closest to the ideal of using Irish naturally and unselfconsciously. However, quite often people who are accustomed to speaking Irish with one another revert to their English mother tongue, for example, when they quarrel; English retains a presence in many Irish language homes and remains the 'reflex' language of strong emotions.

It appears that the Gaeltacht should be a natural point of reference for Irish language enthusiasts; here the language can be heard and practised in its natural environment. However, the interaction between native speakers and Irish language enthusiasts can be fraught with difficulties. As native speakers often do not share the belief that the act of speaking Irish is desirable for its own sake, their use of the language tends to be governed by pragmatism. Native speakers hardly ever explain a word or a phrase in Irish when the other person does not understand, rather, they switch to English. In addition, native speakers do not always understand those who have acquired Irish as a second language. Reasons for the lack of comprehension on the part of the native speaker include the following: the language enthusiast uses archaic words and phrases or employs neologisms unknown to the native speaker ('book Irish'), and uses words or phrases from another dialect which the native speaker does not understand. Furthermore, from the point of view of a native speaker, Irish might not be the appropriate language when talking to a stranger. It is a local and intimate register and a native speaker might feel uncomfortable using Irish when talking to an outsider.

In addition, the attitude of native speakers towards Irish language enthusiasts has changed. In the early days of the revival, a small number of enthusiasts who wished to study the language and related customs visited the Irish-speaking districts. As those visitors had the means and wherewithall to pursue such interests, their relationship to locals was defined by social difference. These visitors were highly regarded by the locals and well esteemed as they could satisfy their curiosity about a very different and cosmopolitan world. Much has changed since then. On the one hand, more people from a broader social spectrum are interested in Irish. On the other hand, the standard of living in the Gaeltacht has risen. Owing to greater mobility and the mass media, the Irish language regions are no longer as remote as they were. Therefore, the lifestyles of language enthusiasts and native speakers have converged.

Locals may not identify with the role of the Gaeltacht as a folk museum. This point is illustrated in Antoine Ó Flatharta's drama *Gaeilgeoirí*. Two Dublin teenagers are staying with Máire, a native speaker in the Connemara Gaeltacht. Máire tells her husband that she was instructed by Éamonn, the teenagers' teacher, not to watch television when the *Gaeilgeoirí* are around. Instead, they should have 'natural' conversations. Her husband, unimpressed by this 'advice', comments (note the mixing of Irish and English in the original quotation):

Ní tithe lóistín atá uaidh Éamonn ach tithe siamsa. Lán le goms ligean orthu gurb é inné inniu agus nach bhfeiceann siad amárach. Hand me down my bodhrán is cuir an television faoin leaba (Ó Flatharta 1986: 20).

Éamonn doesn't need lodgings but houses of entertainment. Full of fools who pretend that yesterday is today and that they don't see tomorrow. Hand me down my bodhrán and put the television under the bed.

In 1992, I was among a group of third-level students who attended an Irish course in the Connemara Gaeltacht, where we stayed with a local family. The teenage boy in the house did not seem to understand any Irish, although we assumed he was pretending. I tried to provoke him in Irish, by calling him an *amadán* ('fool'), but he did not react; my insult appeared to mean nothing to him. Later, he, I and a student who was a native speaker were alone in the living room. While I was reading a book, the teenager and the student conversed with one another – in Irish. I overheard the boy mentioning that *Gaeilge Bhaile Átha Cliath* ('Dublin Irish') was 'stupid Irish'. This incident illustrates the fact that native speakers do not necessarily accept learners as equals and insiders within their group.

The opportunity to speak Irish to locals is now often reduced to small talk with the barman in the pub and the landlady in the B&B; as a consequence, learners often experience difficulty in obtaining linguistic 'input' from native speakers. Many learners reach a fluency which enables them to talk to other language enthusiasts confidently, but they remain too nervous and insecure to talk to native speakers. Some enthusiasts are not overly concerned with this language barrier. In October 1990, an Irish-language article in the Northern Irish newspaper the *Irish News* stated:

Tá an Ghaeltacht beo beathach anseo i mBéal Feirste ach tá cuid acu nach féidir leo bheith sásta gan an fhuilaistriú bhliantúil ó bhóthán éigin i dTír Chonaill nó i gConamara – nó cibe áit a bhfuil an 'blas' ceart nó an 'comhréir' cheart l e [sic] fáil, dar leo (*Irish News*, 1 October 1990).

The Gaeltacht is well alive here in Belfast, but some of them [ie Irish speakers] are unable to be satisfied without their annual blood transfusion from some cabin in Donegal or Connemara – or whatever place has the right 'accent' or 'syntax', according to them.

This article is remarkable for three reasons. First, it uses the term 'Gaeltacht' in the sense of 'Irish-speaking people', including both native speakers and learners. Second, it shows a clear disrespect for the rural Gaeltacht communities. Finally, it propagates a break with native speakers' Irish as a model for learners. The view of the writer is extreme, but nevertheless indicates changing attitudes towards the Gaeltacht in the Irish language movement. For the most part, Belfast language activists speak Irish among themselves. As a consequence, their Irish is heavily influenced by their English mother tongue. This is no longer seen as a deficit; rather, their Irish is redefined as a dialect in its own right – *Gaeilig Bhéal Feirste* or Belfast Irish. Belfast enthusiasts differ from native speakers in that the former often use more neologisms in Irish to describe contemporary objects, such as *cuisneoir* ('fridge') and *luaithreadán* ('ashtray'); native speakers tend to use their English equivalents. Consequently, some enthusiasts may go as far as to claim that better Irish is spoken in Belfast than in the Gaeltacht. Not everyone in the city is happy with this view, comparing such activists with learners of French who only wish to speak their French to other learners. However, most people hold a more pragmatic view:

> Tá daoine agus síleann siad gur chóir do mhuintir Bhéal Feirste a bheith ag caint cosúil le muintir Thír Chonaill. Ach níl an blas sin againne i mBéarla. Sílim féin gur chóir go raibh ár gcanúint féin againn i mBéal Feirste – blas Bhéal Feirste ar ár gcuid Gaeilge. Ach ansin thig le daoine gabháil thar fóir leis sin. Tá a fhios agam, caillíonn siad fuaimeanna na Gaeilge nuair atá siad ag cur fuaimeanna an Bhéarla ar an Ghaeilig, agus níl sin ceart. Tá an dá thaobh ann agus tá líne insan lár.

> There are people who think that the people of Belfast should speak like Donegal people. But we don't have that accent in English. I think that we should have our own dialect in Belfast – Irish with a Belfast accent. But then people can go too far with it. I know, they lose the sounds of Irish when they speak Irish with the sounds of English, and that is not right. There are two sides and in the middle there is a line ('Nuala' during 1995 interview).

Similarly, the rural culture of the Gaeltacht is no longer the ideal for the Irish language culture of Belfast per se. The women in the 'Irish houses' on west Belfast's Shaw's Road once visited an old lady from Donegal who lived locally, in order to learn the vocabulary and phrases related to cookery. It transpired that the styles of cooking, as well as the tools and ingredients she used, differed considerably from those of the younger urban women; they considered her cooking to be 'old-fashioned'. The related language skills could not be transferred as the cultural context differed.

Some Irish language enthusiasts now admit that they find little attractiveness in the rurality of the Gaeltacht. One Irish speaker from Belfast told me that he would rather foster contacts with other Irish speakers in cities such as Cork and Dublin than in the Gaeltacht. Yet those who hold such views also frequently criticise the decline of Irish in the Gaeltacht. From the perspective of language activists who put much effort and time into learning the language, it is beyond comprehension that native speakers abandon their Irish willingly:

> Agus tuigim cén fáth a bhfuil an teangaidh ag dul i laghad sa Ghaeltacht. Ach ag an am cheannann chéanna tá muidinne buailte go trom ag an imirce, tá muidinne buailte go trom ag an dífhostaíocht, tá muidinne buailte go trom ag an droch-tithíochta agus achan sórt. Ach ag an am cheannann chéanna thig linne, agus bhí an cogadh ag gabháil ar aghaidh anseo fosta, ach thig linne an feidhm a bhaint as an Ghaeilig ag an am cheanann chéanna, an bhfuil a fhios agat? So cén fáth nach dtiocfaidh leosan? Ach b'fhearr liomsa gan a bheith ag inse sin dóibhsan. Sin an gnó s'acusan. Agus thig leosan a rogha rud a dhéanamh. Níl sin gnó s'agamsa, an dtuigeann tú?

> And I understand why the language is in decline in the Gaeltacht. But at the same time we are heavily affected by emigration, we are heavily affected by unemployment, we are heavily affected by bad housing and everything. But at the same time we succeeded, and there was also a war going on here, but we succeeded in using Irish at the same time, you know. So why can't they do that? But I prefer not to tell them. That is their business. And they can do whatever they want. That's none of my business, you know. (Eoin, 30 years old, in 1995).

I hope I have shown that, as is the case with Gaelic in Scotland, the function of the Irish language for native speakers differs from that of language activists. In Irish society, north and south, Irish has been established as an additional cultural language for about 100 years. In Belfast, for example, many people take part in the city's Irish language culture in some manner or other. This is not the revival which pioneers of the language movement had envisaged, but nevertheless is a way in which the language lives on. In this context, the Gaeltacht is losing its function for the language movement. Belfast's urban Irish language culture, rather than the Gaeltacht, has become the focus for Irish language enthusiasts in the city and further afield. The differences between an urban subculture and rural lifestyle are too significant for both to form a common identity based upon the language. As the decline of Irish as a native language seems inevitable, the future of the language seems to lie with Irish language activists in the towns and cities of Ireland.

# Aithne na nGael:
# Life after Death?

PHILIP GAWNE

I live in Cregneash, a village on the southern tip of the Isle of Man, which is a place of many lasts, but also a few firsts, particularly for Manx. It is the last place where Manx was spoken as a community language and the last place where we know there was a monoglot Manx speaker, who died around the beginning of the 20th century. Also it was the home of our last traditional native speaker, Ned Maddrell, who died in 1974. Now for the firsts; Annie, my wife, and myself are now living in Ned Maddrell's house and our children are some of the first new or modern native speakers of Manx, as we would call them. Cregneash was also the first place where a serious attempt was made to record the language.

The first recording of Manx in Cregneash was in 1888 when Sir John Rhys, professor of Celtic at Oxford, recorded in note form the speech of Mrs Keggin of Cregneash. The first extensive sound recordings of native Manx speech were made by Professor Carl Marstrander, Department of Celtic, Oslo University. His main informant (which incidentally is the only informant on his surviving recordings) was Harry Kelly of Cregneash. Marstrander's visits to Harry Kelly provided the main impetus for the Manx Museum in establishing Cregneash as an open air Folk Museum. Marstrander's visits and the publicity they received led to Manx Gaelic enthusiasts combing the country for native speakers. By the mid 1940s twenty speakers had been found, five of whom were from or directly linked to Cregneash.

In 1947 Éamon de Valera, Taoiseach of Ireland, paid an official state visit to Man. During a visit to Cregneash where he met Ned Maddrell, de Valera offered the services of the Irish Folklore Commission (IFC) to visit Man and make sound recordings of native speakers. On his return to Ireland, de Valera was told that the IFC had no sound recording unit, so one was obtained, and in April 1948 the IFC arrived in Man to record. Some four hours of recordings were made including recordings of two of the Cregneash speakers.

The Manx are a very pragmatic people; around the beginning of the 19th century we decided to get rid of our language because it was no use to us. Unfortunately, we simultaneously got rid of our confidence, and this has more or less been the state of the Manx people ever since. Up until very recent times the Manx tended to be what they called 'just' the shy'; they did not have the confidence to express themselves, and they developed a very self-critical view of themselves intimating that 'the Englishman knows best, and he does the job so much better than we ever could'. By ridding ourselves of our language we lost so much more.

Since the mid 1960s there has been a tremendous influx of new residents into the Isle of Man, following the introduction of low tax policies and a wave of new resident drives. Prior to these policy initiatives the Manx economy was in a perilous state, with many Manx people having to leave the island to find work. However, the economic benefits accrued from these policies must be weighed against the resultant major social and cultural costs. We have now reached the stage where only 50 per cent of the population of the Isle of Man is Manx-born, including incomers' children who were born on the island. From that position, we have now, I suppose, wakened up to the fact that we have really got to revive our language and hold on to our Gaelic identity if we are not going to be lost as a people altogether. Our Gaelic identity is very important to us in the Isle of Man in this time of great social and cultural flux. There are few things which are recognisably and uniquely Manx and of course Manx Gaelic is one of those things. It is, therefore, an essential element in current attempts to rebuild and redefine our national identity and culture. Encouragingly, government and business, after initial scepticism are beginning to accept this analysis.

Peadar Morgan has raised a number of very interesting points in his paper, many of which do not immediately occur to Manx speakers. In the Isle of Man the Gael, by most definitions I suppose, is dead. Yet after a century of what appeared to be terminal decline there are now quite definite signs of a long life for *Gaelg Vannin* (the Gaelic of Man). At the beginning of the 20th century Manx was still spoken by over 8000 people, or 15 per cent of the population, but by the 1960s this figure had dropped to a little more than 100 speakers. This decline took place despite a sort of semi-official status for Manx, which included promulgating laws in Manx and English, and despite the best endeavours of a few concerned enthusiasts who wished to revive the language.

However, by the time the last traditional native speaker had died in 1974, a grass-roots Gaelic movement had begun to change the fortunes of Manx, and by the 1991 Census we had 643 people claiming to speak Manx, which is just under 1 per cent of the population. Significantly a Gallup survey conducted for the Manx government showed that 3 per cent claimed to speak Manx poorly and 60 per cent knew a few words and phrases in Manx, but most importantly 36 per cent of the population wanted Manx to be taught in schools. Soon afterwards government gave into public pressure and set up a Manx language programme for the schools. The level of provision is woefully small, half an hour a week, and it is unlikely that many fluent speakers will be produced as a direct result of this scheme. However, the scheme has been successful in fuelling the demand for Manx. Children who are unable to get a place in the Manx programme feel cheated of their right to learn their language and parents feel aggrieved that the programme effectively pays lip-service to it. It would appear that this small step by the Manx government has given some degree of security for the future of Manx.

The issue of fluent speakers vis-à-vis native speakers of Manx does not currently present us with many of the problems outlined by Peadar Morgan. We have no traditional native speakers; one speaker learned some of his Manx as a very young boy from his grandmother, but does not claim to be a native speaker as such, and we have five of what we call modern native speakers of 'neo-Manx', as some of the scholars would prefer us to call them. These are young children, two of which are my own, who are being raised as Manx speakers in Manx-speaking homes. About thirty speakers of Manx have learned their Manx primarily from native speakers. The rest of us are all fully-fledged learners who have never met native speakers and have limited access to recordings of their speech, though a high proportion have learned from or been influenced by speakers who learned from native speakers.

Despite considerable efforts by Yn Cheshaght Ghailckagh (Manx Gaelic Society) in the 1950s to record the remaining native speakers, little work has been done on the recordings and only a handful of people have had access to the twenty to thirty hours of recordings. This is a problem which I am currently trying to address through my work with Manx National Heritage.

We do have many tensions within the Manx Gaelic movement, however, which are similar to those mentioned by Peadar, the main one being, 'How Gaelic does Manx have to be?' The great disadvantage of not having a native speaking community is that we have to decide on what period we should base our revived language. Do we go back to 18th- or 19th-century Manx or do we continue from the Manx of the last of the native speakers in the mid 20th century? Fortunately, a compromise has been reached between biblical Manx and late-spoken Manx which seems to suit most tastes, and the great splits in the Cornish language movement have given Manx speakers a timely warning not to get too involved in re-inventing the language.

Our lack of a native-speaking community has some advantages and many other disadvantages. The advantages include a general improvement on the grammar which was used by the native speakers and a re-instatement of Gaelic words where English words had been substituted in later spoken Manx, the most famous example being *corran buigh* ('yellow crescent') instead of banana. Also we do not, unfortunately, have to worry about trying to save native-speaking communities. The time and resources saved by not having this worry is, I suppose, an advantage of sorts!

Disadvantages include a loss of Gaelic accent and an erosion of Gaelic idiom. It is true to say that Irish-speakers sound much more like the native Manx speakers than many Manx learners do now. Despite the brave efforts of some rural pockets of Manx people to retain the Manx accent and dialect the massive influx of non-Manx people has greatly diluted Manx English speech patterns. Consequently most learners come to Manx Gaelic with little or no Manx accent. Another disadvantage is that we have no real base from which to justify the changes which are occurring in the language. The erosion of the use of mutations and an increasing use of English idiom in modern spoken Manx, had been evident in Manx for centuries. However, some academics now dismiss modern spoken Manx as 'neo-Manx', insisting that true Manx died with Ned Maddrell in 1974.

Despite these criticisms, however, there is continued expansion and growing confidence within the Manx Gaelic movement. Efforts are made to simplify and standardise Manx for learners while encouraging more idiomatic Manx in literature. We also strongly believe in using Gaelic neologisms rather than English loan-words. In creating new words we endeavour to generate words from within the Manx language, however, Manxifying Irish and Scottish Gaelic loan words comes a close second. Indeed when Doug Fargher produced his English/Manx dictionary he borrowed extensively from Irish where gaps in the Manx occurred.

Inter-Gaelic co-operation such as this is vital to us mainly for the confidence and new ideas we get from meeting other Gaelic speakers, but also there's a certain degree of 'safety in numbers'. We have only got 600 speakers; it's nice to be able to latch on to the 60,000 or so Scots Gaels, and of course the hundreds of thousands of Irish speakers.

I hope that, if nothing else, my contribution to this conference will highlight that there are three Gaelic worlds, not two. As far as suggestions which have been made for the possible convergence of *Gàidhlig* and Irish, I would recommend Manx; it is a simplified version of both languages (Scottish Gaelic structure with Irish pronunciation), and thus would be the ideal choice, but I'm sure that some people might disagree!

To sum up, worries and arguments over names and standards, Gael, neo-Gael, book-Gaelic, spoken Gaelic, native speaker, fluent speaker, or learner, are important enough to the future of our Gaelic languages. We do wish to revive Gaelic languages, after all, not just *Baarlaghys* (anglicised Manx). However, in Man, much creative time and energy is lost discussing these issues, particularly with regard to countering charges that Manx is dead. It is important that we do not spend all that time and energy debating these issues to the detriment of the real battle to revive Gaelic in each of the three Gaelic countries. We must work positively and actively, not wait around for some expert or official body to give a lead, which in my own experience rarely comes.

# Neighbours in Persistence: Prospects for Gaelic Maintenance in a Globalising English World

Kenneth MacKinnon

## Gaelic in Scotland, Irish in the Six Counties: social perspectives

The present-day Gaelophone language groups in Scotland and the north show demographic and social profiles which are stark witnesses to the economic and social processes which their members and forebears have undergone in recent and historic times. Neither population is demographically 'normal' in terms of age-structure or social class composition. These aspects are illustrated in the accompanying tables, which are discussed in further detail below.

Historically, of course, the two languages had a common origin among the Gaelic peoples who moved from north-eastern Ireland into the western coastlands of Scotland from the period 300–500 AD onwards. Movements have continued to occur 'across the Sheugh' – and the story up to our own times is quite complicated. The present-day non-Gaelic-speaking language groups of the two countries are also related in complex ways to the Gaelic speakers and to one another. But I will leave to others who have specialised in this fascinating process to deal with that story. The present-day Gaelic populations of the two countries is the essential purpose of this paper.

The Gaelic speakers of Scotland are today geographically distributed bi-modally. About 40 per cent are normally resident in Lowland Scotland – and highly urbanised. The remaining 60 per cent are found in the Highlands and Islands – with the principal focus in the Western Isles, Skye and Tiree, which in 1991 were the only areas with a majority Gaelic population. This might be regarded as today's *fìor-Ghàidhealtachd*. This distribution results from such processes as the Highland 'clearance' of the 19th century and the continuing 'economic clearance' of the 20th century. Census distributions since 1881 have shown continued north-western retreat of the language and increasing concentration of migrants in lowland urban areas.

Irish speakers in Northern Ireland were not enumerated between 1911 and 1991. At the beginning of the century there were still residual Gaeltachtaí in mid-Ulster, Antrim and Rathlin, with some native speakers still surviving in isolated areas like the Sperrins. But today there is no surviving Irish-speaking community as such. However, the 1991 results showed their 'ghosts', as Ciarán Ó Duibhín terms them – especially in the local government districts of Dungannon, Newry and Mourne, Magherafelt, Derry, Cookstown and Armagh. Belfast and Derry districts have the largest numerical concentration – arguing also for strongly urban incidence of Irish speakers.

## Distribution by age group

The age distributions of Gaelic speakers in Scotland and of Irish speakers in Northern Ireland are in marked contrast, and the 1991 results are illustrated in Table 12.1 (see p 153). Although Gaelic seems stronger among 3–15-year-olds than 16–24-year-olds, the latter is a smaller age range. These numbers are quite insufficient to reverse the inexorable downward trend of Gaelic speakers across the age-spectrum. In marked contrast, the decline of Welsh-speakers has been reversed in Wales. The 3–15 age group has become the strongest of all these age ranges for the language, and if the trend continues, the language group may be on the way back to demographic normality in the next century. By 1991 the proportion of speakers under 25 years had grown to over one-third of all speakers, which argues for potential demographic maintenance of the language group. Irish speakers in Northern Ireland also show a normalising age-structure. However, in 1991 Irish was stronger among the 25–44 age group numerically and the 16–24 age group proportionately than among under-16s, which argues for the language revival being led by younger adults rather than their children. Nevertheless almost half (48 per cent) of all Irish speakers were under 25 – again with ostensible potential for intergenerational language-maintenance.

There was a quite remarkable parallel between the age distributions of Irish speakers in Northern Ireland and in the Irish Republic – and in particular within the Gaeltacht, as shown in Table 12.2 (see p 154). In each case the parenting age group 25–44 contained the largest proportion of the language group of the age ranges featured, although as a proportion of the whole age group, the incidence of Irish speakers was greatest among the immediately younger 16–24 age group.

Scottish Gaeldom in 1991 presented a dismal contrast to the other

Celtophone language groups, as shown in Table 12.3 (see p 155). The apparently stronger situation among 3–15-year-olds was a feature of the most strongly Gaelic areas only (Western Isles, Skye and Tiree). Even there, it was insufficient to halt language-decline. In both Gàidhealtachd and Galldachd (English-speaking areas) this age range was the weakest of all age ranges for incidence of Gaelic-speakers. The growth of Gaelic-medium education since its inception in 1985 has been a success story – and has shown some real upturns for Gaelic – as in Highland Council areas with Gaelic-medium schooling. These gains have been masked elsewhere, as in the Western Isles where in the 1997–98 school year Gaelic-medium schooling reached only 26 per cent of the primary enrolment. This growth rate will be quite insufficient to prevent a further decennial collapse of Gaelic among young people by 2001. Elsewhere in Scotland any gains in this age range were quite undetectable among the overall losses. For an education-led language revival, Gaelic-medium schooling would need to be expanded six-fold and become universal in the principal Gaelic areas.

## Language, social class and economic activity

Scottish and Six County Gaeldoms are contrasted too by the socio-economic distribution of speakers. These structures are illustrated in the *Northern Ireland Census 1991 Irish Language Report*, and in corresponding special tabulations of Scottish census data. Among Gaelic speakers, compared with non-Gaelic speakers, in Scotland there was a proportional bias towards the intermediate professional and managerial occupational group (Social Class II) in the 1991 census, as there had been in 1981. The bias was reversed among skilled occupational groups (Social Classes IIIN and IIIM), and marginally restored again among partly- and semi-skilled occupational groups (Social Classes IV and V). These differences were statistically significant, as were differences among the economically inactive groups, where there was a bias in favour of Gaelic speakers among the retired, although not among other categories. These differences are in line with research survey findings among Gaelic-speaking communities which found stronger language loyalty among Gaelic-speaking semi-professionals and the semi-/unskilled crofting community core. There were regional differences too. The Western Isles showed an occupational structure biased towards the less prestigious occupations, and towards retirement – both strongly evidencing the greater Gaelic language-loyalty. Professionally-qualified Gaels had gravitated towards the Lowlands, where the bias towards Gaelic speakers in this group became more marked. Within the Highlands, there has been a marked movement of Gaelic-speakers among the semi-professionals and skilled occupations to the Moray Firth area.

Irish speakers in Northern Ireland show some contrasts with this pattern. There was a much stronger bias towards Irish speakers among the intermediate professional and managerial group (Social Class II), and towards the numerically much smaller higher professional and managerial occupational group (Social Class I). Skilled, partly-skilled and unskilled occupational groups (Social Classes III–IV) and those on government schemes reversed the bias. However, among long-term unemployed, bias towards Irish speakers again showed. There were marked differences between the economically inactive in Northern Ireland as compared with Scotland. Students showed very substantial bias towards the acquisition of Irish, as marginally did the 'Other' category (which doubtlessly included the *Jailtacht* phenomenon). The bias was reversed among the retired, permanently sick and disabled, and homecarers. This all argues for a wide measure of 'middle class' or intellectual revivalism, with folk-bilingualism markedly attenuating over age, as does the age-profile in Table 12.1. This is the pattern of a youthful, intellectual middle-class elite-bilingualism in process of formation. It is very much more strongly associated with the Catholic/republican/nationalist and ethnically Gaelic/Irish community than other groups, as shown by the incidence of Irish speakers among the principal religious groupings: 20.6 per cent among Roman Catholics, and 0.5 per cent among main Protestant allegiances.

## Family and community usage

There is no continuing traditional Irish-speaking community as such in Northern Ireland. This may be a pointer to the future for Scottish Gaeldom as well. All is not well within Scottish Gaelic communities today, and there is news too of a crisis of effective family transmission and community usage within the Irish Gaeltachts. In the *Irish Times* (8 February 1998) and *West Highland Free Press* (20 February 1998) the chairman of Údarás na Gaeltachta was reported as saying at a recent 'crisis conference' in Westport, 'The linguistic basis for the Gaeltacht is fast eroding... Even in the strongest parishes... English is the home language of more and more parents. They rely on the schools to give Irish to their children... who relate to each other through English.' Professor Gearóid Ó Tuathaigh regarded neither the state nor language enthusiasts as 'able to stop this erosion, never mind put in place a strategy to renew the language'.

However, within urban Northern Ireland we have watched with growing interest and respect from 'across the Sheugh' the establishment of the neo-Gaeltacht in West Belfast. The earlier development of this has been very ably and informatively charted and explained by Gabrielle Maguire (1991). Perhaps this is to be the future for our Gaelic-language communities in both Scotland

and Ireland? And Northern Ireland has led the way! There have been other and subsequent perspectives on Irish in Northern Ireland (Sweeney 1988; Mac Póilin 1997; McKee 1997). The latter studies have concentrated upon current issues and the politics of language. An update on the lines of Maguire and Sweeney concentrating upon abilities, family and community usage and personal attitudes of the contemporary situation would now be most welcome.

I report here findings from such a recent survey in Scotland: the first national Gaelic use survey 1994–95, organised under the aegis of the Euromosaic Project, which undertook surveys of other EU lesser-used languages on similar lines at that time. I might add that although the European Commission's Task Force Resources Humaines funded these surveys and their coding onto a database, there has yet been no funding for an initiative to analyse and report the results. As organiser of the Gaelic survey, I have permission to analyse and report my own findings. This I have done publicly over the past two years, without response from any development agency or public authority with responsibility for the language, with the exception of CLI (Comann an Luchd Ionnsachaidh – the Gaelic learners' organisation in Scotland) whose director is speaking later at this conference. Despite the appointment of a minister with responsibility for Gaelic with the new government last May, there is yet to be an initiative which looks at the current state of Gaelic in Scotland afresh, and considers, as Professor Ó Tuathaigh advocated, 'a strategy to renew the language'. Perhaps this conference may be a first step – for we are here in the North, with much to learn from you!

Although quoted for area, gender, age and occupation, the Euromosaic National Gaelic Use Survey was small-scale, and cannot therefore claim to be highly representative or reliable. However, what it does show, especially in comparison with earlier surveys (as reported in MacKinnon 1997a, b) should at least enable it to act as a useful pilot of what ought to follow as a more thorough-going study. The sample size of 322 adult Gaelic speakers was divided between 156 respondents in the Western Isles and Isle of Skye, representing the present-day *fìor-Ghàidhealtachd*, (of whom 130 were resident in the Western Isles); and 166 in the rest of Scotland (of whom fifty-eight were located in the mainland Highlands). This was in rough proportion to the present day distribution of Gaelic speakers. The survey instrument was a detailed questionnaire of some 333 questions on language abilities; language use in family, leisure, work and community domains; and on personal attitudes towards Gaelic language maintenance by individuals, Gaelic language bodies and public authorities. Some of the results concerning language-usage levels in the family, work and community domains are reported here.

It is apparent from the results that there has been a very rapid intergenerational language-shift in Scottish Gaeldom. Previous studies have shown earlier stages of this process. Even in the Western Isles the coming generation of potential speakers is rapidly losing its Gaelic, even though there had been some stability until fairly recently. In 1971 and 1981, 67 per cent of children aged 3–15 were Gaelic speaking. In 1991 that fell to 49 per cent – from over two thirds to under one half. Local education policies are insufficient either to halt, let alone reverse the trend. The process shows up graphically in the census results.

Gaelic in the work domain of the present-day *fìor-Ghàidhealtachd* of the Western Isles and Skye was analysed and investigated. Use of Gaelic with bosses was weak. Many may be English monoglots, or if not, use English instrumentally in the workplace. Use of Gaelic with workmates was not much stronger, and weakest of all with subordinates. Use of Gaelic with customers was a little better – but not much. In the Irish Gaeltacht real efforts were made by Údarás na Gaeltachta to change the linguistic culture of the workplace. In Scotland, its equivalent (Highlands and Islands Development Board – now Highlands and Islands Enterprise) initially saw itself as merely providing work – with voluntary bodies such as An Comunn Gaidhealach 'putting Gaelic in people's mouths'. Later it appointed Gaelic-speaking field officers. I have often wondered that, had there been a Gaelic development bank or credit union making low interest loans to young Gaelic speakers with Gaelic business and management education to establish or acquire local small-scale businesses, what a difference there might have been today?

Language use in the community was an important aspect of the study. Within the *fìor-Ghàidhealtachd* the strongest of the domains explored here was with neighbours: 69 per cent reported using Gaelic only or mainly – the only domain which was preponderantly Gaelic. Use of Gaelic only was least reported at church – although together with mainly using Gaelic, this was the second strongest domain with 45 per cent of the respondents. Closely following was conversations with friends in a pub: 41 per cent, and in cultural activities: 40 per cent. Can strategies for revival ever overcome weakness of use within the community? What would need to be done? Could the community's shops and pubs more typically be run by Gaelic-speaking people who used the language with their customers? Could churches reverse their trend away from the language? How could Gaelic be strengthened in any material way in social club and cultural activity life? Strategies would need to address such problems in the voluntary life of the community.

Finally, there had been much change in community use over lifespans. Here the data for the whole of Scotland are essentially reporting on Gaelic speakers, originating in the Gaelic areas and now living throughout the country. In 1994–95 only in the Western Isles and parts of Skye were respondents still living in a majority 'Gaelic-speaking area'. Here, on these measures, use of Gaelic 'frequently' has held up best in public with 90.8 per cent reporting frequent use in streets when a child, and dropping 12.3 percentage-points to 1994–95. Next ranked shops at 86.2 per cent, dropping 16.2 percentage points. Third ranked church with 90.8 per cent, dropping 19.3 percentage points, overtaken in language-loss only by clubs with 66.9 per cent, dropping 26.1 percentage points to 1994–95.

## Prospects for maintenance

So, future prospects do not appear at all encouraging for the maintenance of a living Gaelic speech community in Scotland. Yet today more people are learning the language than ever, more resources are allocated to the Gaelic arts and media, and to Gaelic in education than ever before. Criticisms are sometimes made that with all this money, still the numbers go down. Yet any successes – as with Gaelic in education – may be overwhelmed by losses elsewhere. Those who do show commitment to the language – and their numbers have surely grown – show great commitment. Why do they do so? Gaelic provides identity and a genuine tradition. In a globalising English world, Gaelic is for its speakers, in Gabrielle Maguire's phrase, 'our own language'. We certainly all need a language of wider communication, and in our own time this has certainly now become English world-wide. A previous generation would have felt that to be an argument for abandoning Gaelic. My grandfather, for example, felt you could not keep two languages in your head – despite the fact that he did so successfully, albeit for different purposes. And so do – over many ages – the bulk of this world's peoples. In a globalising English world perhaps we therefore need at least two languages – for different purposes. 'Third-generational return', and re-ethnicisation of the minority 'lesser-used' languages like Welsh, Basque and Catalan goes hand-in-hand with the determination for smaller nation-state languages like Dutch and Danish to maintain themselves. And they are joined by yesterday's major-power languages – like French and German. In the years before England's expansion into Northern Ireland and its ensuing imperial expansion, Richard Mulcaster, an English educator wrote in defence of English-language mother-tongue education:

> '… our English tung… is of small reatch, it stretcheth no further then this Iland of ours, naie not there ouer all… Tho it go not beyond sea, it will serue on this side… for speaking & our pen for writing… But our state is no Empire to hope to enlarge it by commanding over cuntries… tho it be neither

large… nor in present hope of great encrease… yet where it rules, it can (be) as fit for our state, as the biggest can for theirs' (*The Elementarie*, 1582, cited in Gorlach 1991: 229–30.)

Much that Mulcaster said quickly changed: England became an empire and its tongue commanded over other countries worldwide. Today, although England has lost its empire, English commands a global economy. It much what Mulcaster said remains true: English does not even today stretch over the whole isle or isles in these parts of the world. Our own languages have persisted four centuries further on. Who would have thought it then? Our languages have made the new millennium, but will they still serve us well 'on our side' for speaking and writing four centuries hence?

So let us take heart, the world is changing rapidly – so let us change rapidly with it and keep a place in it for 'our own languages'. In a globalising English world we will soon feel, if we do not feel it already, the need for our own discourse, and we do not need to make up a new language or use somebody else's as its vehicle. England today is beginning to realise it has not only lost an empire and world-power status. It has also lost control of its own language: first to America, and the English-speaking societies across the globe, and now to Europe. There is now no single standard English – but maybe an international standard is already in course of formation. Some in England have begun to realise this, and a new psychology of language is developing as a result. The Queen's English Society for example, stands for prescriptive 'British-English' spellings and syntax – and above all that grotesque relic of social superiority 'received pronunciation'. The British Council promotes 'Project 2000' to sell British-English as an alternative to American-English on the world market.

So English too is on the run – and its British variety comes to look more like a lesser-used language every day. It is beginning to struggle to maintain itself. England's adversity was ever Ireland's opportunity – as true linguistically as in *realpolitik*! Today we all need World English (even the English) – and we all need 'our own language' too (even the English!) Indeed we, their neighbours in perversity over the centuries, may even be able to help them, but above all, help ourselves. We celebrate the close contacts and continued exchanges between the Gaelic peoples of the Scottish Highlands and Islands, and Ulster. The mission of Colm Cille, Ulsterman, statesman and saint of the 6th century stands at the inception of this process. Today, fourteen centuries after his death, we have established an initiative to honour his memory and mission, and to renew our own peoples in reconciliation. All Christian traditions in our two countries can acknowledge his mission as a spiritual antecedent of their own, and all our churches commemorate him. Language too can be a healing process in this. Lowland Scots has a Gaelic background – indeed Scotland's conception was as a people of Gaelic identity, which is what 'Scot' originally meant. The Lowland Scots who came to Ireland share in this Gaelic origination and identity. This heritage and tradition is for all our people, and its realisation is part of the process of reconciliation and of liberation for us all. Our two nations are today peoples of three languages: Gaelic, Scots and English. Each has its place in our societies – and doubtless too, today without only one of them, we would be the poorer and no longer the people that we are. May we find an essential and living place for each in our common way of life within the Scotland, the Ulster and the Ireland of the coming millennium.

## Acknowledgements

Permission is acknowledged with thanks, to Euromosaic Project, Research Centre Wales, University of Wales, Bangor for data on National Gaelic Language-Use Survey 1994–95 and printout services. Special thanks are also due to Customer Services, General Register Office (Scotland) for special tabulations on Gaelic language, social class and economic activity, and in particular, Ian Máté, Frank Thomas, Philip Street and Peter Jamieson. The paper also acknowledges support from the University of Hertfordshire, Division of Social Sciences research funds, for media services and computer services undertaken by Wayne Diamond.

Table 12.1  Speakers of Celtic languages in UK countries by age group, 1991 Census

**Gaelic Speakers in Scotland**

| Age Group | No. | As % of all Gaelic Speakers | Whole age group | Gaelic Speakers as % whole age-group |
|---|---|---|---|---|
| 65+ | 16,607 | 25.17 | 767,147 | 2.16 |
| 45-64 | 17,995 | 27.27 | 1,115,411 | 1.61 |
| 25-44 | 17,829 | 27.02 | 1,462,550 | 1.22 |
| 16-24 | 6,455 | 9.78 | 643,139 | 1.00 |
| 3-15 | 7,092 | 10.75 | 821,451 | 0.86 |
| Total 3+ | 65,978 | 0%  5%  10%  15%  20%  25% | 4,809,698 | 0%  1%  2% — 1.37% |

**Welsh Speakers in Wales**

| Age Group | No. | As % of all Welsh Speakers | Whole age group | Welsh Speakers as % whole age-group |
|---|---|---|---|---|
| 65+ | 110,893 | 21.83 | 490,612 | 22.60 |
| 45-64 | 111,165 | 21.88 | 639,217 | 17.39 |
| 25-44 | 113,265 | 22.29 | 779,540 | 14.53 |
| 16-24 | 59,539 | 11.72 | 348,608 | 17.08 |
| 3-15 | 113,236 | 22.29 | 465,646 | 24.32 |
| Total 3+ | 508,098 | 0%  5%  10%  15%  20%  25% | 2,723,623 | 0%  5%  10%  15%  20%  25% — 18.66% |

**Irish speakers in Northern Ireland**

| Age Group | No. | As % of all Irish Speakers | Whole age group | Irish Speakers as % whole age-group |
|---|---|---|---|---|
| 65+ | 9,000 | 6.82 | 199,052 | 4.52 |
| 45-64 | 19,861 | 15.05 | 306,887 | 6.47 |
| 25-44 | 39,784 | 30.15 | 432,921 | 9.19 |
| 16-24 | 27,894 | 21.14 | 229,078 | 12.18 |
| 3-15 | 35,435 | 26.85 | 344,447 | 10.60 |
| Total 3+ | 131,974 | 0%  5%  10%  15%  20%  25%  30% | 1,449,583 | 0%  5%  10% — 9.10% |

*Sources*: 1991 Census Local Base Statistics, Table L67S, Table L67W; 1991 Census Northern Ireland Irish Language Report, Table 1

Table 12.2 Speakers of Irish in the Republic of Ireland by area and age group, 1991 Census

**Irish speakers in the Republic of Ireland (Total)**

| Age Group | No. | As % of all Irish Speakers | Whole age group | Irish Speakers as % whole age-group |
|---|---|---|---|---|
| 65+ | 74,358 | 6.79 | 402,900 | 18.46 |
| 45-64 | 173,105 | 15.80 | 621,683 | 27.84 |
| 25-44 | 292,537 | 26.70 | 958,964 | 30.51 |
| 16-24 | 286,259 | 26.12 | 601,598 | 47.58 |
| 3-15 | 269,571 | 24.60 | 781,861 | 34.48 |
| Total 3+ | 1,095,830 | 0% 5% 10% 15% 20% 25% | 3,367,006 | 0% 10% 20% 30% 40% 50% 32.55% |

**Irish speakers in the Gaeltacht**

| Age Group | No. | As % of all Irish Speakers | Whole age group | Irish Speakers as % whole age-group |
|---|---|---|---|---|
| 65+ | 9,546 | 16.90 | 12,664 | 75.38 |
| 45-64 | 10,609 | 18.79 | 14,554 | 72.89 |
| 25-44 | 14,090 | 24.95 | 21,183 | 66.52 |
| 16-24 | 9,137 | 16.18 | 11,957 | 76.42 |
| 3-15 | 13,097 | 23.18 | 19,205 | 68.14 |
| Total 3+ | 56,469 | 0% 5% 10% 15% 20% 25% | 79,563 | 0% 10% 20% 30% 40% 50% 60% 70% 80% 70.97% |

**Irish speakers in the remainder of the State (Galltacht)**

| Age Group | No. | As % of all Irish Speakers | Whole age group | Irish Speakers as % whole age-group |
|---|---|---|---|---|
| 65+ | 64,812 | 6.24 | 390,236 | 16.61 |
| 45-64 | 162,496 | 15.05 | 607,129 | 26.76 |
| 25-44 | 278,447 | 26.79 | 937,781 | 29.69 |
| 16-24 | 277,122 | 26.66 | 589,641 | 47.00 |
| 3-15 | 256,484 | 24.68 | 762,656 | 33.63 |
| Total 3+ | 131,974 | 0% 5% 10% 15% 20% 25% | 3,287,443 | 0% 10% 20% 30% 40% 50% 31.62% |

*Source*: Republic of Ireland Population Census 1991, Vol 7: Irish Language, Tables 5 and 9A

Table 12.3  Speakers of Gaelic in Scotland by area and age group, 1991 Census

### Gaelic Speakers in Scotland

| Age Group | No. | As % of all Gaelic Speakers | Whole age group | Gaelic Speakers as % whole age-group |
|---|---|---|---|---|
| 65+ | 16,607 | 25.17 | 767,147 | 2.16 |
| 45-64 | 17,995 | 27.27 | 1,115,411 | 1.61 |
| 25-44 | 17,829 | 27.02 | 1,462,550 | 1.22 |
| 16-24 | 6,455 | 9.78 | 643,139 | 1.00 |
| 3-15 | 7,092 | 10.75 | 821,451 | 0.86 |
| Total 3+ | 65,978 | 0%  5%  10%  15%  20%  25% | 4,809,698 | 0%           1%           2% 1.37% |

### Gaelic speakers in the Fìor-Ghàidhealtachd (Western Isles, Skye and Tiree)

| Age Group | No. | As % of all Gaelic Speakers | Whole age group | Gaelic Speakers as % whole age-group |
|---|---|---|---|---|
| 65+ | 6,274 | 25.61 | 7,561 | 82.98 |
| 45-64 | 6,403 | 26.14 | 9,148 | 70.00 |
| 25-44 | 5,852 | 23.89 | 10,820 | 54.09 |
| 16-24 | 2,621 | 10.70 | 4,967 | 52.77 |
| 3-15 | 3,347 | 13.66 | 7,295 | 45.89 |
| Total 3+ | 24,497 | 0%  5%  10%  15%  20%  25% | 39,295 | 0% 10% 20% 30% 40% 50% 60% 70% 80% 61.56% |

### Gaelic speakers in the remainder of Scotland

| Age Group | No. | As % of all Gaelic Speakers | Whole age group | Gaelic Speakers as % whole age-group |
|---|---|---|---|---|
| 65+ | 10,333 | 24.91 | 759,586 | 1.63 |
| 45-64 | 11,592 | 27.95 | 1,106,263 | 1.05 |
| 25-44 | 11,977 | 28.87 | 1,451,730 | 0.83 |
| 16-24 | 3,834 | 9.24 | 683,172 | 0.60 |
| 3-15 | 3,745 | 9.03 | 814,156 | 0.46 |
| Total 3+ | 131,974 | 0%  5%  10%  15%  20%  25%  30% | 4,769,907 | 0%           1%           2% 0.87% |

*Source*: Census 1991 Scotland, SAS/LBS Table 67, Gaelic Language

# Bibliography and further reading

ANDERSON, CHRISTOPHER (1828) *Historical Sketches of the Ancient Native Irish.* Edinburgh: Oliver and Boyd.

ANSDELL, DOUGLAS (1998) *The People of the Great Faith: The Highland Church 1690–1900.* Stornoway: Acair.

BEBBINGTON, DAVID (ed) (1988) *The Baptists in Scotland: A History.* Glasgow: Baptist Union of Scotland.

— (1992) *Evangelicalism in Modern Britain: A History from the 1730s to the 1980s.* Grand Rapids: Baker Book House.

BARNARD, TC (1993) 'Protestants and the Irish Language c. 1675–1725', *Journal of Ecclesiastical History* 44: 2: 243–72.

BLACK, GF (1993 [1946]) *The Surnames of Scotland,* Edinburgh: Birlinn.

BLACK, RI (1998) 'Alastair mac Mhaighstir Alastair: Another flawed giant for Scotland', O'Donnell Lecture given at the University of Edinburgh on 30 May 1998.

BLANEY, ROGER (1996) *Presbyterians and the Irish Language.* Belfast: Ulster Historical Foundation and ULTACH Trust.

BRITISH AND IRISH COMMUNIST ORGANISATION (1973) 'Hidden Ulster' Explored. Belfast: BICO.

BROWN, ALICE; McCrone, David and Paterson, Lindsay (1998) *Politics and Society in Scotland.* Basingstoke: Macmillan.

CAMPBELL, JL (1945) *Gaelic in Scottish Education and Life: Past, Present and Future.* Edinburgh: W and AK Johnston for the Saltire Society.

— (1958) (ed) *Gaelic Words and Expressions from South Uist and Eriskay, collected by the Rev Fr Allan McDonald.* Dublin: Institute for Advanced Studies.

COMUNN NA GAIDHLIG (CNAG) (1997) *Inbhe Thèarainte dhan Ghàidhlig: Secure Status for Gaelic.* Inverness: CNAG.

— (1999) *Gàidhlig plc: Plana Leasachaidh Canain/a development plan for gaelic.* Inverness: CNAG.

CROWLEY, T (1996) *Language in History: Theories and Texts.* London: Routledge.

DAWSON, JANE (1994) 'Calvinism and the Gaidhealtachd in Scotland', in Andrew Pettegree, Alastair Duke and Gillian Lewis (eds) *Calvinism in Europe 1540–1620.* Cambridge: Cambridge University Press.

DE VARENNES, FERNAND (1986) *Language, Minorities and Human Rights.* The Hague: Martinus Nijhoff.

DIECKHOFF, CYRIL (1992) *A Pronouncing Dictionary of Scottish Gaelic.* Glasgow: Gairm. (First published in 1932.)

DURKACZ, VE (1996) *The Decline of the Celtic Languages: A Study of Linguistic and Cultural Conflict in Scotland, Wales and Ireland from the Reformation to the Twentieth Century.* Edinburgh: John Donald Publishers.

FRASER, A (1989) 'Gaelic in primary education: a study of the development of Gaelic bilingual education in urban contexts', unpublished PhD thesis, University of Glasgow.

FRASER PRODUCTION AND CONSULTANCY (1998) *A Review of Aspects of Gaelic Broadcasting, prepared for the Scottish Office Education and Industry Department, Arts and Cultural Heritage Division.* Edinburgh: Fraser Production and Consultancy.

GILLIES, AL (1990) 'An absurd sense of optimism', in A Hetherington (ed) (1990) *Highlands and Islands: A generation of progress.* Aberdeen: University Press.

GILLIES, W (1989) 'The future of Scottish Gaelic studies', in W Gillies (ed) *Gaelic and Scotland.* Edinburgh: University Press.

GORLACH, M (1991) *Introduction to Early Modern English.* Cambridge: Cambridge University Press.

GRAAND, S (1983) 'An investigation into the feasibility of establishing Gaelic /English bilingual primary schools on the mainland of Scotland', unpublished MPhil thesis, University of Glasgow.

GRILLO, R (1989) *Dominant Languages: Language and Hierarchy in Britain and France.* Cambridge: Cambridge University Press.

HERBERT, MÁIRE (1988): *Iona, Kells, and Derry: The history and hagiography of the monastic familia of Columba.* Oxford: University Press 1988 (repr. Dublin: Four Courts Press 1996).

— (1999) 'The legacy of Columba', in TM Devine and JF McMillan (eds) *Celebrating Columba.* Edinburgh.

— (1999) 'Sea-divided Gaels: Constructing relationships between Irish and Scots c. 800–1169', in B Smith (ed) *Britain and Ireland 900–1300.* Cambridge: University Press.

— (2000) '*Rí Érenn, Rí Alban*: Kingship and identity in the ninth and tenth centuries', in Simon Taylor (ed) *Kings, Clerics and Chronicles in Scotland, 500–1297.* Dublin.

HINDLEY, R (1990) *The Death of the Irish Language.* London: Routledge.

HOGG, PW (1992) *Constitutional Law of Canada.* Scarborough: Carswell. (3rd edn).

HUNTER, JAMES (1990) 'A new confidence?', in A Hetherington (ed) *Highlands and Islands: A generation of progress.* Aberdeen: University Press.

— (1995) *The Making of the Crofting Community.* Edinburgh: John Donald.

HUTCHINSON, J (1987) *The Dynamics of Irish Cultural Nationalism: The Gaelic Revival and the Creation of the Irish Nation State.* London: Allen and Unwin.

INTERARTS (1999) *Linguarts: Language and Cultural Policies in Europe.* Barcelona: Interarts Observatory.

JACKSON, KENNETH (1951) 'Common Gaelic' Proceedings of the British Academy 37: 71–97.

KEDOURIE, E (1994) *Nationalism.* Oxford: Blackwell.

KENNEDY, D (1988) *The Widening Gulf: Northern Attitudes to the Independent Irish State, 1919–49.* Belfast: Blackstaff Press.

KERR, EDDIE (1994) 'Our common heritage', carried out by KUDOS on behalf of Naíscoil na Rinne, Derry, unpublished.

McCAUGHEY TP (1989) 'Protestantism and Scottish Highland culture', in JP Mackey (ed) *An Introduction to Celtic Christianity.* Edinburgh: T and T Clark.

McCOY, GORDON (1997) 'Protestant learners of Irish in Northern Ireland', in Aodán Mac Póilin (ed) *The Irish Language in Northern Ireland.* Belfast: ULTACH Trust.

MacDONALD, KD (1968) 'The Gaelic language, its study and development', in DS Thomson and Ian Grimble (eds) *The Future of the Highlands.* London: Routledge.

MACDONALD, MARTIN (1982) Còr na Gàidhlig. *Language, Community and Development: the Gaelic Situation.* Inverness: Highlands and Islands Development Board.

MACDONALD, S (1997) *Reimagining Culture: Histories, Identities and the Gaelic Renaissance.* Oxford: Berg.

MACFARLANE, PATRICK (1834 [1963]) *Iùl a' Chrìosdaidh.* Aberdeen: John Deson and Co. [Stirling: A Learmonth and Son].

MACFHIONNLAIGH, FEARGHAS (1996) 'Creative tensions: Personal reflections of an evangelical Christian and Gaelic poet', *Scottish Bulletin of Evangelical Theology* 14: 1.

MACINNES, JOHN (1951) *The Evangelical Movement in the Highlands of Scotland 1688–1800.* Aberdeen: Aberdeen University Press.

— (1969–70) 'Gaelic spiritual verse', *Transactions of the Gaelic Society of Inverness* 46: 336.

McKEE, VINCENT (1997) *Gaelic Nations – Politics of the Gaelic Language in Scotland & Northern Ireland in the 20th Century.* London: Bluestack.

MACKENZIE, N (1906) 'Bardachd Irteach', *The Celtic Review* 2: 328–42.

MACKINNON, KENNETH (1997a) 'Gaelic as an endangered language – problems and prospects', paper presented to workshop in endangered languages, University of York, 26–27 July.

— (1997b) 'Gaelic in family, work and community domains: Euromosaic

Project 1994–95', paper presented to Fifth International Conference on the Languages of Scotland and Ulster. Aberdeen: University of Aberdeen.

— (1991) *Gaelic: A Past & Future Prospect*. Edinburgh: The Saltire Society.

MACLEOD, FINLAY (1986) *The Gaelic Arts: A Way Ahead*. Edinburgh: Scottish Arts Council.

MACMULLEN, RAMSAY (1997) *Christianity and Paganism in the Fourth to Eighth Centuries*. Yale: Yale University Press.

MACPÓILIN, AODÁN (ed) (1997) *The Irish Language in Northern Ireland*. Belfast: Iontaobhas ULTACH.

— (1994) 'Spiritual Beyond the Ways of Men: Images of the Gael.' *The Irish Review: Defining Borders, Colony, City, Region*. 16 Autumn/Winter 1994, pp 1–22.

MAGUIRE, GABRIELLE (1991) *Our Own Language: An Irish Initiative*. Clevedon: Multilingual Matters.

MALLORY, JP AND MCNEILL, TE (1995) *The Archaeology of Ulster from Colonization to Plantation*. Belfast: Institute of Irish Studies, Queen's University of Belfast.

MEEK, DE (1988a) *Island Harvest: A History of Tiree Baptist Church 1838–1988*. Edinburgh: Tiree Books.

— (1988b) 'The Gaelic Bible', in DF Wright (ed) *The Bible in Scottish Life and Literature*. Edinburgh: St Andrew Press.

— (1992) (ed) *A Mind for Mission: Essays in Appreciation of the Rev. Christopher Anderson (1782–1852)*. Edinburgh: Baptist History Project.

— (1996a) *The Scottish Highlands: The Churches and Gaelic Culture*. WCC Gospel and Cultures Pamphlet 11. Geneva: World Council of Churches.

— (1996b) 'Modern Celtic Christianity', in Terence Brown (ed) *Celticism*. vol 8 of Studia Imagologica: Amsterdam Studies on Cultural Identity. Amsterdam and Atlanta: Rodopi.

— (1997) 'Protestant missions and the evangelization of the Scottish Highlands, 1700–1850', *The International Bulletin of Missionary Research* 21 (2): 67–72.

— (forthcoming) 'The glory of the lamb: The Gaelic hymns of the Rev Peter Grant', in David Bebbington (ed) *Proceedings of the First International Conference on Baptist Studies*.

NEILL, STEPHEN (1979) 'Religion and culture: A historical introduction', in John Stott and RT Coote (1979) (eds) *Gospel and Culture: The Papers of a Consultation on the Gospel and Culture*. Convened by the Lausanne Committee's Theology and Education Group. Pasadena: William Carey Library.

NEWBIGIN, LESSLIE (1995) *The Open Secret: An Introduction to the Theology of Mission*. Michigan and London: SPCK.

NIEBUHR, HR (1952) *Christ and Culture*. London: Faber and Faber.

Ó FLATHARTA, ANTOINE (1986) *Gaeilgeoirí*, Béal an Daingin: Cló Iar-Chonnachta.

Ó HUALLACHÁIN, COLMAN (1994) *The Irish and Irish – a sociolinguistic analysis of the relationship between a people and their language*. Dublin: Irish Franciscan Provincial Office.

Ó MURCHÚ, H (1999) *Irish: Facing the Future. European Languages 8*. Dublin: European Bureau for Lesser Used Languages.

Ó MURCHÚ, M (1985) *The Irish Language*. Dublin: Department of Foreign Affairs and Bord na Gaeilge.

Ó SNODAIGH, P (1973) *Hidden Ulster*. Dublin: Clodhanna Teo.

POLLAK, A (1993) *A Citizen's Enquiry: The Opsahl Report on Northern Ireland*, Dublin: Lilliput Press.

SCHNEIDERMAN, DAVID (ed) 1989 *Language and the State: The Law and Politics of Identity*. Cowansville, Quebec: Les Editions Yvon Blais.

SMITH, AD (1991) *National Identity*. London: Penguin.

PHILLIPSON, RHL (1990) *English Language Teaching and Imperialism*. Tronninge, Denmark: Transcultura.

SPROULL, ALAN (1998) *The Demand for Gaelic Artistic and Cultural Products and Services: Patterns and Impacts*. Glasgow: Caledonia University.

STASSEN, GH, Yeager DM and Yoder, JH (1996) *Authentic Transformation: A New Vision of Christ and Culture*. Nashville: Abington Press.

STOTT, JOHN AND COOTE, RT (1979) (eds) *Gospel and Culture: The Papers of a Consultation on the Gospel and Culture*. Convened by the Lausanne Committee's Theology and Education Group. Pasadena: William Carey Library.

STRINGER, PETER AND ROBINSON, GILLIAN (1991) *Social Attitudes in Northern Ireland,* (1990–91 edn) Belfast: Blackstaff Press.

SWEENEY, KEVIN (1988) *The Irish Language in Northern Ireland 1987*, Northern Ireland Office, Policy Planning and Research Unit.

THOMSON, RL (ed) (1970) *Foirm na nUrrnuidheadh*. Edinburgh: Scottish Gaelic Texts Society.

UA BHRIAIN, ART (1932) 'D'imthig fíor-Gaodhal uainn' *Fèile na nGaideal*, Samhain 1932 (uimhir lxv).

WALL, MAUREEN (1969) 'The decline of the Irish language', in Brian Ó Cuív (ed) *A View of the Irish Language*. Dublin: Stationery Office.

WITHERS, C (1984) *Gaelic in Scotland: the geographical history of a language* Edinburgh: John Donald.

YEATS, WB (nd) quoted B Kiely (1994) *Yeats' Ireland: An Illustrated Anthology*. London: Tiger Books International.

## Government publications

The Scotland Act 1998
Broadcasting Acts of 1990 and 1996
Education (Scotland) Act 1980
Standards in Scotland's Schools (etc.) Bill
International Covenant on Civil and Political Rights
Framework Convention for the Protection of National Minorities

## Stationery Office publications

STATIONERY OFFICE (1990) *The Broadcasting Act 1990*. London: The Stationery Office.
— (1998) *The Scotland Act 1998*. London: The Stationery Office.
COUNCIL OF EUROPE (1992) *European Charter for Regional or Minority Languages*. European Treaty Series No. 148 Strasbourg: Council of Europe Publishing
DEPARTMENT OF HEALTH AND SOCIAL SERVICES REGISTRAR GENERAL, NORTHERN IRELAND (1993) *The Northern Ireland Census 1991, Irish Language Report*. Belfast: HMSO.